Unmasking the Psychopath

Antisocial Personality and Related Syndromes

A NORTON PROFESSIONAL BOOK

Unmasking the Psychopath

*Antisocial Personality
and Related Syndromes*

Edited by

WILLIAM H. REID
DARWIN DORR
JOHN I. WALKER
JACK W. BONNER, III

W · W · NORTON & COMPANY · *NEW YORK* · *LONDON*

Copyright © 1986 by William H. Reid, Darwin Dorr, John I. Walker, Jack W. Bonner

All rights reserved.

Published simultaneously in Canada by Penguin Books Canada Ltd, 2801 John Street, Markham, Ontario L3R 1B4
Printed in the United States of America.

First Edition

Library of Congress Cataloging-in-Publication Data
Main entry under title:

Unmasking the psychopath.

  Includes bibliographies and index.
  1. Antisocial personality disorders. I. Reid,
William H., 1945–   . [DNLM: 1. Antisocial Personality Disorder. WM 190 U58]
RC555.U55 1986   616.85'82   86-715

ISBN 0-393-70025-9

W.W. Norton & Company, Inc., 500 Fifth Avenue, New York, N.Y. 10110
W.W. Norton & Company, Ltd., 37 Great Russell Street, London WC1B 3NU

1 2 3 4 5 6 7 8 9 0

To the memory of Hervey M. Cleckley, M.D.,
and to those he tried to help.

Contents

Introduction: Assaulting the Mask   ix
   William H. Reid

Acknowledgments   xiii
Contributors   xv

I. UNMASKING THE PSYCHOPATH

1. Twenty Years of Experience with the
   Cleckley Psychopath   3
   Robert D. Hare

2. Epidemiology of Antisocial Personality   28
   Remi J. Cadoret

3. The Child Behind the Mask: Sociopathy as
   Developmental Delay   45
   Robert G. Kegan

4. Social Crises and Psychopathy: Toward a
   Sociology of the Psychopath   78
   José Sánchez

5. Ego Dysfunction in Psychopathic Psychiatric Inpatients   98
   Darwin Dorr & Peggy K. Woodhall

6. Human Aggression: A Biological Perspective   132
   Gerald L. Brown & Frederick K. Goodwin

II. TREATMENT APPROACHES

7. Behavioral and Cognitive Treatment of Criminal
   and Delinquent Behavior   159
   William D. Barley

8. Treatment of Antisocial Syndromes:
   The Therapist's Feelings   191
   Larry H. Strasburger

9. Inpatient Treatment of Antisocial Youth   208
   William J. Shamblin, Jr.

10. A Therapeutic Milieu for Treating the Antisocial
    Substance-abusing Adolescent   221
    Richard D. Selman

11. Comprehensive Inpatient Treatment of a Severely
    Antisocial Adolescent   231
    Leo J. Potts, William D. Barley,
    Kathleen A. Jones, & Peggy K. Woodhall

12. Manipulativeness in Entrepreneurs and Psychopaths   256
    Ethel Spector Person

Name Index   275

Subject Index   283

Introduction:
Assaulting the Mask

William H. Reid

The mental health professions, particularly psychiatry, have a problem. Over the years, members of those professions have held themselves out as experts, and sometimes saviors, with respect to the mentally ill in society.

Nowhere was this promise more gratefully embraced by the public than in the antisocial syndromes: psychopathy, delinquency, and criminal violence. We—or at least some of our senior colleagues—extolled the virtues of social and medical science, accepted praise and grant money . . . and did not deliver the answers society expected.

Sometimes this was because of exciting preliminary study results that got much publicity but were not replicated, disappointing and frustrating professionals and laypersons alike. Sometimes excellent, prudent researchers worked too slowly for society's appetite for answers or guidance, and were cast aside. Occasionally, a pseudo-scientist or facile entrepreneur would take the media stage and proclaim his universal "answer" to the psychopathy or delinquency "question." His inevitable failure often embarrassed the mental health professions.

Through all this, a certain quiet group of clinicians and students of human behavior continued to work as they always had, in the traditions of Hervey Cleckley and his contemporary, Georg Stürup. Patients were hard to get and keep in therapy. It was difficult to find payment for treatment, since most of the patients were no longer considered "sick" by the public. Societal anger at, and related fear of, antisocial individuals eroded the prestige of those who would practice or do research among these people. Institutional research and program grant funds were often diverted to other areas.

The authors who have contributed to this book represent, in spirit and often in person, the group who have continued the work. Some of the names in the contributor list are familiar to many readers. Others, not necessarily only newcomers to the field, have published little or have not become known outside their disciplines. But they are the ones who continue the work. They work to understand the patient's biology, his psychology, his behavior, his relationships, and his place in society.

Most of the contributors work daily to do something else, which is fundamental to the health professions, but which is sometimes forgotten by our more academic friends. They work to help the patient, to relieve his pain. The mask of sanity that Cleckley saw and others now recognize hides the psychopath's pathology, which is a source not only of consternation for others but also of pain and sadness for him. The keys to understanding and relief lie beneath the mask. This book gives one a glimpse of some of the work that tries to remove it.

In the first section, *Unmasking the Psychopath*, Robert Hare's chapter reflects work which started long ago on some of the most basic characteristics of characterologic antisocial syndromes. He explains its beginnings in the purely clinical observations of Dr. Cleckley, and outlines apparent physiological differences between the psychopath and others. Remi Cadoret continues the search for biological understanding with a discussion of his studies, and those of others, of familial transmission and epidemiology of antisocial personality.

Robert Kegan expands traditional psychodynamic formulations of psychopathy to what I feel is an eminently logical, and convincing, theory of psychopathic character growth. His work comes close to bridging the gap between biological substrate and eventual "penetrance" of the disorder through aberrant development. José Sánchez opens the door to the topic of social effects on the creation of the psychopath, and his effects on society. Darwin Dorr and Peggy K. Woodhall bring our subject into the clinical arena, where it really counts. Gerald Brown and Frederick Goodwin look to the very chemistry of the brain for their data.

The second section, on *Treatment Approaches* , opens with William Barley's discussion of behavioral and cognitive therapies, some of which he finds specifically useful in the care of antisocial adolescents and adults. Larry Strasburger provides vital information and guidelines on countertransference, the understanding of which is crucial to those who work with patients who are often seen as hateful, malicious, or untreatable.

The chapters by William Shamblin and Richard Selman take the reader into working inpatient models. One sees how the programs work and how the hospital system itself interacts with clinicians and their patients. Leo Potts, William Barley, Kathleen Jones and Peggy Wood-hall then focus on the treatment of one patient, from admission to follow-up. Theirs is a fascinating look at comprehensive clinical intervention, from the viewpoints of several of the many professional disciplines involved.

Ethel Person shows the reader that patients with antisocial character traits do not always present as criminals, delinquents or social outcasts; and by the same token, that not all "successful psychopaths" choose to avoid treatment. Her chapter is the only one in the book that addresses the profession's continuing, if not entirely rational, pessimism about psychodynamic treatment of psychopathy.

The answers are not all here. The editors have not attempted an all-inclusive volume on psychopathy and its treatment. There is nothing in the book about nonmedical community treatment programs, for example, or about the several exciting (to this writer) therapeutic wilderness programs for offenders. Treatments based in correctional settings have been omitted entirely, and perhaps unfairly.

What the editors *have* brought to these pages is a summary of much that we feel is new and clinically relevant to the therapist's task: relief of pain. In my own opinion, the book is one of the first to report significant *integration* of biologic, psychodynamic, cognitive, interpersonal and sociologic approaches to psychopathy. This, in my view, is the beginning of real understanding. When several theories about a phenomenon differ fundamentally, none is likely to be correct. But when one can find points of mutual consistency and support within the theories, they become as soldiers who work together, in this case to assault the patient's mask of sanity.

Finally, this book and the conference out of which much of it arose have been dedicated to the memory of a man who, perhaps more than anyone this century, committed his professional life to the understanding of psychopathy. Hervey Cleckley recognized the profound intrapsychic deficit which lies below the psychopath's façade (Cleckley's "mask") of calm and confidence. Sometimes he carried out his work in the halls of academe. More often he was involved in psychiatric practice, with the people — patients and families — at the center of the practical issues.

Cleckley was one of a handful of men and women who are slowly passing the torch of concern to others. A second, Georg Stürup, a contemporary of Cleckley, recently met with this writer in his Randers, Denmark, home. As he described his decades of work "treating the untreatable" at Herstedvester Institution, he seemed to be saying, "Don't forget these people. They have no one, yet they *are people*. They are desperately lacking and in terrible pain. Those who understand this are so rare; you must not turn your back on them."

Acknowledgments

The conference out of which *Unmasking the Psychopath* arose deserves considerable praise. It was a joint project of Highland Hospital and Duke University, under the coordination of Doctors Bonner and Walker. Many of the speakers are represented in this volume, although each chapter based on an oral presentation has been completely rewritten.

We should like to acknowledge a few of the many fine people who made this book possible. The secretaries in our several offices must not go unsung, especially John A. Walker and Kathy Johnson at the University of Nebraska, and Melba Krisher and Kimberly A. Storrs at Highland Hospital. Facility support by the University of Nebraska and Highland Hospital was appreciated.

Contributors

EDITORS

William H. Reid, M.D., M.P.H.
Medical Director
Colonial Hills Hospital
San Antonio, TX

Darwin Dorr, Ph.D.
Director, Clinical Psychology
Highland Hospital
Asheville, NC

John I. Walker, M.D.
Clinical Professor of Psychiatry
University of Texas Health
  Sciences Center
San Antonio, TX

Jack W. Bonner, III, M.D.
Medical Director
Highland Hospital
Asheville, NC

CHAPTER AUTHORS

William D. Barley, Ph.D.
Director, Cognitive and
  Behavioral Treatment
  Program
Highland Hospital
Asheville, NC

Gerald L. Brown, M.D.
National Institutes of Health
Bethesda, MD

Remi J. Cadoret, M.D.
Department of Psychiatry
Iowa City, IA

Frederick K. Goodwin, M.D.
National Institutes of Health
Bethesda, MD

Robert D. Hare, Ph.D.
Department of Psychology
University of British Columbia
Vancouver, BC

Kathleen A. Jones, O.T.R.
Coordinator, Occupational
  Therapy
Highland Hospital
Asheville, NC

Robert G. Kegan, Ph.D.
Harvard Graduate School of
  Education
Cambridge, MA

Ethel Spector Person, M.D.
Director

Columbia University Center for
   Psychoanalytic Training and
   Research
New York, NY

Leo J. Potts, M.D.
Clinical Director
Highland Hospital
Asheville, NC

José Sánchez, Ph.D.
Political Science Program
Kean College
Union City, NJ

Richard O. Selman, M.D.
Director, Adolescent Substance
   Abuse Program

Highland Hospital
Asheville, NC

William J. Shamblin, Jr., M.D.
Director of Child and
   Adolescent Service
Highland Hospital
Asheville, NC

Larry H. Strasburger, M.D.
Belmont, MD

Peggy K. Woodhall, A.C.S.W.
Director, Social Work
Highland Hospital
Asheville, NC

I

Unmasking the Psychopath

1

Twenty Years of Experience With the Cleckley Psychopath

Robert D. Hare

Hervey Cleckley has had a major impact on the way we think about psychopathy. His work has had a profound influence on empirical research on psychopathy, both by providing a conceptual framework for the disorder and by serving as a rich source of ideas and testable hypotheses. This chapter will summarize that influence and describe Cleckley's personal impact on research.

My original intention was to present an overview of what we know about the psychophysiological correlates of psychopathy. However, several reviews of this literature are already available (e.g., Hare, 1978, 1980a; Raine, 1985; Siddle and Trasler, 1981; Venables and Raine (1985). What I propose to do instead is to illustrate how Cleckley's formal writings and personal encouragement have influenced one person's research on psychopathy over the past 20 years. Emphasis is placed on my attempts to develop reliable and valid procedures for the assessment of psychopathy, with selective accounts of the psychophysiological research in which these procedures were used. Space limitations prevent inclusion of the extensive data gathered on the criminal behaviors of "Cleckley psychopaths"; these include studies of psycho-

The research described in this chapter was supported by Public Health Grant 609–7–163 from the National Health Grants Program of Canada, the Canadian Mental Health Association, and, since 1973, by Grant MT 4511 from the Medical Research Council of Canada. The cooperation of the staff and inmates of the Correctional Service of Canada and of the British Columbia Corrections Branch is greatly appreciated.

pathy and violence (Hare and McPherson, 1984a), the criminal history
of psychopaths (Hare, 1985a; Hare and Jutai, 1983), and the performance of psychopaths following conditional release from prison (Kropp,
Hart, and Hare, 1985).

Most of the research described below was conducted with white male
inmates of federal maximum and minimum security institutions in
British Columbia.

EARLY DAYS

In the early 1960s, the author worked for eight months as a psychologist at the British Columbia Penitentiary, a maximum security institution near Vancouver. It was my first job after receiving an M.A., and
my first exposure to criminals in prison. In retrospect, it is clear that
many of the inmates were psychopaths. However, at the time neither
the professional staff nor the custodial officers showed much interest
in psychiatric categories. When I left to begin study towards a Ph.D.,
I knew quite a lot about criminals and prisons but very little about
psychopathy as a formal construct.

The results of doctoral research on the effects of punishment on human behavior, conducted with university students, were readily interpreted in terms of Mowrer's (1947) two-process theory of avoidance
learning. Mowrer postulated that there were two stages in learning to
avoid punishment. In the first, cues associated with punishment ac-
quire the capacity, through classical conditioning, to elicit conditioned
fear responses. The second stage consists of the reinforcement, by fear-
reduction, of responses that are instrumental in removing the individual
from the fear-producing cues. Punishment can be avoided by making
some other response (active avoidance) or by inhibiting the punished
response (passive avoidance). Because of the importance of anxiety in
Mowrer's theory, it was quite common at the time for researchers to
use self-report anxiety scales to select low and high anxiety groups,
or to compare normal individuals with clinical groups characterized
by high anxiety. While completing my dissertation I began thinking
about the possibility of doing research with individuals who fell at the
lower end of the anxiety continuum. Psychopaths seemed to be the most
obvious choice for this purpose. In reviewing the literature on psychopathy I was particularly impressed by Hervey Cleckley's *The Mask of*

Sanity, then in its third (1955) edition, and by David Lykken's (1957) paper on anxiety and psychopathy.

Cleckley's book was a revelation. In clear, elegant prose he presented richly detailed descriptions of individuals whose personality and behavior were strikingly like those of many of the criminals I had encountered at the B. C. Penitentiary several years before. I was persuaded that psychopathy was a salient, clinical entity and not simply a convenient theoretical construct. Twenty years of research with criminals has reinforced this position.

The clinical basis for Lykken's study was Cleckley's conception of psychopathy. He used a classical conditioning paradigm in which a conditioned stimulus (CS) of five seconds' duration was followed by an unconditioned stimulus (UCS); the CS was a buzzer and the UCS was an electric shock. The conditioned response (CR) was defined as an increase in palmar electrodermal activity that occurred between the onset of the CS and the onset of the UCS. He found that the CRs of psychopathic criminals developed more slowly, and extinguished more rapidly, than those of neurotic criminals and normal noncriminals. He also found that the psychopaths performed poorly on a passive-avoidance learning task; that is, they failed to inhibit a response punished with electric shock. These two findings, interpreted in terms of Mowrer's two-process theory of avoidance learning, offered an explanation for the psychopath's apparent inability to avoid punishment.

By the time I received a Ph.D. in 1963, several lines of research seemed worth following. My first teaching position was in the Psychology Department at the University of British Columbia, and I therefore found it convenient to begin my study of psychopathy at the B.C. Penitentiary, some 20 miles away. After working out administrative details with the warden and his staff, the first problem was how to go about soliciting volunteers. The solution was relatively simple and very effective. A classification officer who was widely respected by both inmates and staff convinced an inmate at the top of the prison hierarchy that the research would have no negative consequences for those who participated, and that it might even be of some use in understanding criminal behavior. The inmate became our spokesman, telling other inmates that the research had his endorsement and that he was planning to take part in it. A large proportion of the inmate population thereupon volunteered their services as subjects.

The second problem was a bit more difficult. It had to do with the methods used to identify those inmates who were psychopaths. There were two main methods available: psychological tests, including self-report inventories, and clinical-behavioral assessments. Self-report inventories, particularly the Minnesota Multiphasic Personality Inventory (MMPI; Dahlstrom and Welsh, 1960), are popular among psychologists because they are easy to administer and score and are capable of providing an operational definition of psychopathy that other investigators can readily understand. Moreover, the inmates do most of the work, in effect diagnosing themselves.

In spite of these advantages I was skeptical about the usefulness of psychological tests in the assessment of criminals. Prison psychologists frequently were required to provide personality profiles of inmates and to make some sort of prediction about how they would do on parole or in some treatment program. The discrepancies between these profiles and what everyone in the prison knew about the inmates in question were often dramatic and sometimes personally embarrassing. Part of the problem was that most inmates were test-wise and saw no reason for revealing anything of real significance to prison staff, unless it was useful for them to do so. An additional problem was that there was no evidence that the methods used to identify psychopathic inmates were valid.

A popular procedure (still used) was to define psychopaths in terms of a particular MMPI profile; several "cookbook" formulas were available for this purpose. For example, elevated scores on the Psychopathic Deviate (*Pd*) and the Hypomania (*Ma*) scales of the MMPI were often used as an operational definition for psychopathy. Many psychologists who were engaged in research on psychopathy, as well as some journal editors and reviewers, preferred operational definitions of this sort, even though there was little evidence that they actually identified inmates who fit clinical conceptions of psychopathy. As a result, the literature was (and still is) cluttered with studies that purported to be about psychopathy but that actually had an uncertain and tenuous relationship to the clinical concept. For these reasons, and also because I wished to do justice to the view of psychopathy reflected in clinical experience, I decided to forego the convenience of self-report inventories when working with criminals and to concentrate on clinical-behavioral assessment procedures.

My initial diagnoses were based on the assumption that clinicians familiar with Cleckley's work and with the clinical views that it reflects (see, e.g., Maughs, 1941; Arieti, 1967; Craft, 1965; McCord and Mc-Cord, 1964; Karpman, 1961) would have little difficulty in deciding whether or not a given criminal was a psychopath, providing that they knew a lot about the individual, were familiar with the ground rules, and were not unduly biased against using diagnostic labels. Psychiatric diagnoses had a bad reputation, but it was also clear that these diagnoses were often made by clinicians with different backgrounds and experience, each of whom used his own conceptual framework and procedure. In my early studies staff psychologists were made thoroughly familiar with Cleckley's work before they were asked to use a list of 12 of his criteria to classify inmates as psychopaths (P) or nonpsychopaths (NP). Agreement among psychologists was generally good (although not quantified), and disagreements were resolved by discussion.

TEMPORAL GRADIENT OF FEAR AROUSAL

The first study with this assessment procedure was influenced by Lykken's (1957) avoidance learning study and by clinical accounts of the psychopath's apparent lack of concern for future events, particularly punishments. A later theoretical paper (Hare 1965a) suggested that psychopaths differ from normal persons in the temporal integration of rewards and punishments (cf., Renner, 1964). The paper argued that psychopathy was characterized by a relatively steep temporal gradient of fear arousal and response inhibition. That is, as the temporal remoteness of punishment increases, the amount of fear elicited by cues associated with the punishment (e.g., thinking about it) decreases more rapidly for psychopaths than it does for others. To the extent that anticipatory fear mediates response inhibition, the psychopath would be unlikely to inhibit a response for which the reward is immediate and the anticipated punishment is remote in time.

In a laboratory test of the temporal gradient of fear arousal hypothesis (Hare, 1965b), palmar skin conductance (mediated by the sympathetic nervous system) was recorded while an inmate watched the numbers 1 to 12 appear in sequence before him; each number appeared for three seconds. He was told that when the number 8 appeared he would receive a strong electric shock to the fingers. As predicted, increases in skin conductance prior to the shock were smaller, and began later, for inmates in Group P than for those in Group NP. That is, even though only a brief time span was involved, psychopaths did not show any increase in fear (as reflected in skin conductance) until just before the shock was to be delivered.

A related study using the same assessment procedure (Hare, 1966) asked prison inmates to choose between an immediate electric shock to the fingers and one that was delayed 10 seconds. There was some evidence that normal persons preferred to receive an immediate punishment (electric shock) rather than one that was delayed (Cook and Barnes, 1964), probably because waiting for something umpleasant to occur can be as bad as, or worse than, the event itself. I reasoned that psychopaths, with their steep temporal gradient of fear arousal, would not really care about when they received the shock, whereas other criminals would prefer immediate shock to one that was delayed. This is precisely what happened: 88% of the choices made by Group NP, but only 56% of the choices made by Group P, were for immediate shock; a noncriminal group chose immediate shock 79% of the time. It appeared that psychopaths, unlike most people, did not find it particularly distressing to wait for some unpleasant event.

RATINGS OF PSYCHOPATHY

In the next few studies we added a middle or mixed group (M) of inmates who met some of the Cleckley criteria but who did not qualify for inclusion in Group P. Rather than rely on staff personnel to make the diagnoses, we began to make them ourselves. This procedure of placing inmates into one of three groups was later replaced with a global clinical rating scale. In making these ratings, each inmate was ordered along a 7-point scale according to the extent to which his personality and behavior over a long period were consistent with Cleckley's conception of psychopathy. The ratings were based on interview and case-history information and were very reliable (interrater correlations of around .90). For research purposes, psychopaths (P) were generally identified by mean ratings of 6–7 and nonpsychopaths (NP) by mean ratings of 1–3. The remaining inmates constituted a middle or mixed group (M).

PATTERNS OF AUTONOMIC ACTIVITY

This 7-point rating system was used in a classical conditioning study that produced some unexpected results (Hare and Quinn, 1971). Recall that Lykken (1957) was able to relate poor electrodermal conditioning in psychopaths to their apparent inability to avoid punishment. In this case, it was assumed that electrodermal activity (e.g., increases in skin conductance) reflected fear arousal. Other studies of electrodermal activity in psychopaths (see reviews by Hare, 1978; Raine, 1985; Siddle and Trasler, 1981; Venables, 1985) are consistent in finding that psychopaths are indeed poor electrodermal conditioners when the UCS is a noxious stimulus.

The study involved two types of UCS: electric shock and color slides of nude females. Three different tones or conditioned stimuli, each 10 seconds long, were presented 16 times each in random order. One tone was always followed by a strong electric shock, one by a two-second presentation of a slide, and one was not followed by anything. In addition to electrodermal activity, we recorded heart rate, respiration rate, and vasomotor (digital and cephalic) activity. The results were quite dramatic: Group NP developed large conditioned electrodermal responses in anticipation of shock, whereas Group P completely failed to do so; Group M fell between these extreme groups, though much closer to Group P than to Group NP. Similar results were obtained with slides of nude females as the UCS, although in this case the differences among groups were not nearly as large.

In contrast, there were no differences among groups in the extent to which conditioned heart rate and digital vasomotor responses developed. All three groups acquired conditioned cardiovascular responses in anticipation of both the shock and the slides. That is, the psychopaths showed poor electrodermal, but good cardiovascular, conditionability. The results with the shock UCS posed a problem for the position that psychopaths show little fear arousal in anticipation of an unpleasant event; the electrodermal results were consistent with this position but the cardiovascular ones were not. We of course recognized that cardiovascular responses are complexly determined and that, in the particular procedure used, they may have reflected something other than fear arousal (Hare, 1972a). Two subsequent studies suggested that this may indeed have been the case.

In the first of these studies (Hare and Craigen, 1974), we recorded skin conductance, heart rate, and respiratory activity from inmates engaged in a two-person mixed-motive game — a game in which one individual's actions have clear outcomes for himself and for the other individual involved. On each trial one inmate (referred to as A) had to choose the intensity of electric shock to be delivered to himself and to the other inmate (referred to as B). The weaker the shock chosen by A for himself, the stronger the shock received by B, and vice versa. B was then given a chance to retaliate. A 10-second warning tone preceded delivery of each shock; each inmate thus knew precisely when he and the other inmate would receive a shock. Compared with nonpsychopaths (NP), psychopaths (P) gave small skin conductance responses, but large heart rate responses (acceleration followed by deceleration), in anticipation of shock delivered to themselves or others.

In the second study (Hare, Frazelle, and Cox, 1978), skin conductance and heart rate were recorded from inmates while the numbers 1–9 were counted out loud; the count took 24 seconds and was followed by a very loud noise. Again, psychopaths gave relatively small skin conductance responses, but large heart rate responses, in anticipation of an unpleasant stimulus.

MODULATION OF SENSORY INPUT

The results of these three studies are difficult to interpret if one assumes that increases in skin conductance and heart rate each reflect the same thing, in this case, fear arousal. However, it is possible that cardiovascular activity plays an important role in the modulation of sensory input. Lacey (1967; Lacey and Lacey, 1974) has argued that heart rate deceleration and decreased pressure in the carotid sinus serve to increase cortical arousal and to facilitate "sensory-intake," whereas heart rate acceleration and increased carotid pressure are associated with decreased cortical arousal and "sensory-rejection." Similarly, heart rate deceleration is part of the orienting response (OR) associated with increased sensitivity to the environment, while heart rate acceleration is part of the defensive response (DR) associated with decreased sensitivity to the environment. Transient (phasic) changes in heart rate may therefore influence or reflect the way in which sensory input is modulated (see Coles, Jennings, and Stern, 1984, for critical discussions of the Lacey model). Presumably, anticipatory heart rate acceleration is part of an adaptive process that helps the individual to cope with, "tune-out," or otherwise reduce the impact of premonitory cues and the impending aversive stimulus.

I have argued elsewhere (Hare, 1972a, 1978) that the psychopath's pattern of electrodermal and cardiovascular activity in anticipation of an unpleasant event may reflect the operation of an active coping mechanism (large increases in heart rate) and, as a consequence, the inhibition of fear arousal (small increases in skin conductance). If so, situations that have great emotional impact for most people may be of little concern to psychopaths. Moreover, they may have difficulty in avoiding punishment because the cues that would help them to do so are tuned out and the mediating effects of anticipatory fear are greatly reduced.

In evaluating this model of defensive coping in psychopaths, Venables (1985) concluded that the postulated sequence of events was tenable from a physiological point of view; that is, the increase in heart rate occurred quickly enough to have a modulating effect on skin conductance responses. Fowles (1980) has suggested that the data could be understood by postulating that psychopathy is associated with a weak or deficient behavioral inhibition system, which results in reduced electrodermal activity in response to threatening stimuli and increased heart rate when active coping responses are made.

Whatever the merits of these models, it should be emphasized that other interpretations of the results are possible. Moreover, we have no direct evidence that the psychopath's pattern of electrodermal and cardiovascular activity actually reflects the operation of an active coping process. Until appropriate empirical data are available, this process is really only an inference drawn from physiological activity, the psychological implications of which are not well understood.

Still, it is interesting that Yochelson and Samenow (1976), though working from a psychodynamic perspective, came to somewhat the same conclusion about habitual criminals, many of whom were probably psychopaths. Their description of the "cutoff" process by which habitual criminals inhibit fear and eliminate danger signals is compatible with the physiological coping mechanism that I have postulated for psychopaths.

There are other similarities between these physiological and psychodynamic models. For example, the results of two studies, one involving electrodermal and cardiovascular activity (Hare, 1982), the other electrocortical activity (Jutai and Hare, 1983), suggest that psychopaths may use active coping mechanisms when the nature of the situation forces them to pay attention to warning cues, but that under other conditions they may be able to focus attention on things of immediate interest, effectively ignoring warning cues and other stimuli not of immediate interest to them. Yochelson and Samenow came to a similar conclusion: They suggested that the habitual criminal's restricted vision allows him to focus attention on one thing at a time and to exclude everything else.

If psychopaths are able to deal effectively with unpleasant signals and events, the origins of this ability are unclear. Rotenberg (1978) has argued that most of the behaviors referred to as psychopathic reflect various "differential insensitivities"; they may be socially functional or dysfunctional, and result from specific formal or informal desensitizing-socialization experiences (in much the same way that medical students become desensitized to autopsies). There is no indication of what these experiences might be or how people from a wide variety of backgrounds can, from a very early age, show signs of what will ultimately emerge as a common core of personality traits and behaviors. My own view is that the psychopath's social insensitivities and core attributes are more the result of constitutional (perhaps genetic) factors than the result of experience (see also Mednick and Christiansen, 1977; Mednick and Moffit, 1985; Schulsinger, 1974).

BEHAVIOR UNDER STRESS

Incidentally, the argument that psychopaths may be very good at focusing attention has some implications for the popular clinical belief that they are likely to be calm and cool under stress or in an emergency. An unusual ability to focus attention may or may not be a good thing, depending on the extent to which the cues required to handle things effectively are also the ones that are attended to. For example, some psychopaths were considered to be fearless fighter pilots during World War II, but in the excitement of battle they often failed to keep track of details (fuel supply, where they were, the position of other planes in their own squadron, etc.) that were important for their own survival as well as that of their comrades.

The electrocortical study by Jutai and Hare (1983) suggests that psychopaths tend to distribute their attentional resources in favor of stimuli that are most salient and interesting to them, at the expense of other less interesting, but nevertheless task-relevant, stimuli. That is, cues necessary for efficient performance of a task could easily be missed. The results of a second electrocortical study (Hare, Jutai, and Connolly, 1985) in fact suggest that psychopaths may have difficulty in allocating their attentional and processing resources between the competing demands of two tasks. It appears that rather than distributing resources between tasks they focus attention on the one that is most interesting to them. To generalize these laboratory findings to real life, one should be very reluctant to entrust his safety to a psychopath unless he can be certain that the task-relevant cues are the only ones the psychopath finds interesting.

PERCEPTUAL-COGNITIVE FACTORS

My recent interest in cognitive processes in psychopaths is part of a gradual shift away from emphasis on autonomic nervous system activity as primarily an indicant of emotional arousal. Research and theory on psychopaths have made heavy use of such constructs as fear and anxiety, usually inferred from paradigms in which aversive or painful stimulation was used and electrodermal activity recorded. Some investigators have used the results of these studies to suggest that psychopaths may not have the physiological capacity for experiencing fear or anxiety; that is, it is sometimes assumed (often implicitly) that small electrodermal responses to aversive events and threatening situations reflect not only an absence of fear but also a functionally hyporesponsive or "sluggish" autonomic nervous system.

However, there is ample evidence that psychopaths are quite capable of giving normal electrodermal (and other autonomic) responses under appropriate conditions (see Hare, 1968, 1978). Anomalies in the autonomic responses of psychopaths are more likely a reflection of the particular motivational and cognitive demands placed on them, than of an autonomic nervous system that does not function properly. Moreover, it would be misleading to assume that electrodermal activity, even when recorded in a context containing elements of threat, is necessarily associated with fear arousal or apprehension. Most autonomic responses, including electrodermal ones, are relatively nonspecific, and can be elicited by a wide range of nonthreatening events (including interest, surprise, cognitions, etc.).

DETECTION OF DECEPTION

Lie detection is an example of the sort of problem that can occur when these considerations are not taken into account. In one study (Raskin and Hare, 1978), prison inmates were either "guilty" or "innocent" of committing a mock crime (taking $20 from a drawer). They were then given a field-type interview and a control-question polygraph examination by the senior author of the study. Each inmate was instructed to deny having taken the money. If the polygraph examination found an inmate to be "innocent," he was either allowed to keep the money if he was in the "guilty" group or given $20 if he was in the "innocent" group. Clinical folklore and previous research on autonomic activity in psychopaths suggested that the psychopaths should have had little difficulty in "beating the polygraph." However, deception was just as readily detected in the psychopaths as it was in the other inmates. "Guilty" psychopaths, like other "guilty" inmates, gave larger electrodermal and heart rate responses to the relevant questions than to the control questions.

Although this may mean that the psychopaths became emotionally aroused or anxious when responding to the relevant questions (e.g., "Did you take that $20?"), it is more likely that the physiological activity reflected cognitive responses to a psychologically significant question. In this regard, it is interesting that the heart rate response elicited by the relevant and control questions included an initial period of acceleration in both "guilty" and "innocent" subjects. This initial acceleration was probably associated with the preparatory and motor responses involved in answering the question. In the "innocent" subjects this increase in heart rate was followed by a return to the pre-question baseline. However, in "guilty" subjects the initial acceleration was followed by a period of deceleration to a point well below the pre-question baseline.

We suggested that this deceleration was part of an attentional process (cf., Lacey, 1967) in which the subject attempted to determine the examiner's response to his deception. This decelerative response was larger in psychopaths than it was in the other inmates, suggesting that they may have been unusually attentive to cues emanating from the examiner. Presumably the polygraph examination was a challenge for them, and they wanted to get as much information as possible on how well they were doing (in this case, by attempting to use their ability to "read" people).

Two things are worth pointing out here. In the first place, the implications that laboratory studies of lie detection have for real-life situations (where the stakes are considerably higher) are uncertain. Secondly, even if psychopaths are generally emotionally unresponsive and unlikely to give normal physiological responses in situations that others find unpleasant or threatening, it is still quite possible that a polygraph examination can be structured so that psychopaths will give differential responses to the perceptual-cognitive demands associated with relevant and control questions.

A 22-ITEM CHECKLIST FOR PSYCHOPATHY

Returning to assessment issues, the global 7-point rating scale, though reliable, valid, and useful, was not without its problems. It was often difficult for others to evaluate our assessment and to determine precisely what went into a particular rating. At the same time, the rating procedure required an extensive knowledge of the concept of psychopathy, particularly as expressed by Cleckley, and the ability to integrate large amounts of interview and case-history data into a single score. This does not mean that other investigators were not able to use our procedures successfully. For example, Dengerink and Bertilson (1975) used the 7-point scale with 92 inmates of a prison in which we had conducted some of our research. They obtained an interrater reliability of .92. We had previously rated some of the same inmates; the correlation between their ratings and ours was .88, indicating that the procedure was replicable across investigators. Nevertheless, there was a clear need for a more objective assessment procedure, preferably one tailored for prison populations, where most of the research on psychopathy is carried out.

The initial work on the development of such a procedure began in 1978 (see Hare, 1980b, 1985b, for details). Because we wished to retain the essence of psychopathy embodied in Cleckley's work, we began with an analysis of his 16 criteria for psychopathy; they are presented in Table 1, along with some statistical data discussed below. In order to determine the psychometric properties of this list, we used interview and case-history data to rate 143 prison inmates on each of the 16 characteristics. A 3-point scale was used for this purpose, with 0 indicating that the characteristic definitely was not present or did not apply, 1 indicating some uncertainty about whether or not it applied, and 2 indicating that it definitely was present or applied.

The distribution of scores, though approximately normal, had a slight negative skew. The total scores ranged from 6 to 32 (mean = 22.8; median = 24.0; standard deviation = 5.67). Coefficient alpha, which takes into account the number of items and the average correlation among them, was .80, indicating reasonably good internal consistency. However, some of the characteristics (2, 3, 14) had very low correlations with the total score (see Table 1) and probably do not belong in the list, at least when it is used with a criminal population. A principal components analysis and varimax rotation of the 16 items yielded five factors; only the first two are described here. Factor 1 (defined by items 9, 10, 12, 5, 6, 15) reflected what most clinicians consider to be at the core of psychopathy: an inability to develop warm, genuine relationships with others, a lack of empathy, and a callous disregard for the rights and feelings of others. Factor 2 (defined by items 16, 4, 8) reflected an unstable, transient lifestyle, with an absence of long-

TABLE 1

Sixteen Characteristics of the Psychopath Listed by Cleckley

Characteristic	Correlation with total score[a]
1. Superficial charm and good intelligence	.26
2. Absence of delusions and other signs of irrational thinking	− .02
3. Absence of "nervousness" or psychoneurotic manifestations	.05
4. Unreliability	.42
5. Untruthfulness and insincerity	.65
6. Lack of remorse or shame	.43
7. Inadequately motivated antisocial behavior	.53
8. Poor judgement and failure to learn by experience	.32
9. Pathologic Egocentricity and incapacity for love	.76
10. General poverty in major affective reactions	.71
11. Specific loss of insight	.36
12. Unresponsiveness in general interpersonal relations	.59
13. Fantastic and uninviting behavior with drink and sometimes without	.36
14. Suicide rarely carried out	.21
15. Sex life impersonal, trivial and poorly integrated	.44
16. Failure to follow any life plan	.33
Coefficient alpha = .80	

Note. From Cleckley (1976). The statistical analyses are based on data from 143 male prison inmates.
[a]Corrected for overlap.

term plans and commitments. Several statistical analyses indicated that our global diagnoses of psychopathy were determined primarily by the characteristics represented by these two factors.

We began development of a new scale for use with criminals by listing all of the traits and behaviors that we felt were explicitly or implicitly used in making a global assessment of psychopathy (see Hare, 1980b). A series of statistical analyses determined that our clinical judgments could be represented effectively by 22 items (since reduced to 20 items; see Table 2). Each item was scored on a 3-point scale, with 0 indicating that the item did not apply, 1 indicating some uncertainty about whether or not it applied, and 2 indicating that it did apply to the inmate. Although some of the items in the checklist involved complex behaviors and required difficult clinical inference, early indications were that the scale was highly reliable. For example, the interrater reliability of total scores for 143 inmates was .93 and coefficient alpha was .88. Principal components analysis of the items yielded five factors which were highly correlated with the factors derived from the Cleckley criteria; the first canonical correlation between the two sets of factors was .90.

Subsequent research with the 22-item checklist confirmed its high reliability. For example, Schroeder, Schroeder, and Hare (1983) evaluated the checklist in terms of both generalizability (G) theory and classical test theory indices of reliability. G theory (see Jackson and Paunonen, 1980) provides a single index of the reliability of measurement, whereas classical test score theory may require that many indices of reliability (e.g., inter- and intrarater reliability, internal consistency) and their relative importance be determined. The generalizability coefficient (GC) for 301 inmates studied over five years was .90. The GC is an intraclass correlation coefficient that ranges from 0 to 1 and is interpreted in much the same way as a reliability coefficient.

A 20-ITEM REVISED PSYCHOPATHY CHECKLIST

In spite of the success of the 22-item scale, we have recently revised it slightly in order to make it easier for others to use. The items in the Psychopathy Checklist (as the 20-item version is called) are presented in Table 2. A manual (Hare 1985c) containing a complete description of the items and scoring procedures is available on request. The two versions of the checklist are substantively identical, have virtually the same psychometric properties, and classify inmates in the same way.

TABLE 2

Items in the Revised (20-item) Psychopathy Checklist

1. Glibness/superficial charm
2. Grandiose sense of self-worth
3. Need for stimulation/proneness to boredom
4. Pathological lying
5. Conning/manipulative
6. Lack of remorse or guilt
7. Shallow affect
8. Callous/lack of empathy
9. Parasitic lifestyle
10. Poor behavioral controls
11. Promiscuous sexual behavior
12. Early behavior problems
13. Lack of realistic, long-term plans
14. Impulsivity
15. Irresponsibility
16. Failure to accept responsibility for own actions
17. Many short-term marital relationships
18. Juvenile delinquency
19. Revocation of conditional release
20. Criminal versatility

From Hare (1985c).

Because most of our research thus far has involved the 22-item version, it forms the basis for the results presented below.

COMPARISONS AMONG ASSESSMENT PROCEDURES

A recent study illustrates the difficulties that can arise when one investigator uses these clinical-behavioral procedures while another uses self-report inventories. In this study (Hare, 1985d), 274 male prison inmates were assessed for psychopathy with a variety of different methods. The clinical-behavioral procedures were the 22-item checklists, global ratings of psychopathy on a 7-point scale, and diagnoses of Antisocial Personality Disorder (APD) in accordance with criteria listed in the American Psychiatric Association's (1980) *Diagnostic and Statistical Manual of Mental Disorders* (DSM-III). The self-report inventories included the MMPI, the Socialization (*So*) scale from the California Psychological Inventory (Gough, 1969), and an experimental 29-item self-report psychopathy (*SRP*) scale based on the 22-item checklist. In addition, two composite scales used by several investigators were derived from the *So* scale and the *Pd* and *Ma* scales of the MMPI. These composite scales were the sum of the *Pd* and *Ma* scores (*Pd* + *Ma*), and the *Pd* score minus the *So* score (*Pd* − *So*).

The interrater reliability of the ratings and the checklist scores were, respectively, .90 and .89. The kappa coefficient of agreement (Fleiss, 1981) between the two clinicians who made the diagnoses of APD was .79; that is, 79% of the joint diagnoses were in agreement, with chance excluded. It is clear that the three clinical-behavior measures were very reliable. The self-report inventories were somewhat less reliable. Coefficient alpha for each scale was as follows: *SRP* scale, .80; *So* scale, .73; *Pd* scale, .65; *Ma* scale, .67. The reliabilities of the composite scales were not computed.

Table 3 presents the correlations among measures (above diagonal) and the kappa coefficients of agreement between extreme groups (below diagonal). The largest correlations were among the three clinical-behavioral measures, and particularly between the ratings and checklist. Correlations among the self-report measures, and between the clinical-behavioral and self-report domains, were generally small. A principal

TABLE 3

Correlations Between Psychopathy Assessment Procedures (Above Diagonal) and Kappa Coefficients of Agreement Between High and Low Psychopathy Groups (Below Diagonal)

Variable	1	2	3[a]	4	5	6	7	8[b]	9[b]
1. Rating	.	.80	.57	.28	.21	.22	− .29	.27	.36
2. Checklist	.93	.	.67	.38	.26	.27	− .32	.35	.33
3. DSM-III[a]	.71	.79	.	.35	.29	.21	− .37	.33	.44
4. SRP	.31	.42	.44	.	.26	.36	− .53	.40	.49
5. Pd	.16	.27	.37	.36	.	.14	− .34	—	—
6. Ma	.26	.42	.18	.40	.15	.	− .31	—	.27
7. So	.41	.42	.46	.52	.44	.44	.	− .42	—
8. Pd + Ma[b]	.31	.46	.36	.52	—	—	.53	.	—
9. Pd − So[b]	.40	.37	.56	.54	—	.29	—	—	.

Note. Adapted from Hare (1985d). DSM-III = 3rd edition of *Diagnostic and statistical manual of mental disorders* (APA, 1980); SRP = Self-report psychopathy scale; *Pd* = MMPI Psychopathic Deviate scale; *Ma* = MMPI Hypomania scale; *So* = Socialization scale.
[a]Correlations involving DSM-III (0 versus 2 diagnoses of APD) are point-biserial.
[b]Correlations and kappa coefficients between composite measures and their components are omitted.

components analysis of the correlation matrix confirmed the independence of the two domains: Two factors emerged, one defined entirely by the clinical-behavioral measures and the other entirely by the self-report measures.

The kappa coefficients reveal the extent to which the different assessment procedures agreed on the actual classification of inmates. Each distribution of assessment scores was divided into approximate thirds to form groups representing low, medium, and high psychopathy. The two extreme groups from one distribution were then compared with the corresponding groups from another distribution. The kappa coefficients in Table 3 represent the agreement between assessment procedures on which group (low or high) inmates should be classified into. They indicate the proportion of joint decisions about group assignment (made by a given pair of procedures) that were in agreement beyond chance. Diagnostic agreement among the clinical-behavioral measures was very good, whereas agreement among the self-report inventories, and between the clinical-behavioral and self-report domains, was poor.

A proponent of the MMPI would argue that it is not reasonable to use only one or two scales (e.g., the *Pd* and *Ma* scales) for the diagnosis of psychopathy. But this is precisely what the majority of investigators who use the MMPI to select research subjects do. Nevertheless, in order to put the MMPI to a fair test I evaluated a number of standard cookbook procedures for identifying psychopaths on the basis of profiles of scores on the validity and clinical scales. None of these procedures was very successful in picking out inmates who would be considered to be psychopaths according to the clinical-behavioral procedures.

Somewhat better results were obtained when the 13 basic MMPI validity and clinical scales were entered into a discriminant analysis and used to classify inmates into low and high psychopathy groups formed on the basis of clinical-behavioral measures. In one analysis, for example, a linear combination of the 13 MMPI scales was able to classify correctly 72.9% of the inmates into low and high checklist groups. However, the kappa coefficient between predicted and actual group membership was only .45, with 27.6% false positives and 26.8% false negatives.

The results of this particular study may help to explain why the research literature on psychopathy is often confusing and contradictory: Self-report inventories simply do not sort subjects in the same way that clinical-behavioral procedures do. Even among the latter, agreement is not perfect. For example, the 22-item checklist and DSM-

III diagnoses of APD managed to classify a large proportion of inmates into the same groups (kappa coefficient of .79). This is not surprising— each procedure placed considerable emphasis on case-history evidence of antisocial and criminal behaviors. However, the checklist differs from DSM-III in that it also considers personality traits, whereas DSM-III focuses almost exclusively on a list of antisocial acts, some of them trivial. In practice, this means that DSM-III has difficulty in identifying individuals who fit the classic picture of psychopathy but who manage to avoid early or formal contact with the criminal justice system (see Millon, 1981). Certainly many of Cleckley's patients would not have met the criteria for a DSM-III diagnosis of APD. At the same time, some of the individuals who do receive a diagnosis of APD are not psychopaths in the sense that the term is used here.

Returning to the 22-item psychopathy checklist, there is now ample evidence that it is a valid and useful measure of psychopathy in criminal populations. For example, checklist scores are strongly related to criminal activities, violence, institutional behavior, and outcome on conditional release, including parole (Hare, 1985a; Hare and McPherson, 1984a; Kropp, Hart, and Hare, 1985; Wong, 1985).

CEREBRAL SPECIALIZATION FOR LANGUAGE

The checklist has also been used in our recent studies of electrocortical activity and language processing. Although the primary impetus for the latter studies was Cleckley's speculation that psychopaths suffer from a deep-seated semantic disorder, we were also influenced by Flor-Henry's (1976) assertion that the left hemisphere of psychopaths and schizophrenics was damaged or dysfunctional. There is certainly something odd about the way in which psychopaths use language. For example, their behavior is often strikingly inconsistent with their verbalized thoughts, feelings, and tensions. I suspect that more than simple lying, deceit, and dissimulation are involved here; there may be something pathological about the structure and dynamics of the psychopath's language processes.

Cleckley long held that the speech of psychopaths appears to be a mechanically correct artifact that masks a semantic disorder in which the formal, semantic, and affective components of language are dissociated from one another. The nature of this putative disorder was not made clear, but we might surmise that it involves unusual or abnormal interactions among the cortical, subcortical, and limbic mechanisms responsible for the integration of verbal, emotional, and social behavior. However, before speculating further along these lines we need to obtain basic data on the ways in which psychopaths use language. One way of doing so is to use procedures that permit inferences to be made about cerebral asymmetries in the organization of language. These include dichotic listening, in which different verbal stimuli are presented simultaneously to each ear, and the divided visual field (DVF) technique, in which verbal stimuli are presented in the right visual hemifield (RVF) or in the left visual hemifield (LVF). Right ear and RVF advantages are typically obtained with verbal material (see Beaumont, 1982; Bryden, 1982), presumably because of left-hemisphere specialization for language.

In an early study with the DVF technique (Hare, 1979), prison inmates were asked to identify 3-letter words that appeared for 80 milliseconds in either the LVF or the RVF, 1.5 degrees to the left or right of a central fixation point. The rationale for this procedure was that visual stimuli presented in a given hemifield project directly to the contralateral hemisphere. The study assumed that if the left hemisphere of psychopaths is dysfunctional, performance should be less lateralized in favor of the RVF-left hemisphere than it is in normal people.

There were in fact no differences between psychopaths and other criminals in performance of the task; both groups identified words presented in the RVF more accurately than they did words presented in the LVF. Nevertheless, the task required only simple recognition of common words, and I suggested that group differences might emerge with tasks that require a greater degree of semantic involvement.

In commenting on these results, Cleckley (personal communication, April 24, 1980) said that although the study "did not indicate a specific defect in the psychopath of the dominant hemisphere, I have sometimes wondered if fairly recent concepts about our bicameral brain may eventually be developed and with much additional knowledge finally throw some better light on the mystery of why the psychopath, who apparently has so many assets, can misuse them or fail to use them sensibly. . . . Are there ways to investigate the possibility of subtle deficits of integration between some recently surmised functions of the nondominant hemisphere and those of the dominant hemisphere?" Some of our recent research (described by Hare and Connolly, 1985) suggests that there may indeed be subtle deficits, or at least anomalies, in the interhemispheric organization of the psychopath's language processes.

In one study (Jutai and Hare, 1985) we used a more semantically complex version of the DVF task described above. We presented concrete nouns in either the LVF or the RVF under three conditions. One condition involved simple recognition of the sort used in the previous study. The other two conditions required semantic elaboration. That is, the inmate had to decide whether a given word was a member or exemplar of a specified semantic category, in one case quite concrete and in the other abstract. We expected that differences between psychopaths and others would be most likely to occur on the abstract categorization task. The words appeared for 80 milliseconds and were located 1.5 degrees to the right or left of a central fixation point. The subjects were all consistently right-handed males; they included 39 prison inmates, divided into three groups (P, M, NP) on the basis of scores on the 22-item psychopathy checklist, and 25 noncriminals.

The results were in line with expectation and can be summarized as follows. The performance of the noncriminals was consistent with the literature on lateralized information-processing tasks; that is, the task that required the most semantic elaboration (the abstract categorization task) produced the largest RVF-left hemisphere advantage. Among the criminals only the performance of the psychopaths (P) stood out. For them, the abstract categorization task produced a marked LVF-*right hemisphere* advantage, whereas their performance on the other tasks was not much different from that of the noncriminals. Some interpretations of this curious finding are offered following a brief description of results from another lateralized information-processing task, dichotic listening.

In this study (Hare and McPherson, 1984b) we presented two sets of words through stereophonic headphones, one set to the left ear and the other simultaneously to the right ear. Because the dominant projections from each ear are to the contralateral hemisphere, and because the left hemisphere is usually specialized for language, verbal stimuli presented to the right ear typically are more accurately identified than are those presented to the left ear; that is, a right ear advantage is obtained. The subjects were 146 male inmates, divided into three groups (P, M, NP), and 159 male noncriminals. They were instructed to report, after each trial, any words that they could identify. The noncriminals and Group NP showed a strong right ear advantage, whereas Group P (and to a lesser extent, Group M) showed only a slight right ear advantage. That is, the performance of the psychopaths was less lateralized than that of the other subjects. Even when the psychopaths were instructed to focus attention on one ear at a time, their right ear performance did not improve.

It is not possible to draw any firm conclusions from these two studies, but the consistency of the results suggests that psychopaths may differ from others in the cerebral organization of some perceptual and cognitive processes. One hypothesis worth investigating further is that in psychopaths the left hemisphere is not as specialized for language as it is in normal individuals. Another possibility is based on evidence that perceptual asymmetries on lateralized information processing tasks, as well as some personality characteristics and psychopathological processes, may be related to hemispheric differences in arousal (Hellige, 1983; Levy, 1983; Tucker, 1981). For example, relatively high left hemisphere arousal may be associated with rightward perceptual tendencies and with enhanced right ear and right visual field advantages. For some unknown reason psychopaths may be characterized by asymmetrically low left hemisphere arousal (cf. Tucker, 1981). This asymmetric arousal hypothesis is not necessarily incompatible with the hypothesis that language is weakly lateralized in psychopaths.

Even if these hypotheses are tenable, they are not readily translated into adequate explanations for the complex behavior of psychopaths. About all one can do at this point is offer some speculations. For example, if psychopaths are not strongly lateralized for language, or if their dominant hemisphere is asymmetrically underaroused, they may tend to use cognitive strategies and to exhibit overt behaviors that rely little on verbal, logical, and sequential operations (see Tucker, 1981). At the same time, language should play a relatively ineffective role in the regulation of their behavior (cf., Schalling, 1978). Both possibilities may have some bearing on Cleckley's suggestion that psychopaths have a deep-rooted semantic disorder in which the normal connections between semantic and affective components of language are missing or dysfunctional. Some of our current research is directed toward these issues.

REFERENCES

American Psychiatric Association (1980). *Diagnostic and statistical manual of mental disorders* (3rd ed.). Washington, DC: Author.

Arieti, S. (1967). *The intrapsychic self.* New York: Basic Books.

Beaumont, J. G. (Ed.). (1982). *Divided visual field studies of cerebral organization*. New York: Academic Press.

Bryden, M. P. (1982). *Laterality: Functional asymmetry in the intact brain*. New York: Academic Press.

Cleckley, H. (1976). *The mask of sanity* (5th ed.). St. Louis, MO: Mosby.

Coles, M. G. H., Jennings, J. R., and Stern, J. A. (1984). *Psychophysiological perspectives: Festschrift for Beatrice and John Lacey*. New York: Van Nostrand Reinhold.

Cook, J. O., and Barnes, L. W. (1964). Choice of delay of inevitable shock. *Journal of Abnormal and Social Psychology, 68,* 669–672.

Craft, M. J. (1965). *Ten studies into psychopathic personality*. Bristol: John Wright.

Dahlstrom, W. M., and Welsh, G. S. (1960). *An MMPI handbook: A guide to use in clinical practice and research*. Minneapolis, MN: University of Minnesota Press.

Dengerink, H. A., and Bertilson, H. S. (1975). Psychopathy and physiological arousal in an aggressive task. *Psychophysiology, 12,* 682–684.

Fleiss, J. L. (1981). *Statistical methods for rates and proportions*. New York: Wiley.

Flor-Henry, P. (1976). Lateralized temporal-limbic dysfunction and psychopathology. *Annals of the New York Academy of Sciences, 280,* 777–797.

Fowles, D. C. (1980). The three arousal model: Implications of Gary's two-factor learning theory for heart rate, electrodermal activity, and psychopathy. *Psychophysiology, 17,* 87–104.

Gough, H. G. (1969). *Manual for the California Psychological Inventory*. Palo Alto, CA: Consulting Psychologists Press.

Hare, R. D. (1965a). A conflict and learning theory analysis of psychopathic behavior. *Journal of Research in Crime and Delinquency, 2,* 12–19.

Hare, R. D. (1965b). Temporal gradient of fear arousal in psychopaths. *Journal of Abnormal Psychology, 70,* 442–445.

Hare, R. D. (1966). Psychopathy and choice of immediate and delayed punishment. *Journal of Abnormal Psychology, 71,* 25–29.

Hare, R. D. (1968). Psychopathy, autonomic functioning, and the orienting response. *Journal of Abnormal Psychology*. Monograph Supplement, 73, 1–24.

Hare, R. D. (1972a). *Dissociation of conditioned electrodermal and cardiovascular responses in psychopathy*. Paper presented at the annual Meeting of the Society For Psychophysiological Research, Boston.

Hare, R. D. (1972b). Psychopathy and physiological responses to adrenalin. *Journal of Abnormal Psychology, 79,* 138–147.

Hare, R. D. (1978). Electrodermal and cardiovascular correlates of psychopathy. In R. D. Hare and D. Schalling (Eds.). *Psychopathic behavior: Approaches to research*. Chichester, England: Wiley.

Hare, R. D. (1979). Psychopathy and laterality of cerebral function. *Journal of Abnormal Psychology, 88,* 605–610.

Hare, R. D. (1980a). Psychopathy. In H. Van Praag, M. Lader, O. Rafaelson, and E. Sacher (Eds.). *Handbook of biological psychiatry*. Part II. New York: Marcel Dekker.

Hare, R. D. (1980b). A research scale for the assessment of psychopathy in criminal populations. *Personality and Individual Differences, 1,* 111–119.

Hare, R. D. (1982). Psychopathy and physiological activity during anticipation of an aversive stimulus in a distraction paradigm. *Psychophysiology, 19,* 266–271.

Hare, R. D. (1985a). Criminal Psychopaths. In J. Yuille (Ed.). *Police selection and training: The role of psychology*. Dordrecht, The Netherlands: Martinus Nijhoff.

Hare, R. D. (1985b). A checklist for the assessment of psychopathy. In M. H. Ben-

Aron, S. J. Hucker, and C. D. Webster (Eds.). *Clinical criminology.* Toronto: M and M Graphics.

Hare, R. D. (1985c). *The Psychopathy Checklist.* Unpublished manuscript, Department of Psychology, University of British Columbia, Vancouver, Canada.

Hare, R. D. (1985d). Comparison of procedures for the assessment of psychopathy. *Journal of Consulting and Clinical Psychology, 53,* 7–16.

Hare, R. D., and Connolly, J. F. (1985). In S. Mednick and T. Moffit (Eds.). *Biology and crime.* Cambridge: Cambridge University Press.

Hare, R. D., and Craigen, D. (1974). Psychopathy and physiological activity in a mixed-motive game situation. *Psychophysiology, 11,* 197–206.

Hare, R. D., Frazelle, J., and Cox, D. N. (1978). Psychopathy and physiological responses to threat of an aversive stimulus. *Psychophysiology, 15,* 165–172.

Hare, R. D., and Jutai, J. W. (1983). Criminal history of the male psychopath: Some preliminary data. In K. T. Van Dusen and S. A. Mednick (Eds.). *Prospective studies of crime and delinquency.* Boston: Kluwer-Nijhoff Publishing.

Hare, R. D., Jutai, J. W., and Connolly, J. F. (1985). *Psychopathy and allocation of attentional resources during performance of a dual-task.* Manuscript submitted for publication.

Hare, R. D., and McPherson, L. M. (1984a). Violent and aggressive behavior by criminal psychopaths. *International Journal of Law and Psychiatry, 7,* 35–50.

Hare, R. D., and McPherson, L. M. (1984b). Psychopathy and perceptual assymetry during verbal dichotic listening. *Journal of Abnormal Psychology, 93,* 141–149.

Hare, R. D., and Quinn, M. J. (1971). Psychopathy and autonomic conditioning. *Journal of Abnormal Psychology, 77,* 223–235.

Hellige, J. B. (1983). Hemisphere X task interaction and the study of laterality. In J. B. Hellige (Ed.). *Cerebral hemisphere asymmetry: Method, theory, and application.* New York: Praeger.

Jackson D. N., Paunonen, S. V. : Personality structure and assessment (1980). in M. R. Rosenzweig and L. W. Porter (Eds.), *Annual Review Of Psychology,* Vol. 31, Palo Alto, CA: Annual Reviews, Inc.

Jutai, J. W., and Hare, R. D. (1983). Psychopathy and selective attention during performance of a complex perceptual-motor task. *Psychophysiology, 20,* 146–151.

Jutai, J. W., and Hare, R. D. (1985). *Psychopathy and cerebral asymmetry in semantic processing.* Manuscript submitted for publication.

Karpman, B. (1961). The structure of neurosis: With special differentials between neurosis, psychosis, homosexuality, alcoholism, psychopathy, and criminality. *Archives of Criminal Psychodynamics, 4,* 599–646.

Kropp, R., Hart, S., and Hare, R. D. (1985). *Psychopathy and performance after conditional release from prison.* Manuscript in preparation.

Lacey, J. I. (1967). Somatic response patterning and stress: Some revisions of activation theory. In N. H. Appley and R. Trumbell (Eds.). *Psychological stress: Issues in research.* New York: Appleton-Century-Crofts.

Lacey, B. C., and Lacey, J. I. (1974). Studies of heart rate and other bodily processes in sensorimotor behavior. In P. A. Obrist, A. H. Black, J. Brener, and L. V. Dicara (Eds.). *Cardiovascular psychophysiology: Current issues in response mechanisms, biofeedback, and methodology.* Chicago: Aldine-Atherton.

Levy, J. (1983). Individual differences in cerebral hemisphere asymmetry: Theoretical issues and experimental considerations. In J. B. Hellige (Ed.). *Cerebral hemisphere asymmetry: Method, theory, and application.* New York: Praeger.

Lykken, D. T. (1957). A study of anxiety in the sociopathic personality. *Journal of Abnormal and Social Psychology, 55,* 6–10.

McCord, W., and McCord, J. (1964). *The psychopath: An essay on the criminal mind.* Princeton, NJ: Van Nostrand.

Maughs, S. B. (1941). Concept of psychopathy and psychopathic personality. Its evolution and historical development. *Journal of Criminal Psychodynamics, 2,* 329–356.

Mednick, S. A., and Christiansen, K. O. (Eds.). (1977). *Biosocial bases of criminal behavior.* New York: Gardner Press.

Mednick, S. A., and Moffit, T. (Eds.). (1985). *Biology and crime.* Cambridge: Cambridge University Press.

Millon, T. (1981). *Disorders of personality; DSM-III: Axis II.* New York: Wiley.

Mowrer, O. H. (1947). On the dual nature of learning—a reinterpretation of conditioning and problem-solving. *Harvard Educational Review, 17,* 102–148.

Raine, A. (1985). Antisocial behavior and social psychophysiology. In H. Wagner (Ed.). *Bodily changes and social behavior: Theory and experiment in social psychophysiology.* London: Wiley.

Raskin, D. C., and Hare, R. D. (1978). Psychopathy and detection of deception in a prison population. *Psychophysiology, 15,* 126–136.

Renner, K. E. (1964). Conflict resolution and the process of temporal resolution. *Psychological Reports, 15,* 423–438. Monograph Supplement No. 2.

Rotenberg, M. (1978). Psychopathy and differential insensitivity. In R. D. Hare and D. Schalling (Eds.). *Psychopathic behavior: Approaches to research.* Chichester, England: Wiley.

Schalling, D. (1978). Psychopathy-related personality variables and the psychophysiology of socialization. In R. Hare and D. Schalling (Eds.). *Psychopathic behavior: Approaches to research.* Chichester, England: Wiley.

Schroeder, M. L., Schroeder, K. G., and Hare, R. D. (1983). Generalizability of a checklist for assessment of psychopathy. *Journal of Consulting and Clinical Psychology, 51,* 511–516.

Schulsinger, F. (1974). Psychopathy: Heredity and environment. In S. A. Mednick, F. Schulsinger, J. Higgins, and B. Bell (Eds.). *Genetics, environment, and psychopathology.* Amsterdam: North Holland/Elsevier.

Siddle, D. A. T., and Trasler, G. B. (1981). The psychophysiology of psychopathic behavior. In M. J. Christie and P. G. Mellett (Eds.). *Foundations of psychosomatics.* London: Wiley.

Tucker, D. M. (1981). Lateral brain function, emotion, and conceptualization. *Psychological Bulletin, 89,* 19–46.

Venables, P. H. (1985). Autonomic nervous system factors in criminal behavior. In S. A. Mednick and T. Moffit (Eds.). *Biology and crime.* Cambridge: Cambridge University Press. In press.

Venables, P. H. and Raine A. (1985). Biological theory. In B. McGurk, D. Thornton, M. Williams (Eds.). *Theory and practice: Applying psychology to imprisonment.* London: Her Majesty's Stationery Office.

Wong, S. (1985). *The criminal and institutional behaviors of psychopaths.* Program Branch User Report, Ministry of the Solicitor General of Canada, Ottawa, Canada.

Yochelson, S., and Samenow, S. (1976). *The criminal personality.* Vol. I. New York: Jason Aronson.

2

Epidemiology of
Antisocial Personality

Remi J. Cadoret

Antisocial personality or sociopathy is one of the better defined personality disorders. Its description and course have been charted in a number of longitudinal studies. As defined in DSM-III, antisocial personality is a potpourri of behaviors ranging from criminal activity to impulsiveness, aggressivity, social irresponsibility, and early indulgence in sex, alcohol, and illicit drugs. There is no guarantee that antisocial personality as currently defined in DSM-III is a homogeneous condition. Indeed, there is evidence that it is possible to subdivide groups of antisocials, delinquents or criminals into more homogeneous subgroups (Blackburn 1971; Karpman 1947; Peterson, Quay, and Tiffany, 1961). For example, one study of alcoholic sociopaths has shown two subgroups: one with many symptoms of psychiatric illnesses, including multiple somatic complaints; the other group having few such symptoms (Whitters, Troughton, Cadoret, and Widmer, 1984).

Both the heterogeneity and the multitude of behaviors classed as characteristic of antisocials increase the difficulty of determining how much heredity and environment contribute to the etiology of antisocial personality. The varied and lifelong manifestations of antisocial personality are reflected in the studies of etiology and of epidemiology. Most investigators have selected their samples on the basis of some outstanding characteristic, such as juvenile delinquency (Glueck and Glueck, 1968), criminality (Mednick, Gabrielli, and Hutchings, 1984), or referral for treatment in a psychiatric setting (Robins, 1966). Thus, selection factors and resultant biases are found in many studies.

Other confounding factors also confuse the epidemiologic and etiologic picture of antisocial personality. Alcoholism and substance abuse occur frequently in antisocials (Lewis, Robins, and Rice, 1985; Virkkunen, 1979) and indeed constitute some of the criteria for antisocial personality. Yet alcohol abuse has been shown in a variety of studies (Goodwin, 1979) to have a genetic factor in its etiology. How, then, can the confounding factor of alcohol abuse be separated from factors leading to antisocial personality? The picture is confused further by the association of alcoholism with crime (Guze, Wolfgram, and McKinney 1968). Studies of inheritance of criminality could well be looking at the inheritance of alcoholism instead, unless the factor of alcohol abuse and its inheritance were controlled. In this chapter we will apply the foregoing considerations to the evidence for a genetic factor in the etiology of antisocial personality.

EPIDEMIOLOGY OF ANTISOCIAL PERSONALITY

Recent population studies in several major American cities (including some rural areas in one survey) have begun to detail the prevalence and distribution of antisocial personality as determined from DSM-III criteria (Regier *et al.*, 1984). Results of population surveys from this study in three urban sites are shown in Table 1. The overall lifetime prevalence is in the range of 2–3% (Table 1, line 1). The results from all three sites show the usual male predominance of the diagnosis (Table 1, line 2), with male to female ratios varying from 4 : 1 to 7.8 : 1. There appears to be little reliable difference due to race (Black vs non Black, Table 1, line 3), but consistently lower prevalence of antisocials among college graduates (Table 1, last line), a finding which is compatible with the marked tendency of antisocials to drop out early from formal schooling.

In the St. Louis sample urban versus "rural" breakdowns were made which showed that the highest lifetime prevalences occurred in the central city population: 5.7% of 983 core city inhabitants met DSM-III criteria, in contrast to 3.1% of 1267 inner suburb and 2.4% of 740 small town dwellers. The reason for this distribution is not clear but

TABLE 1

Lifetime Prevalence of Antisocial Personality Diagnosis
in Three Urban Areas
(% antisocial ± standard error)

New Haven, CT 1980–1981 N = 3,058		Baltimore, MD 1981–1982 N = 3,481		St. Louis, MO 1981–1982 N = 3,004	
Total 2.1 ± 0.3		Total 2.6 ± 0.3		Total 3.3 ± 0.5	
Male	Female	Male	Female	Male	Female
N = 1,292	N = 1,766	N = 1,322	N = 2,159	N = 1,202	N = 1,802
3.9 ± 0.6	0.5 ± 0.2	4.9 ± 0.7	0.7 ± 0.2	4.9 ± 0.7	1.2 ± 0.3
Black	Not Black	Black	Not Black	Black	Not Black
N = 334	N = 2,708	N = 1,182	N = 2,299	N = 1,158	N = 1,846
1.7 ± 0.6	2.1 ± 0.3	2.3 ± 0.5	2.7 ± 0.4	3.9 ± 0.9	3.1 ± 0.5
College	Other	College	Other	College	Other
N = 839	N = 2,218	N = 303	N = 3,174	N = 416	N = 2,498
0.9 ± 0.4	2.5 ± 0.4	1.5 ± 0.8	2.7 ± 0.3	2.3 ± 1.0	3.4 ± 0.5

Adapted from Robins et al., 1984

could represent drift of antisocials to core city environments and/or the operation of predisposing factors in the core city milieu.

Antisocial behavior, delinquency, criminality, and alcoholism have always been associated in families (Guze, Wolfgram, and McKinney, 1968; Jonsson 1967; Robins, 1966; West and Farrington 1977). Some have also described conditions such as increased prevalence of hysteria (Briquet's syndrome) in families of criminals or antisocials (Guze, Wolfgram, McKinney, and Cantwell, 1967). The overlap between alcohol abuse and antisocial behavior is a large one and will be considered in a later discussion of adoption studies. Some idea of the overlap between antisocial personality and alcohol abuse is contained in a study by Lewis et al. (1985) of 223 urban Black men in St. Louis. They found that 119 of the men studied met criteria for antisocial personality, 57.1% of whom were alcoholic. Only 15.4% of the 104 non-antisocial men were alcoholic. Their study also showed the usual association of antisocial behavior in families and a correlation of proband diagnosis with parent diagnosis (Table 2). In this table the two types of proband diagnoses (alcohol abuse and antisocial personality) are separated. Alcohol abuse in probands seems to be related more to familial alcohol problems (column 3, compare lines 1 and 3 versus lines 2 and 4). Antisocial personality is more related to familial antisocial behaviors (column 2, compare lines 1 and 2 versus lines 3 and 4). This specificity of inheritance will be developed later when adoption studies are discussed.

Many familial factors have been associated with antisocial personality (Anolik, 1983): parental personality problems, poor parental discipline and child supervision (Fischer, 1983; Robins, 1966), discord between parents and broken homes (Robins, 1966; West and Farrington, 1977), larger sibship size (Fischer, 1984). In almost all of these studies the genetic and environmental factors have been confounded in that delinquents or antisocials shared the parental environment. Careful studies of adoptees help separate genetic from environmental factors.

Evidence for genetic factors in psychiatric conditions usually comes from studies of twins or adoptees, or correlations of known genetic traits with behavioral pathology in linkage or association studies (Rosenthal, 1970). There are no studies relating criminality, delinquency or antisocial personality to known genetic traits, so linkage or association data are not available (as they are, for example, with depression and linkage to the X-chromosome in bipolar affective disorder) (Cadoret and Winokur, 1975). Evidence from adoptee studies is heavily relied upon herein for the following reasons: 1) All of the twin studies deal with criminality (Mednick and Christiansen, 1977), which,

TABLE 2

Familial History of Antisocial Behavior and Alcohol Problems
in Male First-degree Relatives and Their Relationship to
Proband Diagnosis of Alcohol Abuse (ALC)
and Antisocial Personality (ASP)

Proband Diagnosis		% Relatives with Antisocial Behaviors	% Relatives with Alcohol Problems
ASP(–)	ALC(–)	19/88 = 21.6%	13/87 = 14.9%
ASP(–)	ALC(+)	5/16 = 31.2%	6/16 = 37.5%
ASP(+)	ALC(–)	24/68 = 35.3%	11/65 = 16.9%
ASP(+)	ALC(+)	24/51 = 47.1%	16/51 = 31.4%

Adapted from Table 4 in Lewis et al., 1985.

though highly visible and characteristic of antisocial personalities, is not sufficiently diagnostic to enable conclusions to be drawn as to heritability of sociopathy in general; many sociopaths never have criminal convictions. 2) In the last decade a large amount of research has been done with adoptees in studying the inheritance of criminality, antisocial behavior, and antisocial personality. Although none of these studies addresses directly the inheritance of antisocial personality, the preponderance of evidence indicates a genetic factor in the etiology of antisocial behavior and antisocial personality.

ADOPTION STUDIES RELEVANT TO INHERITANCE OF ANTISOCIAL PERSONALITY

The Adoptee Method

In general, there are two designs which use adoptees to separate genetic from environmental factors. In both, adoptees separated from biologic parents at or close to birth and raised with nonbiologic relatives form the principal ingredient. In one design, the starting point is psychopathology in the adoptee; the evidence for similar psychopathology in biologic and adoptive parents is studied. In the second design, the starting point is psychopathology in the biologic parent, and adopted-away children are studied for similar psychopathology. In both designs controls are included: in the first, adoptees without psychopathology; in the second, biologic parents without psychopathology. Both methods have been used in research on antisocial behavior and criminality and both have been successful in showing correlations between biologic parental conditions and those of their adopted-away children.

Using the second design, several investigators (Bohman, Cloninger, Sigvardsson, and von Knorring, 1982; Cadoret and Cain, 1981) have been able to show that certain environmental conditions are factors in antisocial or criminal behavior. Despite careful preadoption screening, many adoptive homes turn out to have adverse factors such as psychopathology in parents or sibs. One of the advantages of the second adoption approach is the lack of bias introduced by selecting individuals who needed treatment as in the first design; results are more similar to a population study.

Evidence for Genetic Inheritance of Adolescent Antisocial Behavior

There are several studies relating antisocial behavior in biologic parents to antisocial behavior or conduct disorders in adolescents. In a study of 367 adoptees, Cadoret and Cain (1981) reported that adolescent antisocial behaviors were increased in males who had alcoholic biologic relatives, and in females who had antisocial biologic relatives. Males appeared to be more affected than females by environmental factors such as exposure to an adverse adoptive home where alcohol, antisocial, or other psychiatric problems were present. One other environmental factor predicted increased adolescent antisocial behavior: exposure to discontinuous mothering during the first year of life, such as occurred when infants were placed in an institution-type setting at a state university. College students in home economics cared for the infants there on a rotating basis so that in the course of several months an infant had a wide variety and range of "mothers" (Pease and Gardner, 1958).

Further analyses of these same adoption data found evidence for significant gene-environment interaction (Cadoret and Cain, 1982). In the presence of a genetic background of either alcoholic or antisocial parent, an adverse adoptive home environment resulted in a significantly greater increase in adolescent antisocial behavior than would have been expected on the basis of simple addition of the environmental and genetic factors (Cadoret, 1982). The importance of both genetic and environmental factors in the genesis of adolescent antisocial behavior was confirmed in an independent data set (Cadoret, 1985), in which similar biologic backgrounds (alcoholic and antisocial) predicted increased adolescent antisocial behavior. Evidence for gene-environment interaction was also found. However, the ultimate importance of gene-environment interaction in mediating *adult* antisocial behavior remains to be demonstrated.

Evidence for Genetic Inheritance of Adult Antisocial Behavior, Criminality, or Antisocial Personality

In a study of biologic and adoptive parents of adoptees with personality disorders, Schulsinger (1977) found an increase in sociopathy (defined in a Schneiderian sense) in their biologic parents, compared to the controls (parents of non-personality-disordered adoptees). All types of personality disorders were included in the sociopathy, including the antisocial. No excess of sociopathy was found in the adoptive parents. This would suggest, but not prove, the lack of environmental factors, since there is no evidence in Schulsinger's reports of any correlations between adoptive parent sociopathy and adoptee outcome.

Adoption studies of adult personality traits in general have been equivocal. Loehlin, Horn, and Willerman (1981) reported little personality resemblance among family members, when related either biologically or adoptively. However, in their study of a subsample of well-measured children there was more evidence of heritability of, especially, extraversion. Scarr, Webber, Weinberg, and Wittig (1981), in a similar study of adoptees, found that personality resemblance among biological relatives was greater than among adopted relatives for certain traits: introversion-extraversion, neuroticism, and an activity preference measure, a finding consistent with genetic heritability. However, the estimated heritabilities were lower than found in studies of twins, suggesting that twin studies may exaggerate the degree of genetic control of personality. These latter two studies suggest that genetic factors are important in adult personality, and the Schulsinger study suggests that abnormal or deviating personalities correlate with biologic parent personality deviations.

There are two adoption studies relating adult adoptee antisocial personality to biologic backgrounds of either criminality or antisocial types of behavior. Crowe (1974) studied adopted-away children of females who were imprisoned for felonies. Since the majority of convicted felons are diagnosable as having antisocial personality (Guze et al., 1967), this study provides more direct evidence for inheritance of antisocial personality. Crowe found a greater incidence of antisocial personality in the offspring of the convicted felons than in control adoptees who did not have a felon as a mother.

In an analysis of adult adoptees, Cadoret (1978) found that adoptees from backgrounds in which antisocial behaviors occurred in relatives were more likely to be diagnosed as having antisocial personality. Unfortunately, the exact diagnoses of the biologic parents were not available for this analysis. Several other conditions were found more frequently in the adult adoptees from antisocial behavior backgrounds, e.g., mood swings and the presence of audible thoughts. This finding suggests that types of psychopathology other than antisocial behavior may be part of the antisocial inheritance. This view is supported by a number of family studies and statistical model-fitting to patterns of illness in family trees, showing that antisocial personality and such conditions as hysteria (Briquet's sydrome) are related (Cloninger, Reich, and Guze, 1975). Some support for the relationship between antisocial personality and hysteria has been reported from two separate adoption studies. Both found that female adoptees from biologic backgrounds of antisocial behavior had higher rates of unexplained medical symptoms reminiscent (but not diagnostic) of hysteria (Cadoret 1978; Cadoret, Cunningham, Loftus, and Edwards, 1976).

Criminality, an aspect of antisocial behavior with high visibility, has been used in the Scandinavian adoption studies. For a number of years, Mednick and his associates have utilized the registries of Denmark to correlate criminality in biologic parents with criminality in adopted-away offspring. Mednick et al. (1984) reported a significant correlation between adoptees and their biological parents with respect to convictions for property crimes, but not with respect to crimes of violence. They found no significant correlation between adoptee and adoptive parent court convictions. This group has also reported the effect of "genetic" social class and adoptive parent social class upon crime (Van Dusen, Mednick, Gabrelli, and Hutchings 1983). Male adoptee crime varied inversely as a function of both genetic and environmental social class.

Just as crime and antisocial personality are interrelated, crime and antisocial personality are both related to alcohol abuse and dependency. The importance of the relationship between criminality and alcohol abuse has been documented by Bohman and coworkers (Bohman, 1983; Bohman et al., 1982; Cloninger, Bohman, and Sigvardsson, 1981; Sigvardsson, Cloninger, Bohman, and von Knorring, 1982) and forms the basis for their analysis of a large adoption study of registered criminality and alcoholism in Sweden. They found that criminality alone in biologic parents tended to increase the risk of criminality in adopted-away sons but not to increase their alcohol abuse. On the other hand, alcohol abuse alone in the biologic parents increased the risk of alcohol abuse, but not criminality, in those sons. Parents manifesting both criminality and alcohol abuse seemed heterogeneous, in that sons showed increased risk for alcohol abuse but not for both alcohol abuse and criminality. These investigators concluded that different genetic and environmental antecedents influenced the development of criminality, depending on the presence or absence of alcohol abuse. In their study, criminality without alcohol abuse was characterized by petty property offenses. This type of criminality in an adoptee was associated with criminality in a parent and is consistent with the findings of the Mednick et al. Danish study cited above (1984). In contrast, when an adoptee had alcohol abuse, criminality in the biologic parent was related to severity of alcohol abuse in that parent and not with criminality in the son, suggesting that criminality was more symptomatic of alcoholism. Criminality related to alcohol abuse was usually more repetitive, as well as more violent and damaging to other people.

Environmental factors were also important in criminality. The Bohman et al. studies found that unstable preadoptive placement increased the risk for petty criminality. In contrast, low social status of adoptive parents predicted increased alcohol-related criminality. In an analysis of gene-environment interaction, Bohman (1983) reported that 40% of adoptees with both genetic and environmental predisposing factors were present were registered for petty criminality, in contrast with 6.7% with the environmental factor only and 12.1% with the genetic factor only. Adoptees with neither genetic nor environmental factors present had only a 2.9% criminal registration. These results are consistent with a non-additive interaction predicting a higher than expected rate for ciminality when both genetic and environmental predisposing factors occur together. Earlier work from the Danish adoptee cohort has shown that criminality in adoptees was increased by placement in an adoptive family in which a parent had a criminal record (Hutchings and Mednick, 1974). Thus two independent studies show environmental effects for antisocial behavior.

The Bohman study (1983) also found that criminality in women was related to criminality in a biologic parent and that criminality rates were much higher in women's relatives than in the male sample. This suggests that there may be a threshold effect, with liability for petty criminality lower in men than in women.

Because alcohol abuse and its associated behaviors are often antisocial in quality (and are part of the DSM-III criteria for antisocial personality), many alcoholics can appear to be quite antisocial but not necessarily meet criteria for antisocial personality. Vaillant (1983) describes cases of this type in his studies of alcoholism. However, in many more cases alcohol abuse is one of the more common behaviors of those with antisocial personality (Hesselbroch et al., 1984; Lewis, Rice, and

Helzer, 1983; Lewis et al. 1985; Stabenau, 1984; Virkkunen, 1979). In view of the demonstrated heritability of alcohol abuse in adoption studies (Bohman, Sigvardsson, and Cloninger, 1981; Cadoret, Cain, and Grove, 1980; Cadoret and Gath, 1978; Cloninger et al., 1981; Goodwin, Schulsinger, and Hermansen, 1973), it is possible that estimates of heritability of antisocial personality may reflect the heritability of alcohol abuse. This is likely since several of the studies cited above report increased adolescent conduct disorder predicting alcohol abuse in adult adoptees (Cadoret et al., 1981) or increased adolescent and childhood antisocial behaviors in alcohol abusing adoptees (Goodwin et al., 1975).

The factor of alcohol abuse was controlled in a recent adoption design by Cadoret, O'Gorman, Troughton, and Hayward (1985), who showed that antisocial behavior in a biologic parent predicted an increase in adoptees with later adult antisocial personality diagnoses. Alcohol problems in biologic parents predicted increased alcohol abuse in the adopted-away children but not antisocial personality. This model of inheritance of antisocial personality is shown in Figure 1 for a male sample of adoptees. Females were found to follow a similar model, with similar odds ratios for the different relationships. In this particular male sample, one environmental factor, alcohol problems in the adoptive family, increased alcohol abuse in the adoptee; but no environmental factors were found which increased antisocial personality. The model with the environmental factor added is shown in Figure 2. This study demonstrates that even when alcohol abuse and its genetic inheritance are controlled in a statistical model, antisocial personality is found to have a genetic background which is different from that of alcohol abuse, and that environmental factors are of additional importance.

SUMMARY OF AND INTERPRETATION OF FINDINGS

The results of adoption studies show that adolescent antisocial behaviors can be linked to genetic antecedents of alcohol abuse and antisocial behavior. The importance of genetic etiology is supported by a recent twin study of self-reported delinquent behavior in which correlations of delinquent behaviors in monozygotic twins were higher than in dizygotic twins (Rowe, 1983).

Adult criminality which is a manifestation of antisocial personality

Figure 1. Diagram of "Basic" Model

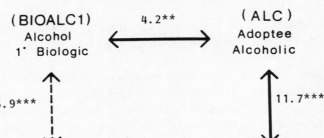

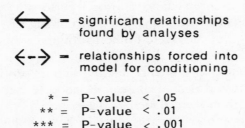

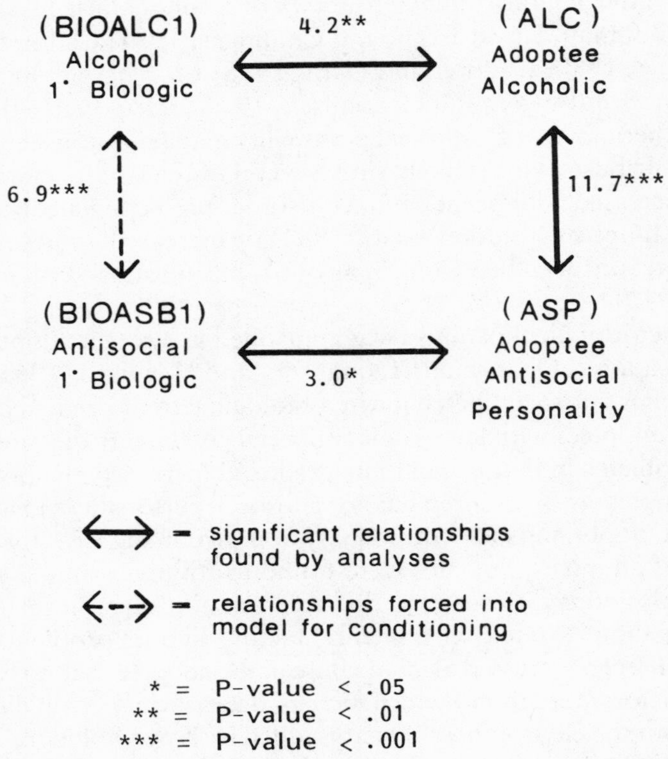

(BIOALC1)
Alcohol
1° Biologic
4.2**
(ALC)
Adoptee
Alcoholic
6.9***
11.7***
(BIOASB1)
Antisocial
1° Biologic
3.0*
(ASP)
Adoptee
Antisocial
Personality
= significant relationships found by analyses
= relationships forced into model for conditioning
* = P-value < .05
** = P-value < .01
*** = P-value < .001

Adapted from Cadoret et al., 1985

Explanation of figures: Arrows are used to show relationships between the factors in the model. Dotted arrows are relationships which are forced into the model to control for selective placement. Solid arrows are significant relationships or correlations found by the computer program. The strength of the correlation is indicated by the odds ratio which appears beside the arrow. Odds ratios of greater than one indicate positive correlation of the factors connected by the arrows. For example, in Figure 1, the odds ratio of 4.2 between BIOALC1 and ALC means that a given biologic first degree relative with alcohol problem the adoptee is 4.2 times more likely to be an alcohol abuser than if the biologic parent did not have an alcohol problem. Each odds ratio is corrected for the other relationships in the model; that is, other relationships are controlled.

(also of alcoholism—another inherited behavior) has been shown by Mednick and coworkers to have a genetic etiology; the Bohman et al. group has been able to document this relationship while controlling for alcohol abuse and dependency.

Figure 2. Diagram of "Basic" Model with Addition of Environmental Term

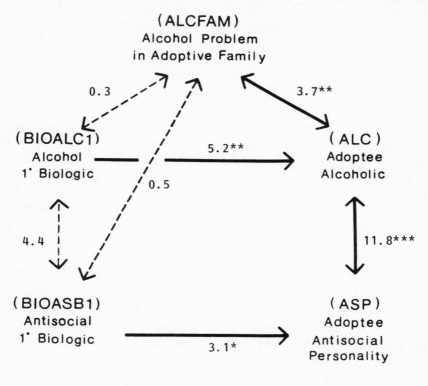

(ALCFAM)
Alcohol Problem
in Adoptive Family

0.3

3.7**

(BIOALC1)
Alcohol
1° Biologic

5.2**

(ALC)
Adoptee
Alcoholic

0.5

4.4

11.8***

(BIOASB1)
Antisocial
1° Biologic

3.1*

(ASP)
Adoptee
Antisocial
Personality

⟵ = significant relationships
found by analyses

⟵-- = relationships forced into
model for conditioning

* = P-value < .05
** = P-value < .01
*** = P-value < .001

Adapted from Cadoret et al., 1985

Antisocial personality in adults has been shown to be related to biologic relatives conficted of crime (Crowe, 1974), and in a separate study
(Cadoret et al., 1985) to biologic relatives with antisocial behavior (although not diagnosable as having antisocial personality by DSM-III
criteria). The latter study also controlled for inheritance of alcohol
abuse. Thus, while there is no direct connection demonstrated between
biologic relatives with antisocial personality and adult adoptees with
the same diagnosis, the preponderance of evidence would suggest that
there is a direct relationship. Further support for this position comes
from the fact that biologic predisposition for antisocial behavior pre-
dicts higher numbers of adolescent antisocial behaviors, and higher
numbers of the latter predict adult antisocial personality (Robins, 1966;
Rutter, 1984). Family studies (Vaillant, 1983) and adoption studies
(Bohman, 1983; Cadoret et al., 1985) show independent and different
biologic backgrounds for antisocial behavior and alcoholism, suggesting a specificity of inheritance.

Some of the adoption studies (those of Mednick and Bohman) have
described environmental factors which affect criminality. The adoption method may underestimate the importance of environmental factors, since adoptive homes are carefully selected and are not likely to
represent extremely adverse environmental circumstances, such as very
large sibships (Fischer, 1984) and parents who are poor supervisors
(Fischer, 1983). From a preventive standpoint, evidence from several
studies of gene-environment interaction is extremely important. Avoidance of combinations of biologic backgrounds with certain environmental factors could result in marked lowering of antisocial behavior or
of criminality (Cadoret, 1982). Gene-environment interaction is of particular interest to students of the interactionism school of human development (Magnusson and Allen, 1983), which holds that behavior
is part of "the continuously ongoing, bidirectional, person-situation
interaction in which the person is the intentional active agent." How
this viewpoint is applicable to the etiology of psychopathology, antisocial and criminal, is discussed by Rutter (1983).

Sex differences have been found suggesting that similar genetic factors may predispose to female antisocial behavior and criminality, but
that female environmental factors may be different from those found
with males (Cadoret and Cain, 1981). One study showed that female
criminals have a higher loading of criminal relatives, suggesting that

a differential threshold might be involved in female psychopathology (Cloninger et al., 1978).

The Gene Pool

In considering behavior traits with genetic etiologies, it is necessary to wonder what forces maintain these behaviors in the gene pool, especially when the genes responsible apparently lead to negative social consequences. A variety of theoretical positions can be called upon to explain the ubiquity and apparent durability of the genes responsible for antisocial behavior.

One explanation, from the field of sociobiology, holds that antisocial behavior can be considered one end of a continuum of adoptive strategies aimed at maximizing reproductive fitness (thus maintaining or even increasing the genes involved). The sociobiologist would regard the greater sexual promiscuity of the sociopath as evidence of increased "fitness" to leave more genes like its own surviving into the next generation. The antisocial reproductive strategy would involve maximizing the number of offspring by copulating with multiple mates, in preference to mating with one individual and putting energy and effort into helping a few offspring survive (MacMillan and Kofoed, 1984).

Another basic theoretical aspect of psychobiology relevant to the question of sociopathy is the concept that organisms indulge in altruism in order to insure survival of their genetic material (Wilson, 1975). How this behavior can apply to antisocial individuals, who are usually regarded as self-centered and not particularly self-sacrificing, seems paradoxical. However, a new theory has been developed which evolved from the idea that similar kin selection is a form of altruism. This genetic similarity theory proposes "that a gene insures its own survival by acting so as to bring about the reproduction of any organism in which copies of itself are found" (Rushton, Russell, and Wells, 1984). Since antisocial behavior is generally rather blatant, recognition is no problem and could lead to selective mating or other social action destined to maintain or increase the gene pool. Thus, it is possible that antisocial personality, however self-defeating it appears to some observers, provides an effective behavioral vehicle for propagation of its etiologic genes.

REFERENCES

Anolik, S. (1983). Family influences upon delinquency: Biosocial and psychosocial perspectives. *Adolescence, 18,* 489–498.

Blackburn, R. (1971). Personality types among abnormal homicides. *British Journal of Criminology, 11,* 14–31.

Bohman, M. (1983). Alcoholism and crime: Studies of adoptees. *Substance Alcohol Actions Misuse, 4,* 137–147.

Bohman, M., Cloninger, C., Sigvardsson, S., & von Knorring, A. (1982). Predisposition to petty criminality in Swedish adoptees. I. Genetic and environmental heterogeneity. *Archives of General Psychiatry, 39,* 1233–1241.

Bohman, M., Sigvardsson, S., & Cloninger, R. (1981). Maternal inheritance of alcohol abuse: Cross-fostering analysis of adopted women. *Archives of General Psychiatry, 38,* 965–969.

Cadoret, R. (1978). Psychopathology in adopted-away offspring of biologic parents with antisocial behavior. *Archives of General Psychiatry, 35,* 176–184.

Cadoret, R. (1982). Editorial: Genotype-environmental interaction in antisocial behavior. *Psychological Medicine, 12,* 235–239.

Cadoret, R. (1985). Genes, environment and their interaction in the development of psychopathology. In J. Sakai & T. Tsuboi (Eds.). *Genetic aspects of human behavior.* Tokyo, New York: Aino Hospital Foundation, Igaku-Shoin.

Cadoret, R., Cain, C., & Grove, W. (1980). Development of alcoholism in adoptees raised apart from alcoholic biologic relatives. *Archives of General Psychiatry, 37,* 561–563.

Cadoret, R., & Cain, C. (1981). Environmental and genetic factors in predicting adolescent antisocial behavior in adoptees. *Psychiatric Journal of the University of Ottawa, 6,* 220–225.

Cadoret, R., & Cain, C. (1982). *Genetic-environmental interaction in adoption studies of antisocial behavior.* Proceedings of the Third World Congress on Biological Psychiatry. Amsterdam: Elsevier/North Holland.

Cadoret, R., Cunningham, L., Loftus, R., & Edwards, J. (1976). Studies of adoptees from psychiatrically disturbed biological parents: III. Medical symptoms and illnesses in childhood and adolescence. *American Journal of Psychiatry, 133,* 1316–1318.

Cadoret, R., & Gath, A. (1978). Inheritance of alcoholism in adoptees. *British Journal of Psychiatry, 132,* 252–258.

Cadoret, R., O'Gorman, T., Troughton, E., & Haywood, E. (1985). Alcoholism and antisocial personality: Interrelationships, genetic and environmental factors. *Archives of General Psychiatry, 42,* 161–167.

Cadoret, R., & Winokur, G. (1975). X-linkage in manic-depressive illness. *Annual Review Medicine, 26,* 21–25.

Cloninger, C., Bohman, M., & Sigvardsson, S. (1981). Inheritance of alcohol abuse: Cross-fostering analysis of adopted men. *Archives of General Psychiatry, 38,* 861–868.

Cloninger, C., Christiansen, K., Reich, T., et al. (1978). Implications of sex differences in the prevalences of antisocial personality, alcoholism, and criminality for familial transmission. *Archives of General Psychiatry, 35,* 941–951.

Cloninger, C., Sigvardsson, S., Bohman, M., & von Knorring, A. (1982). Predisposition to petty criminality in Swedish adoptees. II. Cross-fostering analysis of gene-environment interaction. *Archives of General Psychiatry, 39,* 1242–1247.

Cloninger, C., Reich, T., & Guze, S. (1975). The multifactorial model of disease transmission. III. The familial relationship between sociopathy and hysteria (Briquet's syndrome). *British Journal of Psychiatry, 127*, 23–32.

Crowe, R. (1974). An adoption study of antisocial personality. *Archives of General Psychiatry, 31*, 785–791.

Fischer, D. (1983). Parental supervision and delinquency. *Perception and Motor Skills, 56*, 635–640.

Fischer, D. (1984). Family size and delinquency. *Perception and Motor Skills, 58*, 527–534.

Glueck, S., & Glueck, E. (1968). *Delinquents and nondelinquents in perspective*. Cambridge, MA: Harvard University Press.

Goodwin, D. (1979). Alcoholism and heredity. *Archives of General Psychiatry, 36*, 57–61.

Goodwin, D., Schulsinger, F., & Hermansen, L. (1973). Alcohol problems in adoptees raised apart from alcoholic biological parents. *Archives of General Psychiatry, 28*, 238–243.

Goodwin, D., Schulsinger, F., Hermansen, L., Guze, S., & Winokur, G. (1975). Alcoholism and the hyperactive child syndrome. *Journal of Nervous Mental Disorders, 160*, 349–353.

Guze, S., Wolfgram, E., McKinney, J., Cantwell, D. (1967). Psychiatric illness in the families of convicted criminals: A study of 519 first-degree relatives. *Diseases of the Nervous System, 28*, 651–659.

Guze, S., Wolfgram, E., & McKinney, J. (1968). Delinquency, social maladjustment and crime: The role of alcoholism (a study of first degree relatives of convicted criminals). *Diseases of the Nervous System, 29*, 238–243.

Hesselbrock, M., Hesselbrock, V., Babor, T., Stabenau, J., Meyer, R., & Weidenman, M. (1984). Antisocial behavior, psychopathology and problem drinking in the natural history of alcoholism. In D. W. Goodwin, K. T. Van Dusen, and S. A. Mednick (Eds). *Longitudinal Research in Alcoholism*. (Chap. 12) Boston: Kluwer-Nyhoff Publising. 197–214.

Hutchings, B., & Mednick, S. (1974). Registered criminality in the adoptive and biological parents of registered male adoptees. In S. A. Mednick, F., Schulsinger, J. Higgins, and B. Bell (Eds.) *Genetics, Environment, and Psychopathology*. Amsterdam: North Holland Publishing Co. 215–230.

Jonsson, G. (1967). Delinquent boys, their parents and grandparents. *Archives of Psychiatry, Scandinavian Supplement, 195*, 43.

Karpman, B. (1947). Passive parasitic psychopathy: Toward the personality structure and psychogenesis of ideopathic psychopathy. *Psychoanalytic Review, 34*, 102–118, 198–122.

Lewis, C., Rice, J., & Helzer, J. (1983). Diagnostic interactions: Alcoholism and antisocial personality. *Journal of Nervous Mental Disorders, 160*, 105–113.

Lewis, C., Robins, L., & Rice, J. (1985). Association of alcoholism with antisocial personality in urban men. *Journal of Nervous Mental Disorders, 173*, 166–174.

Loehlin, J., Horn, J., & Willerman, L. (1981). Personality resemblance in adoptive families. *Behavior Genetics, 11*, 309–330.

MacMillan, J., & Kofoed, L. (1984). Sociobiology and antisocial personality: An alternative perspective. *Journal of Nervous Mental Disorders, 172*, 701–706.

Magnusson, D., & Allen, V. (1983). An interactional perspective for human development. In D. Magnusson and V. L. Allen. (Eds). *Human Development: An interactional perspective*. New York: Academic Press. 3–31.

Mednick, S., & Christiansen, K. (1977). *Biosocial bases of criminal behavior*. New York: Gardner Press.

Mednick, S., Gabrielli, W., Jr., & Hutchings, B. (1984). Genetic influences in criminal convictions: Evidence from an adoption cohort. *Science, 224*, 891–894.

Pease, D., & Gardner, D. (1958). Research on the effects of non-continuous mothering. *Child Development, 29*, 141–148.

Peterson, D., Quay, H., & Tiffany, T. (1961). Personality factors related to juvenile delinquency. *Child Development, 32*, 355–372.

Regier, D., Myers, J., Kramer, M., Robins, L., Blayer, D., Hough, R., Eaton, W., & Locke, B. (1984). The NIMH epidemiologic catchment area program: Historical context, major objectives, and study population characteristics. *Archives of General Psychiatry, 41*, 934–941.

Robins, L. (1966). *Deviant children grown up: A sociological and psychiatric study of sociopathic personality*. Williams and Wilkins.

Robins, L., Helzer, J., Weissman, M., Orvaschel, H., Gruenberg, E., Bruche, J., Jr., & Regier, D. (1984). Lifetime prevalence of specific psychiatric disorders in three sites. *Archives of General Psychiatry, 41*, 949–958.

Rosenthal, D. (1970). *Genetic theory and abnormal behavior*. New York: McGraw-Hill.

Rowe, D. (1983). Biometrical genetic models of self-reported delinquent behavior: A twin study. *Behavioral Genetics, 13*, 473–489.

Rushton, J., Russell, R., & Wells, P. (1984). Genetic similarity theory: Beyond kin selection. *Behavior Genetics, 14*, 179–193.

Rutter, M. (1983). Statistical and personal interactions: Facets and perspectives. In D. Magnusson and V. L. Allen. (Eds.) *Human Development: An Interactional Perspective*. (Chap. 17). New York: Academic Press. 295–319.

Rutter, M. (1984). Psychopathology and development. I. Childhood antecedents of adult psychiatric disorder. *Australia, New Zealand Journal of Psychiatry, 18*, 225–234.

Scarr, S., Webber, P., Weinberg, R., & Wittig, M. (1981). Personality resemblance among adolescents and their parents in biologically related and adoptive families. *Journal of Personal and Social Psychiatry, 40*, 885–898.

Schulsinger, F. (1977). Psychopathy: Heredity and environment. In S. A. Mednick and K. O. Christiansen (Eds.) *Biosical Bases of Criminal Behavior*. (Chap. 6) New York: Gardner Press. 109–141.

Sigvardsson, S., Cloninger, C., Bohman, M., & von Knorring, A. (1982). Predisposition to petty criminality in Swedish adoptees. III. Sex differences and validation of the male typology. *Archives of General Psychiatry, 39*, 1248–1253.

Stabenau, J. (1984). Implications of family history of alcoholism, antisocial personality, and sex differences in alcohol dependence. *American Journal of Psychiatry, 141*, 1178–1182.

Van Dusen, K., Mednick, S., Gabrielli, W., Jr., & Hutchings, B. (1983). Social class and crime in an adoption cohort. *Journal of Criminal Law Criminology, 74*, 249.

Vaillant, G. (1983). *The natural history of alcoholism*. Cambridge: Harvard University Press.

Virkkunen, M. (1979). Alcoholism and antisocial personality. *Acta Psychiatric, Scandinavian Supplement, 59*, 493–501.

West, D. & Farrington, D. (1977). *The delinquent way of life*. London: Heineman.

Whitters, A., Troughton, E., Cadoret, R., & Widmer, R. (1984). Evidence for clinical heterogeneity in antisocial alcoholics. *Comprehensive psychiatry, 25*, 158–164.

Wilson, E. (1975). *Sociobiology: The new synthesis*. Cambridge: Harvard University Press.

3

The Child Behind the Mask: Sociopathy as Developmental Delay

Robert G. Kegan

One of the more poignant lines in Cleckley's elegant and humble book-long observation of the "psychopath" (1941) is his statement toward the end that such persons "do not make the ordinary meaning of human experience." Just what meaning they do make remained for Cleckley a puzzle. What puzzled Cleckley nearly 50 years ago is still puzzling to us today. Although this chapter promises no definitive solution, it does amount to an argument for the existence of a new clue, and one which comes from a possibly unexpected quarter.

Piagetian developmental psychology generally has been thought to confine itself to the logical cognition of children or adolescents, and — even within this domain — to limit its study to "normal," nonpathological phenomena. But over the past 20 years a "Piagetian paradigm" has slowly begun to emerge extending study throughout the lifespan and attending to regular forms and processes of the mental organization of cognitive, social-cognitive, interpersonal and intrapersonal experiencing. Piaget's original demonstration that the child is a "philosopher" has begun to grow into a science of the *person* (child, adolescent and adult) as philosopher. "Philosophy" has been differentiated into its familiar parts; research programs are underway which study the person as natural, non-self-conscious logician and epistemologist (Basseches, 1984; Broughton, 1978; Perry, 1970), ethicist (Gilligan,

For their helpful responses to earlier drafts of this chapter, the author expresses grateful acknowledgment to Sophie Freud, Ann Fleck Henderson, Laura Rogers, and William H. Reid.

1982; Kohlberg, 1981, 1984), theologian, (Fowler, 1981; Parks, 1986), ontologist (Kegan, 1982; Loevinger, 1976), and aesthetician (Gardner, 1982; Parsons, 1983). Indeed, since Cleckley's weary aside about the non-ordinary way the subjects of his book make meaning, a whole branch of psychology has emerged which takes as its central preoccupation precisely the question of the forms and processes of an individual's meaning-making (Kegan, 1982).

Much more recently, this psychology (called variously "structural-developmental," "constructive-developmental," or "cognitive-developmental ego psychology," because it attends to the development of the meaning-constructive aspects of personality) has begun to consider psychiatric or psychopathological phenomena.

Studies which look at specific psychiatric syndromes in light of developmental organization have not, with one exception, found strong relationships between given syndromes and given levels of development. For example, developmental studies of clinical depression (Kegan, 1979) or borderline character disorder (Noam, 1984) do not indicate that persons with these diagnostic labels tend to be at a given level of development; rather, the results argue for a more polymorphic perspective on what has been previously regarded as a monolithic diagnostic category.

The one exception to this trend is sociopathy. Persons diagnosed sociopathic (or antisocial personality) overwhelmingly illustrate the same developmental diagnosis. I shall temporarily hold the reader in suspense as to the specific developmental position persons diagnosed sociopathic seem to fit. Instead I shall first inquire as to whether one does not find the sociopath "unmasked" in the following sequence of normal qualitative organizations of mental experience. This chapter will then briefly review preliminary, but nonetheless suggestive, research findings as to the relationship between sociopathy and a given developmental stage. Finally, a variety of implications for a revised view of sociopathy, when it is regarded as a specific and unusual form of "developmental delay," will be considered.

NORMAL DEVELOPMENT IN THE MAKING OF MEANING:
A SYNTHETIC VIEW

Psychologists in the tradition of Piaget (1937) and Werner (1940) believe they can identify distinct aspects of mental organization and follow the way these develop (become more differentiated and more integrated) over one's lifespan. Table 1 sketches normal forms of development in each of several domains—logical-cognitive, social-cognitive, intrapersonal-affective—over three eras from early childhood through adolescence. In *The Evolving Self* (Kegan, 1982), I suggested a single, "deep structure" evolving over the course of personality development, the various forms of which may give rise to the different mental organizations these theorists describe. Although this remains a controversial claim and its empirical exploration is at an early stage, it is heuristically useful to see these three eras presented as if each were a distinctly different epistemology giving rise to a set of capacities which share a common, underlying principle of mental organization.

The process of development in the making of meaning involves, with each new era of development, a qualitative transformation, which has been variously described as a process of "decentration" (Piaget, 1937), the overcoming of a former egocentrism (Elkind, 1974), and an emergence from embeddedness (Schachtel, 1959). These descriptions refer to mental reorganization in which what was the entire "structure" or system of organization becomes an element of a more encompassing and comprehensive structure or system. All these descriptions speak to development or adaptation, the differentiation of the organism from that which was the very principle of its organization (subject), which thereby becomes an element (or object) integrated into a new principle of organization (the new subject).

As the infant gradually evolves from its globally undifferentiated state, coming to some beginning relationship to (rather than embeddedness in) its sensing and moving, it creates a first, rudimentary distinction between a "me" and a "not me," granting to objects an existence independent of its immediate experience of them. This begins the first era described here, at about two years of age. In disembedding itself from its reflexes (of sensation and physical movement) the two-year-old comes to "have" the reflexes (as *object*) rather than "be" them (as *subject*). The new self is embedded in a subjectivity which coordinates these reflexes, namely, the "perceptions" and the "impulses" (see Table 2). The tremendous cognitive and emotional lability of the preschool child is suggested to be a function of this new embeddedness. The child is able to recognize things as separate from itself, but those things remain *subject to* the child's perception of them; i.e., if the child's perception of an object changes, he experiences a change in the object itself.

This is the essence of Piaget's stage of "preoperational thinking."

TABLE 1
Three Eras of Meaning Organization

	ERA #1 (Normal age: roughly 2–6 years)	ERA #2 (Normal age: roughly 6–14 years)	ERA #3 (Normal age: roughly 14–indeterminant)
Logical-Cognitive Domain	*Can*: recognize that objects exist independent of one's own sensing of them ("object permanence") *Cannot*: distinguish one's own perception of an object from the actual properties of the object; construct a logical relation between cause and effect (Piaget's stage of "preoperational thought")	*Can*: grant to objects their own properties irrespective of one's perceptions; reason consequentially, i.e.: cause and effect, construct a narrative sequence of events, relate one point in time to another; construct fixed categories and classes into which things can be mentally placed *Cannot*: reason abstractly; subordinate concrete actuality to possibility; make generalizations; discern overall patterns; form hypotheses; construct ideals (Piaget's stage of "concrete operational thought")	*Can*: reason abstractly; i.e., reason about reasoning; think hypothetically and deductively; form negative classes (e.g., the class of all not-crows); see relations as simultaneously reciprocal *Cannot*: systematically produce all possible combinations of relations; systematically isolate variables to test hypotheses (earliest form of Piaget's stage of "formal operations")

Socio-Cognitive Domain	*Can:* recognized that persons exist separate from oneself *Cannot:* recognize that persons have their own purposes independent of oneself; take another person's point of view as distinct from one's own (Kohlberg's stage of "heteronomous morality")	*Can:* construct own point of view and grant to others their distinct point of view; take the role of another person; manipulate others on behalf of one's own goals; make deals, plans, strategies *Cannot:* take own point of view and another's simultaneously; construct obligations and expectations to maintain mutual interpersonal relationships (Kohlberg's stage of "instrumentalism")	*Can:* be aware of shared feelings, agreements, and expectations which take primacy over individual interests *Cannot:* construct a generalized system regulative of interpersonal relationships and relationships between relationships (Kohlberg's stage of "interpersonal concordance")
Intrapersonal-Affective Domain	*Can:* distinguish between inner sensation and outside stimulation *Cannot:* distinguish its impulses from itself; i.e., is embedded in, or driven by, its impulses (Kegan's "impulsive self")	*Can:* drive, regulate, or organize impulses to produce enduring dispositions, needs, goals; delay immediate gratification *Cannot:* internally coordinate more than one point of view or need organization; distinguish its needs from itself (Kegan's "imperial self")	*Can:* internalize another's point of view in what becomes the *co-con*struction of personal experience, thus creating new capacity for empathy and sharing at an internal, rather than merely transactive, level; coordinate more than one point of view internally, thus creating emotions experienced as internal subjective state rather than social transaction *Cannot:* organize own states or internal parts of self into systematic whole; distinguish self from one's relationships (Kegan's "interpersonal self")

49

Sources: Kegan, 1982; Kohlberg and Gilligan, 1972; Lickona, 1976

TABLE 2

Balances of Subject and Object as the Common Ground of Several Developmental Theories

	Stage 0 Incorporative	Stage 1 Impulsive (Era 1)	Stage 2 Imperial (Era 2)	Stage 3 Interpersonal (Era 3)	Stage 4 Institutional	Stage 5 Individual
Underlying structure (subject vs. object)	S – Reflexes, (sensing, moving) O – None	S – Impulses, perceptions O – Reflexes (sensing, moving)	S – Needs, interests, wishes O – Impulses, perceptions	S – The interpersonal, mutuality O – Needs, interests, wishes	S – Authorship, identity, psychic administration, ideology O – The interpersonal, mutuality	S – Interindividuality, interpenetrability of self systems O – Authorship, identity, psychic administration, ideology
Piaget	Sensorimotor	Preoperational	Concrete operational	Early formal operational	Full formal operational	Post-formal Dialectical?
Kohlberg	–	Punishment and obedience orientation	Instrumental orientation	Interpersonal concordance orientation	Societal orientation	Principled orientation
Loevinger	Pre-social	Impulsive	Opportunistic	Conformist	Conscientious	Autonomous
Maslow	Physiological survival orientation	Physiological satisfaction orientation	Safety orientation	Love, affection, belongingness orientation	Esteem and self-esteem orientation	Self-actualization
McClelland/ Murray	–	–	Power orientation	Affiliation orientation	Achievement orientation	Intimacy orientation
Erikson	–	Initiative vs. guilt	Industry vs. inferiority	Affiliation vs. abandonment?	Identity vs. identity diffusion	–

50

Source: Kegan, 1982

The young child may think an amount of water becomes more water when poured into a taller, thinner glass. He is unable to hold his perception of the liquid in one container with his perception of the same amount of liquid in the taller, thinner container. He cannot separate himself from his perceptions.

What is true of the young child's cognitions about the physical world is as true of his or her social cognitions. The inability to grant to physical objects the independence of their properties from one's perception of them is paralleled by the social egocentrism of this era, in which the young child is unable to distinguish other people's point of view from his own, or to take the role of another. The young boy who has only one male sibling can correctly answer that he has a brother, but he does not understand that his brother has a brother. He cannot take the point of view of his brother and see that his brother does have a brother and it is he! This social egocentrism constrains the nature of the young child's moral meaning-making as well, since he is unable to consider the meaning of another's acts independently of his own point of view. The ideas of separate intentions and cause-and-effect are not yet constructed.

This embeddedness in the perceptions (physical or social) is paralleled by an embeddedness in the structurally equivalent psychological category, the "impulse" (perceptions of one's "insides"). The preschooler has poor "impulse control," it is suggested, not because he lacks some quantitative countering force, but because his underlying subject-object organization is composed in a way qualitatively different from that of most 10-year-olds who *do* have impulse control. Impulse control requires the mediation of one's impulses (i.e., impulses as *object*); but the impulses are immediate (i.e., *subject*) in this subject-object balance. When I am *subject to* my impulses, their non-expression raises an ultimate threat; they risk who I am.

Similarly, the preschooler's inability to hold two perceptions together is paralleled in his or her inability to hold two feelings about a single thing together—he is unable to hold together either the same feelings about a thing over time, which creates the "enduring disposition" (the psychological structure I call "needs, interests, wishes" in Table 2), or competing feelings at the same time. This suggests why the preschooler lacks the capacity for ambivalence. It also suggests that the tantrum—the classic expression of distress in this era—is an example of a system overwhelmed by internal conflict. There is no self yet which can serve as a context upon which the competing impulses can play themselves out; the impulses are the self, are themselves the context.

The extremely varied assortment of phenomena suggesting transformations between the ages of five and seven finds a unifying context if we consider that a more general evolution in the underlying construction of subject and object may be occurring (Kegan, 1985)—particularly one in which the structures of "perception" and of "impulse" become elements or objects within a new subjectivity. Consider findings as apparently disparate as these: 1) Children on the early side of the five-to-seven shift seem to need rewards that are fairly immediate, sensual, and communicating of praise. Children on the older side seem to feel more rewarded by the information that they have been correct. 2) Children who lose a limb or become blind before they are through the shift tend not to have phantom limb responses or memories of sight; children on the other side of the shift do. The capacity to take their impulses and perceptions as an *object* of their meaning-making not only brings an end to the lability of the earlier subject-object relation, but also brings into being a new subject-object relation that creates a more endurable self. The new self is a system of its own that does its own praising, so to speak, but needs the information that it is correct as confirmation; it is a system which can *store* memories, feelings, and perceptions (rather than immediately *being* them), so that a feeling arm or a seeing eye lives on in some way.

One way of characterizing this new subject-object relationship (Era 2—the Imperial balance; see Table 2) is in terms of the construction of the *role*. This is true whether one is speaking of the social-cognitive capacity to take the role of another person or the affective differentiation within the impulse life of the family (which permits one to take his or her appropriate role as a "child" relative to a "parent" rather than "being" his impulse life bound up with another). A distinguishing feature of this new subject-object relationship is that the child seems to "seal up" in a sense; there is a self-containment that was not there before. The mother no longer finds herself engaged in the middle of conversations the child has begun all by himself; the child no longer lives with the sense that the parent can read his private feelings. He has a private world, which he did not have before.

It is not just the physical world that is being conserved, but internal experience, too. With the constitution of the "enduring disposition" there comes as well the emergence of a self-concept, a more or less consistent notion of a *me,* of *what I am.*

With the capacity to take command of one's impulses (to have them, rather than be them) can come a new sense of freedom, power, independence — agency, above all. Things no longer "just happen" in the world; with the capacity to see behind the shadows, to "come in" with the data of experience, the child now has something to do with what happens. The end of Kohlberg's first moral stage, where authority is all powerful and right, is probably brought on by this construction of one's own authority.

The new liberation carries new risks and vulnerabilities. If the child now affects the world, then whether things go badly or well is a question of what he can do. Looming over a system whose hallmark is newly won stability, control, and freedom is the threat of the old lability, loss of control, and what now appears as the old subjugation from without. How much of the control and manipulation others experience when they are the object of this meaning-making balance is a matter of the child's efforts to save himself from the threat, real or imagined, of ungovernable and overwhelming impulse life? Every new balance is a triumph over the constraints of the past evolutionary truce, but a limit with respect to later development.

What are the limits of Era #2, the "Imperial I"? For one, the child cannot feel feelings that might arise out of a simultaneous consideration of his own impulse-coordinating and another's. To do so would require impulse-coordinating as an object, which is precisely the limit of this evolutionary balance. This means that if he betrays a confidence, for example, because it suits his needs to do so, he does not experience whatever it is one experiences when one simultaneously considers one's own impulse-coordinating and another's (often called "guilt"). He may experience concern about whether the betrayed person will find out, and what the consequences will be. He is able to see that the other person has needs and interests, and that he may be angry, but how the other person will feel is not a part of the very source of his own feeling or meaning-making. For the latter to be so would require integrating one needs-perspective with another, which would be not just an additive but a qualitative reconstruction of the balance in which he hangs.

Such a reconstruction entails not just a new level of social perspective, but a new organization and experience of interior life as well.

When one's own needs and another's are not integrated, the former cannot hold the other imaginatively and so must seek to hold him in some other way. Being unable to hold the other imaginatively, he is left to await or anticipate the actual movements or happenings of others in order to keep his world coherent. The creation of guilt, or the development of conscience, may seem to some a terrible burden and a terrible loss; but it is also quite liberating, as it frees one of having to exercise so much control over an otherwise unfathomable world. It frees one of the distrust of a world from which he is radically separate.

Without the internalization of the other's voice in one's very construction of self, how one feels is much more a matter of how external others will react, and the universal effort to preserve one's integrity will be felt by others as an effort to control or manipulate.

When others are known by the subject-object structure of Era #2 (Tables 1 and 2), they are subject to its projecting onto them its embeddedness in its needs. The individual in Era #2 constitutes the other as one by which he either meets or does not meet his needs, fulfill his wishes, pursue his interests, confirm his self-competence. Instead of seeing his needs, he sees *through* his needs. Instead of coordinating competing needs and experiencing this conflict internally, he projects half the conflict onto the other and makes him into the antagonistic holder of a competing view. This may be experienced by the other as manipulation, being imperialized, or an authority battle of wills. In order for the Era #2 individual to keep his balance, he must control, or at least predict, the behavior of other people who, in carrying around their own agendas separate from the child, make it impossible for him to gauge reality and know the consequences of his actions. What makes the subject-object structure "imperial" is the absence of a shared reality. This names the structural limits of the second era, common to latency-age children.

A qualitatively new organization of meaning—a new subject-object relation—typically begins to emerge around adolescence, the third era to be discussed here (see Tables 1 and 2). From the purely cognitive point of view, this represents the emergence from an embeddedness in the concrete, the actual, the given, the fact, and their subordination (or coordination) within a new system of the *meta*physical, the possible, the hypothetical, the general. This first appearance of abstract thinking is arguably a function of the capacity to *abstract from* (i.e., make object) the particular, the stable organization of which was the triumph of the earlier epistemology. Abstract thinking relativizes the particular givens to a qualitatively bigger field which subtends them, relates them, generalizes from them.

Something structurally similar is happening at the same time in the realms of interpersonal and intrapersonal meaning-organization. With the emergence from an embeddedness in one's own need system, one no longer *is* one's needs; one *has* needs. In having them one can now coordinate, or integrate, one need system with another, and in so doing, bring into being that need-mediating reality which we refer to when we speak of the "interpersonal," or mutuality (the new subject of Era #3). The ability to coordinate independent points of view allows one, for the first time, to take another person's independent purposes into account at the same time one is considering one's own. Indeed, what *is* one's own comes gradually to entail the integration of both points of view, which is what we mean by interpersonalism or mutual reciprocity. Like all epistemological evolutions, this one comes gradually, and during the transition, when one is still more the old self than the new, the internal integration of this point of view can feel most like an unwelcome intrusion on the more independent world of unilateral self-determination, self-control, and personal agency. ("I feel like other people are being knit into me," one adolescent in the midst of this transition told us.) When the new subject-object balance is fully evolved, the other point of view becomes a part of oneself.

The construction of the "moral" also shifts dramatically as a result: Right action no longer consists of that which instrumentally satisfies one's needs; human relations are no longer viewed in marketplace terms; elements of fairness, sharing, and reciprocity are no longer only present in a pragmatic, "you scratch my back and I'll scratch yours" sort of way; others are no longer valuable only by virtue of their helping one meet one's needs. Within the new epistemology of Era #3, maintaining the expectations of valued others and earning their approval become important in their own right, regardless of the immediate consequences. Good behavior is what pleases or helps others; guilt, as internal self-punishment (rather than anxious anticipation of what external others might do) is created for the first time. Era #3 represents the psychological birth of the adult-like form of moral conscience.

Finally, the same structural evolution brings about a reorganization of intrapersonal experiencing. The emerging capacity to coordinate points of view within oneself leads to the creation of inner subjectivity and feelings experienced as inner states rather than social negotiations. During the transition into this new subject-object structure, one can feel bewildered by the new complexity of holding a multiplicity of points of view internally (rather than projecting them) and this often manifests itself as adolescent moodiness. As this becomes a more familiar internal organization, the epistemology of Era #3 leads to affective life which is fundamentally more intimately related to others, since the empathic introjecting of other points of view amounts to a kind of co-constructing and co-experiencing of inner experience. Of course, the epistemology of Era #3 is constrained by its own subjectivity and the possibility of evolutions beyond this subject-object balance is the story of adult development (Fowler, 1981; Kegan, 1982; Parks, 1986; Vaillant, 1977). For the purposes of the present chapter, however, these three eras are sufficient.

AN EMERGING EMPIRICAL FINDING:
THE CORRESPONDENCE OF SOCIOPATHY AND ERA #2

Despite the fact that the second epistemology described in the previous section is more commonly associated with the meaning-making of children between the ages of seven and 13, it may strike a familiar chord to anyone who has had experience with persons of any age diagnosed as sociopathic. If persons diagnosed as sociopaths actually do share this epistemological system, a host of implications follows, both for our understanding of their capacities and constraints and for considerations of treatment. But before we turn to such implications, it is fair to ask if there is any evidence that sociopaths tested with respect to their natural epistemology do in fact show up with scores more common to preadolescents.

The answer is that a full-scale empirical exploration of the several testable strands of constructive development has not been undertaken with persons diagnosed as sociopathic. But such a study deserves to be undertaken, especially in light of the highly suggestive impression beginning to take shape from the accumulating pieces of empirical evidence that do exist. These are reviewed in this section under three categories: 1) studies with samples of persons not formally diagnosed as sociopathic but presumed largely to be diagnosable as sociopathic (i.e., certain kinds of "delinquent populations"); 2) studies relating a varie-

ty of clinical diagnostic categories (including "sociopathy") to developmental variables; and 3) studies relating diagnosed sociopaths with
developmental variables.

1) Delinquency and Development Studies

There have been several studies of delinquency populations with constructive-developmental measures (such as Kohlberg's moral judgment
measure or Loevinger's measure of ego development). These studies
generally suggest a strong relation between (non-politically-motivated)
delinquency and the second epistemology (Kohlberg's "Stage 2," Loevinger's "Delta" or "pre-conformist"). Frank and Quinlan (1976), e.g.,
found a group of high-school-age delinquent girls (mean age = 16) to
be 92% at Loevinger's "stage 2" (preconformist"). For comparison,
Noam et al. (1984) cite Gold's study (1980) of a normal, nondelinquent, high school sample (actually a year or two *younger* than Frank
and Quinlan's sample), in which the breakdown is: Stage 2 — 54%;
Stage 3 — 36%; Stage 4 — 9%). Jennings, Kilkenny, and Kohlberg (1983)
cite several studies relating delinquent populations to measures of moral
development. For example, Kohlberg (1958) compared a sample of
10 adolescent delinquent males and 12 adolescent nondelinquent males
(matched on age, IQ, and socioeconomic status (SES)). Mean moral
stage scores for the two samples (reported so that "200" significes exactly Stage 2, "250" in the middle between Stage 2 and Stage 3, etc.)
were 224 for the delinquent sample and 293 for the nondelinquent sample. Hickey (1972) did a similar study comparing 20 delinquent males
(average age 19.3) with 14 nondelinquent males (average age 19.9)
(samples matched on age, IQ, and SES). Mean moral stage scores were
260 for the delinquent group and 319 for the nondelinquent group.
Kohlberg and Freundlich (1973) compared 13 adolescent delinquent
males with 13 adolescent nondelinquent males (samples matched on
age, IQ, and SES); mean moral stage scores were 206 for the delinquent group and 282 for the nondelinquent group. Hudgins and Prentice (1973) compared 10 adolescent delinquent males with 10 controls
(matched on age, IQ, race, SES, and geographic area); mean moral
stage scores were 208 for the delinquent sample and 252 for the nondelinquent sample.

These studies are impressive in their agreement that adolescent delinquents tend more toward the second epistemology and that adoles-

cent nondelinquents tend more toward the third. Since the studies are confined to a period in the lifespan when many "normals" will themselves be at or just beyond Stage 2, it is all the more notable that small samples of same-aged subjects yield such striking differences. An untested inference is that this "gap" would widen between a delinquent older sample and an age-matched normal sample. We do not *know* if these delinquent samples are sociopathic (the delinquent offenses are repetitive car theft, burglary, robbery by assault, repeated court appearances), but we know that sociopathic patterns often begin in early adolescence. If these samples are sociopathic, what we might be seeing in these studies is that point in epistemological development where sociopathic and "normal" trajectories diverge.

2) Clinical Diagnoses and Developmental Measures

A few studies have looked developmentally at psychiatric inpatient populations in which subjects spanned ages from adolescence through 60 and carried a variety of clinical diagnoses. Vincent and Vincent (1979) assessed the ego development (via the Loevinger measure) of 100 inpatients who were also grouped (via MMPI) into neurotic, psychotic, character-disordered, and normal categories. Ages ranged from 18 to 60. The character-disordered group (which we can only presume included those diagnosed as sociopathic, since Vincent and Vincent do not report the specific diagnoses within groups) was much more likely to be at Loevinger's second stage than were all the other groups, which tended to be at the third stage and beyond.

Kegan (1979) assessed the moral stage (via the Kohlberg measure) of 38 consecutively admitted psychiatric inpatients and divided them into three groups: those at Stage 2 or transitional from 2 to 3; those at Stage 3 or transitional from 3 to 4; those at Stage 4 or transitional from 4 to 5. Age of subjects ranged from 14 to 70. Clinical diagnoses included: obsessive-compulsive, sociopathic, borderline, psychotic depression, depressive neurosis, simple schizophrenia, paranoid schizophrenia, anorexia nervosa, paranoid psychosis, adolescent adjustment reaction, schizo-affective psychosis, and manic-depression. Of the 38 subjects, four were diagnosed sociopathic. Three of these had moral stage scores in the Stage 2 or transitional from 2 to 3 group; one was in the Stage 3 or transitional from 3 to 4 group.

These two studies are not blockbusters; in the first instance we cannot even be certain we are talking about sociopathy, and in the second the numbers are small. But they are intriguing and suggestive along a similar line.

3) Sociopathy and Developmental Measures

As reported in Jennings, Kilkenny, and Kohlberg (1983), Jurkovic and Prentice (1977) compared samples of 12 "psychopathic" delinquent boys, 12 neurotic delinquent boys, 12 "subcultural" delinquent boys, and 12 "normals" (matched by age [mean = 15.7], IQ, SES, length of institutionalization). Psychopaths differed significantly in stages of moral judgment with each of the other three groups (e.g., psychopaths' score − 216 vs. normals' score − 260), while there were no significant differences between any other two groups. Using Cleckley's criteria, Fodor (1973) distinguished 30 psychopathic delinquents from 30 nonpsychopathic delinquents (matched by sex [male], age [16], IQ, and race), and assessed stage of moral judgment using Kohlberg's measure. His findings were as follows: 24 psychopathic delinquents were found to be at Stages 1 or 2, and only six at Stages 3 or 4, while 15 nonpsychopathic delinquents were at Stages 1 or 2, and 15 at Stages 3 or 4. The apparent greater tendency of the psychopathic group to be at Stage 1 or 2 was found to be statistically significant ($X^2 = 5.94$, $p < .02$).

No one of the entire 11 studies reviewed here is necessarily startling by itself, nor does the group as a whole prove anything conclusive about the relation between sociopathy and epistemological level. The cumulative effect, however, of the studies' unequivocal finding of association between sociopathic or sociopathic-like phenomena and the second epistemological stage described in the previous section does seem to point supportively to the unusual premise that sociopathy may be a specific kind of developmental delay.

SOCIOPATHY AS DEVELOPMENTAL DELAY: IMPLICATIONS

When the hypothesis is entertained that sociopathy is a form of developmental delay — specifically, a delay or arrest at the level of latency in the evolution of one's underlying epistemology — several implications present themselves, which I have grouped here into three categories: 1) a number of otherwise disparate characterizations and observations of the sociopathic personality come together into a more coherent organization; 2) a number of characterizations and observations of the sociopathic personality appear to reveal more about the frame of mind of the attributor than that of the sociopath; and 3) consideration of sociopathy in the context of lifelong processes of development suggests that the sociopath is someone who has never had an adolescence, that sociopathy may be "outgrown" rather than "cured," and that treatment should be considered in terms of facilitating that growth.

1) *A number of otherwise disparate characterizations and observations of the sociopathic personality come together into a more coherent organization.* There exists a host of commonly and sensibly accepted indicia of sociopathy; there does not exist a host of plausible explanations as to why such characteristics should group themselves together. One test of the promise of such a formulation is to assess how much of the available evidence gathers to it—how much can it take account of, and how little does it have to stretch or contort itself to do so? If the formulation can take account of a great deal, then it introduces the possibility of the qualitatively better understanding of a phenomenon that comes from knowing not only more and more signs of its expression, but the source itself *of* those signs.

It would seem that nearly every one of the most common features of sociopathy can be associated with one or the other of the three aspects of mental organization discussed in the previous section: cognitive; social-cognitive or interpersonal; and affective or intrapersonal. In general, these sociopathic features amount to deficits or peculiarities in one or the other of these three aspects of mental organization. But in each case it can be argued that the "principle of constraint" giving rise to the deficit or peculiarity is that of the second epistemology described in the previous section.

Consider, for example, these features of sociopathy, all of which reflect on the realm of interpersonal or social-cognitive meaning-making. The sociopath is said to be: a con-man, manipulative, a facile and convincing liar, selfish, callous, charming, disarmingly capable of understanding others and their motives well, naive, a blamer of others rather than oneself, an irresponsible parent, unable to sustain consistent work involvement, unaccepting of ordinary social norms with respect to lawful behavior or meeting financial or other agreements and social contracts, incapable of significant loyalty or enduring attachment of warmth and responsibility to others. The argument of the present chapter is not only that all of these things could be said of many a 10-year-old, but that there is a reason why such things could be said of both (some) 10-year-olds and (all) sociopaths. And that reason is that they share a common developmental position in the evolution of natural epistemological structures.

The ability to construct one's own point of view (and recognize that others are constructing their own as well) and the *in*ability to coordinate these points of view (to construct the self or the other not only in terms of one's point of view, but in terms of the relation of one point of view to another)—this simultaneous achievement and constraint—is consistently implicated in these social-relational features of sociopathy. This epistemological state need *not* express itself in antisocial behavior (especially in the presence of effective social models and social control) but even the best behaved 10-year-old is a *kind* of con-man whose con is sanctioned, monitored, perhaps even created, by its "pigeon." Well-behaved or not, the 10-year-old is a prisoner of an epistemology that includes others on behalf of his own goals and purposes. This epistemology allows him to take others into account to the extent of providing them with the sense they are understood, so there *is* a kind of empathy of which the 10-year-old is capable, although the intent of such considerations has to do with the pursuit of one's own goals and purposes, which, if one is expecting otherwise, could be seen as selfish, callous, manipulative, deceptive, or even dishonest.

The 10-year-old's sealed-up epistemology (compare with the *previous* epistemology) lets him know he *can* have an unintrudable world of his own—private, secret, and unexposing of the differences between what he knows to be true and what he says to be true. Since the same epistemology is also without the burdensome in-dweller of another's internalized point of view ("conscience"), he is perfectly able to make use of his privacy in pursuit of his goals and purposes. If he can lie with certainty that bad (external) consequences will not follow, he will do so. Because he does not orient to the other's point of view in the very construction of the self (but only *a posteriori* for the operation of the self), his interpersonal relationships are essentially built on benefits (and fairly immediate benefits) to himself.

This same epistemological situation speaks to why: the sociopath does not construct the kind of relationships a diagnostic manual would characterize as significantly deep, loyal, or responsible (one has to construct *mutually* reciprocal relations, minimally the third epistemology, in order to form relations of this sort); he blames others rather than himself when in difficulty (since he does not internalize others' points of view, antagonistic reactions *to* them, which by the third epistemology would be expressed as guilt, get expressed as external, social embattlement); he would be an irresponsible parent, employee, law-maintainer, or debtor (each of these requires the ability to coordinate one's own needs with another's in a fashion that will allow one to relativize or subordinate one's immediate goals to the broader context of interpersonalism). A 10-year-old's ill-equippedness to be parent, employee, or debtor is not a social problem only because we as a society effectively and with remarkable unanimity forbid 10-year-olds to be parents, employees, or debtors. Indeed, responsible parents who know nothing explicitly about "natural epistemologies" make differential diagnoses (between the second and third epistemologies) when they decide if a particular adolescent is equipped to play even the temporary parenting role of babysitter.

An identical analysis can be made of descriptive features of sociopathy in the other realms (cognitive and affective/intrapersonal), as well. Cognitively, the sociopath is said to be both highly intelligent and pathetically naive; he is capable of extraordinarily intricate plotting, holding a variety of pieces of information in his head at once, but at the same time he seems not to engage in long-term planning and can set off almost impulsively with no clear goal in mind; in description after description the sociopath's thinking is called unusual, but most observers agree he is not psychotic and does not have a thought disorder in the usual sense of the word. Emotionally, in addition to the already discussed lack of capacity for a kind of depth in his relationships, he is said to be incapable of guilt, and asexual or non-relationally motivated in sexual encounters; also, lurking beneath the controlled surface there is a capacity for high irritability and even aggression.

It will come as no surprise by now if I suggest that the sociopath's "thought disorder in the non-usual sense" is what Piaget called "concrete operations." In conceding that persons diagnosed as sociopathic do not have psychotic-like thinking, what is being recognized, I believe, is that, different as the individual's thinking is from what we expect of adolescents or adults (the third epistemology or beyond), it does not have the features of associationism, irrationality, nonlinearity, highly intuitive or imagistic or fantasy-embedded thinking which is characteristic of both psychotic thinking and the thinking of children between the ages of two and five (the first epistemology).

Concrete thinking is both capable of holding several pieces of information together and incapable of subordinating the actual to the realm of the possible (which is required for the construction of long-range plans, patterns or generalizations). It is not enough to say that some sociopaths are highly intelligent; studies must look carefully into the nature or shape of this intelligence. Brilliant 10-year-olds have higher IQs and are more apt to appear to us as "highly intelligent" than normal 35-year-olds, even though the former cannot think abstractly and the latter can. If we talk further with the brilliant 10-year-old and the normal 35-year-old, or in a different way, we will come to see that, yes, the 10-year-old is very intelligent, *but also very naive*, exactly what is said of the person diagnosed as sociopathic. In my view, the delicious essence of the famous exchange between bank robber Willy Sutton and a newspaper reporter is that everyone else thought his answer funny but Willy Sutton was completely sincere:

"Why do you rob all these banks, Willy?"

"Because that's where they keep the money."

A quite similar exchange took place recently when a judge was preparing to sentence a man who repeatedly ordered meals at restaurants, ate them, and then was unable to pay for them. Prior to sentencing, the judge sought to inquire into the motives of the unhappy man before him. "Tell me," he said, "what's going on with you? I mean, why do you *do* this?" The man thought for a moment and then answered with obvious sincerity, "Well, Judge, I go in and order the meals because I'm hungry. And then I don't pay for them because I don't have any money."

The judge was seeking, no doubt, some report of inner states, perhaps even of inner conflict, but in any case some verbal consequence of self-reflection. But perhaps he did not receive it because no "self" was there before him organized in such a way that "reflection" would lead to a report of internal conversation (psychological states, experienced and expressed as such, grow out of a coordination of points of view within the self). If the man were constrained by the second epistemology, "self-reflection" would amount to a narration of logically sequential behaviors, which is just what the judge got.

The same constraint also makes it impossible to feel genuine guilt; the word may be in one's vocabulary but what it means (to a person diagnosed as sociopathic and to a 10-year-old alike) is anxious anticipation of what others might do. Real guilt is itself an internal psychological conversation and the second epistemology cannot conduct such an internal conversation.

The attribution that sociopaths are asexual or engage in sex as means to ends (rather than for the experience or nurturance of an interpersonal relationship) is especially interesting from the point of view that sociopathy is a developmental delay at an epistemological level more appropriate to latency. That their sexual behavior should be on behalf of their own goals, plans, or needs is, of course, consistent with the epistemological point of view taken here, but that they should often actually be *a*sexual seems even to be latency-like in ways not obviously related to underlying epistemology.

In sum, it appears that a great many of the most commonly attributed features of sociopathy — features that do not have an immediately obvious correlation — take on a logical coherence when considered as expressive of the capacities and constraints of the second epistemology described in the previous section. As this lends greater credence to our formulation, we are led then to some *re*considerations of common descriptions of sociopathy, and finally, to some preliminary considerations for treatment from this perspective.

   2) A number of characterizations and observations of the sociopathic personality appear to reveal more about the frame of mind of the attributor than that of the sociopath. Among the most common attributions made to the sociopath are the following: a) The sociopath is amoral; b) the sociopath is impulsive and/or goalless; c) the sociopath's inner life is hollow; d) the sociopath is manipulative. Each of these deserves to be reconsidered as potentially an artifact of the lens through which the sociopath is being observed.

If the sociopath is organizing the world according to the epistemology of Kohlberg's second stage of moral judgment (and the previous section has demonstrated that this possibility already has some empirical support), then the sociopath can only be said to be *amoral* when the speaker unwittingly confines the moral universe to those organizations of reality beyond stage two. At best the sociopath can be said to be morally retarded, but even this characterization risks missing the very real way in which the sociopath is an active participant in the moral world. Most eight-to-10-year-olds organize the moral world according to this same logic, and while most adults recognize there is something different about their own notions of right and wrong and that of a nine-year-old child's, they do not call the nine-year-old amoral. Further, they recognize that the nine-year-old's participation in the world of fairness-governed social relationships is already markedly different from what it was five or six years earlier when "there was just no reasoning with him at all." We would do far better in dealing with a person diagnosed as sociopathic by understanding the systematicity and coherence of meaning-making that he *does* have, rather than only defining those capacities he does *not* have or those worlds (e.g., "conventional" or "principled" morality) from which he is (at this time) excluded.

Perhaps the following two examples, one of a child's thinking (Kegan, 1982, pp. 46–48) and the other of a sociopath's (Kegan, 1982, pp. 172–3) will make clearer how the sociopath can be said to be both morally arrested and possessed of a moral logic which is genuinely his own rather than pretended to.

A group of school children read a story called "The New Kid" by Murray Heyert. The city block and the nearby playing field form the universe of the story, which opens with the choosing of sides for baseball. This ritual is a humiliating one for Marty; he is always chosen last and relegated to the outfield. He prays fervently that no ball will leave the infield, much less come his way. But, as it happens, at the crucial moment the ball soars toward Marty who, sprouting extra arms, fails the chance and costs his side the game. As he trudges in from the field his teammates heap abuse upon him. We get the impression that this is not only an awful experience for Marty, but a rather common one. He isn't Willy Mays. Then one day a new kid appears on the block. He's little. His clothes are too nice. His socks match. There are buckles on his shoes. All bad signs. In other words, he may be more of a wimp than Marty. He is invited to the ballfield and sides are chosen. For the first time Marty is not the least favored. The new kid is put in the outfield. He belongs to the same religion as Marty and prays that nothing will be hit to him, but as luck (or artistic license) would have it, the new kid must handle the crucial, last-inning blow. He fails spectacularly—not merely at catching it, but at running after it, grasping it, and throwing it. He returns from the field with his chin on his knees, and who should begin—who should lead, who should sustain — the round of humiliating invective, but Marty himself!

When the children were asked the moral of this story, their answers ran something like this:

> The story is saying that people may be mean to you and push you down and make you feel crummy and stuff, but it's saying things aren't really all that bad because eventually you'll get your chance to push someone else down and then you'll be on top.

It seems clear that what we are looking at here is not so much what kids know, but *how* they know. However harsh their interpretation might sound (or, for that matter, actually be), theirs was a staunchly and explicitly moral formulation. It was not an amoral position they adopted or an immoral one. They spoke their point of view with a righteous sense that indeed we were touching here on solemn matters of right and wrong, and, as any moralist might, they were champion-ing the right as they saw it. The students' analyses of the story have an undeniable ring of reciprocity to them, even if they strike us as an odd, or logically circular, sort of reciprocity. It is a kind of reciprocity that seems to let slip away just the different pieces that need to be held together — for example, that Marty, better than anyone, should know how the new kid felt. This refusal to let yourself be the context in which the two sides are joined is reminiscent of a famous Groucho Marx ex-change: "What if everyone felt the way you did?" "Well then," says Groucho, "I'd be a fool to feel otherwise!" What is funny or exasper-ating in Groucho's ability to purposely slip out of a kind of meaning he is capable of making is actually quite close to a structure of mean-ing the normal school child has no choices about. The children revealed an understanding of how Marty felt (he felt awful when picked on; he was happy and relieved to have someone else to pick on) and of how the new kid felt (he felt awful when picked on, too, but he'd have his chance). What the children could *not* do was consider simultaneous-ly the way each felt, orienting each to the other. But even this lesser ability for simple, one-way reciprocity, the ability to "take the role" of another, is a product of many years of evolution (Selman, 1980).

Roxanne is an inmate in a woman's correctional institution (Blakeney and Blakeney, 1977). She has prostituted herself, shoplifted, picked pockets, stolen other people's welfare checks, used other people's credit cards. She feels that stealing is generally wrong ("stealing is the worst thing I do"), except when it is necessary to meet one's needs ("stealing is okay when you need the money for yourself"). On the other hand, she feels that people who shoplift for the fun of it are definitely wrong, and that people who sleep around a lot are "whores." ("It's wrong if you're not getting paid for it.") She defends another's check-stealing on the grounds that "if she didn't steal the money she woulda got put out, right? So that made it fair to her, then. I wouldn't have thought about jail then. I'd have stole it and it would have been fair 'cause it was for my needs. It would be right to steal it at the time and you don't think about coming to jail. When you're cashing checks, you don't think about getting caught." The only thing that makes it not right, in other words, is that one is sure to be caught for it and sent to jail, but she can understand how, under the pressure of need, one would not exercise what is implicitly one's "best judgment"—that is, don't steal in situations where you are likely to be caught. When she is asked if it would be fair for someone else who faced the same kind of needs to steal her check, she says, "No. That wouldn't be fair." As Blakeney and Blakeney say, the logic seems to be that "it is right for me to take someone's check *because I need it*, and it is wrong for someone to take my check *because I need it*," a position that is at least consistent if it is not mutually reciprocal.

While the sociopath's moral logic is not the same as our own (most likely!), I suggest we will do better to see that it *is* a moral logic. We will better understand how his world *is* holding together, which is a question that must precede that of how it *should* hold together. Understanding the logic and order of the sociopath's morality also helps us to see an epistemological past that has been outgrown (not just a future that has been too long resisted). Better recognizing an outgrown epistemological past amounts to recognizing strengths and previous constraints of mind that have been overcome.

In this context we are naturally led to reconsider also the common characterization that the sociopath is impulsive or goalless. This characterization, too, bespeaks an unwitting comparison to psychological organizations of *desire* expressive of the third epistemology or beyond. It may be true that sociopaths cannot organize their desires in such a way that frustration, for example, registers as an inner state of disappointment rather than as socially transacted embattlement; but such an organization of desire is a far cry from that of the earlier epistemology which *is* genuinely driven by its moment-to-moment feelings and literally incapable of suspending a wish through time (i.e., a "goal"), let alone plotting a strategy to fulfill it.

If sociopaths are organized at the second epistemological level they are capable of driving (rather than being driven by) their moment-to-moment feelings, constructing concrete goals and plans for fulfilling them. If sociopaths were genuinely goalless, no one would complain of being manipulated by them. It is true that these goals can be short-term, highly concrete and not related to any self-identified overall life plan, but that again is the difference between the second epistemology and those which follow. For example, the person diagnosed as socio-pathic may want a pack of cigarettes and, finding that he has no money, snatch a purse in order to get the cigarettes. While it is understanda-ble how such behavior leads one to call the sociopath "impulsive" or "action-oriented," it is important to distinguish it from the person who is walking down the street with no intentions and in the presence of a snatchable purse finds himself unable to inhibit the impulse to take it. The sociopath's "action orientation" is about *planful* action, not merely (as in the case of the first epistemology) *motoric* action. The sociopath can sit still, inhibit immediate aims, defer gratification. In-deed, if he did not have these abilities (which most latency-age chil-dren also have), people would not confuse him with an adult even with his adult-looking body (which most latency-age children do not have, and which has more to do with why latency-age children are not con-fused with adults than people realize).

The sociopath's vaunted "hollowness" may similarly reflect more upon the instruments of measurement than the object being measured. To a fisherman with inch-square netting the ocean is devoid of fish smaller than an inch. It is true that when one gains sufficient rapport so that a sociopath will honestly reveal his feelings, what one hears is an unabashed orientation to others as supplies to the self. As dem-onstration of the essential "hollowness" he saw, Cleckley gave the ex-ample of a young suitor who admitted he placed no feelings of impor-tance on his relationship to his intended; the whole idea of marriage was lacking in meaning to him, he said himself, unless of course what one was talking about was really a merger, say, of two wealthy, dynas-tic families!

In another instance, a seasoned clinician is fond of the way he helped an intern give up her naive notion that a sociopath could be possessed of (non-hollow) feelings of loyalty, warmth, and inclusion within some family or clan with which he positively identified. The patient, who happened to be both black and a thief, had been asked if there was anyone from whom he would not steal, and he had replied warmly, seriously, and sincerely that he would never steal a purse from a black woman. The intern took this as a sign of loyalty to one's group and sympathy for another until the seasoned clinician asked the man why it was he would never steal the purse of a black woman. "Because," he said, "no sense maybe getting caught for no money."

It is true, if the sociopath organizes his experience according to the second epistemology, that he does not construct an interpersonal world; he does not identify with those points of view with which he can empathize; they do not become a part of an internal, co-constructive process of "interpersonal" experiencing. He takes the point of view of a (more likely to be poor) black woman—not for the purpose of establishing or renewing his shared bond with her, but for the purpose of making a judgment about what will be most enhancing for the self's prosecution of its needs.

While this may be the case, it can only be said to be "hollow" from some more evolved point of view. It looks hollow to us because we construct a "bigger" inner world, and when we "try on" the sociopath's world within ourselves it doesn't fill *us* up; it leaves *us* feeling empty or hollow! So we then attribute hollowness to the sociopath! But this may not be the sociopath's experience of his inner world at all; nor need it be the only perspective for us to take.

In fact, this is the same world as that of a normal eight- or 10-year-old, and, although most sensitive parents realize their children would be tempted to sell them for a cold drink on a hot day, they do not think of the rather shortsighted self-interestedness of their children as a sign of "hollowness." Indeed, the latency-age child (Erikson's "industrial" child "on the make" [1963]) is *full* of plans and goals and organized wants, and he or she is quite ready to make use of anyone or anything that can be pressed into service as a tool on behalf of accomplishing these ends. The inner world may be concrete; it may be more filled with persons-as-tools than persons-as-sharable-psychologies; but it is not empty or hollow. If a caterpillar doesn't know its future has wings, it hardly experiences itself as land-bound.

This leads quite naturally to a reconsideration of a last and hardest-to-alter characterization of the sociopath: the sociopath as *manipula-*

tive. Maybe the sociopath's inner world is *not* hollow, since it is filled with persons-as-supplies or persons-as-tools; but to feel *ourselves* made use of as tools on behalf of someone else's project feels to us as if we are being manipulated. And of course, in a sense we are. The implication of considering sociopathy as an arrest in the evolution of epistemological structures is not so much to deny that the sociopath is manipulative as it is to suggest more about what that manipulation involves.

The first suggestion is that *it is choiceless*. A great deal of our anger at being manipulated arises out of our inference that the person could do otherwise. What we are calling the sociopath's manipulation may really be an expression of the way he is epistemologically constrained to hold the world (of which we are an important part) together. Without the internalization of others' voices in one's very construction of self, how one feels is much more a matter of how actual external others will react, what they will or will not do in consequence of what one does. One's emotional situation is thus always changing, depending on the actions and reactions of others, who are not easily decipherable since their interior life cannot be constructed any more complexly than one can construct one's own. If the limits of one's epistemology make it impossible for one to hold the other interiorly or imaginatively (the shared reality, the essence of mutuality), one must seek to hold and regulate the other externally, which the other experiences as being manipulated.

3) Consideration of sociopathy in the context of lifelong processes of development suggests that the person diagnosed as sociopathic is someone who has never had an adolescence, that sociopathy may be "outgrown" rather than "cured," and that treatment should be considered in terms of facilitating that growth. The message in arguing for sociopathy as a specific form of developmental delay is *not* that persons diagnosed as sociopathic are nice, normal 10-year-olds living in adult-looking bodies. And the implication of pursuing a better understanding of how they do make meaning is *not* that persons diagnosed as sociopathic will be much helped if we just extend them the kindness of our empathically accurate understanding. If the formulation of developmental delay has any promise, its implication is that persons diagnosed as sociopathic are as far away from nice, normal 10-year-olds as autistic children are from the wholesome and normally undifferentiated state of infancy. The implication is that something has gone terribly wrong with the normal processes of development at a highly conspicuous cost to those who are connected to the individual, but at an equally high, if less conspicuous, cost to the individual himself, who can only maintain his psychological configuration by continuously moving against the forward motion of his own life. This is enormously hard work and the sociopath needs help in giving it up.

Such help would amount to recreating the formal aspects of those unself-consciously therapeutic processes (primarily, parenting and peer culturing) which naturally facilitate the evolution from latency into adolescence. I will address here two of these, which do not ordinarily occur for persons diagnosed as sociopathic: *the protection of latency*, and *the promotion of adolescence*.

The person diagnosed sociopathic is not just someone who has never had an adolescence; he has also never had a protected latency. The much vaunted increased independence, self-assurance, and initiative of the latency-age child is actually quite fragile and provisional, and in all wholesome situations it is exercised within a context that protects it through constant monitoring by competent adults. Put most simply — in wholesome situations some competent adult has a 10-year-old's precise whereabouts in mind at all times. To an extent we little realize we keep a 10-year-old on a very short leash. If he or she is not at home or at school or at the home of a friend or under some other direct supervision, he or she is usually either on the way to direct supervision (walking to school), within close reach of direct supervision (outside playing in some specified locale), or essentially free on a very circumscribed pass issued by direct supervision. Ten-year-olds are generally not long let out of an adult's sight (or, by phone, hearing). For very good reason we have provided for our 10-year-olds an environment that, first of all, can be described as one of nearly seamless monitoring or containment. We don't realize it, but it is true.

If we thought seriously about what the world would be like if we let 10-year-olds out of this containment, we might better understand what the world is like for those who live around a sociopath; and if we thought seriously about what the world of a 10-year-old who has *lost* this containment is like, we might better understand what the world is like for a sociopath. The first treatment implication of this developmental line of reasoning is thus: *Although most persons diagnosed sociopathic are neither suicidal or homicidal, they cannot be successfully treated without being hospitalized, institutionalized, or otherwise integrated into a self-conscious community that will exercise monitoring responsibilities 24 hours a day.*

However much the 10-year-old may object to his constant surveillance, what he comes to experience in its competent exercise is the safety of his containment. He experiences auxiliary psychological equipment, there to assist him in his central internal task, the containment of his own impulses. Thus, the naturally therapeutic environment is not only watching, but ready to take action on behalf of its central goal—the protection of latency. At bottom such action protects by convincing the child not only that there are others who care for him who are stronger than he is but also that they exercise their power on behalf of values, purposes, and convictions.

Power, influence, and control are words that make people uncomfortable, especially in a context such as parenting, which is first of all about *love*; but effective parental loving of a 10-year-old must include competent executive functioning, a child's sure sense that someone is in charge who believes in something and will stand up for those beliefs. Ten-year-olds are in the process of learning to exercise control over themselves so that they can pursue their own goals with a new measure of independence and self-sufficiency, so that they can take pleasure in the competent exercise of social roles (child, peer, pupil) and participation in social institutions. A child at this age is most in need of inclusion and recognition in social institutions which he or she experiences as fair, committed to some shared purposes, and, above all, led by persons who are models of the executive command which is first on the child's own psychological agenda. The most intimate institution in which the child participates is the family, and the most visceral and instructive lessons the child receives in effective self-leadership come from the ways she or he experiences *being* led. In a family with a 10-year-old someone must be clearly in charge and it had better not be the 10-year-old.

Power, authority, and control make many people uncomfortable, in part because they have seen so many arbitrary and abusive exercises of power (especially at the governmental and corporate levels) that they come to feel that all exercises of power must be intrinsically arbitrary or deleterious. On the contrary, the exercise of power as a parent is itself intrinsic to effective loving and effective leadership. Thus, a second implication for treatment is: *An effective therapeutic community for the person diagnosed as sociopathic is hierarchical not egalitarian, clearly distinguishing the leaders from the led; leadership stands for, fosters, and invites participation in community-wide vlaues and purposes, at the same time recognizing and preserving distinctions in membership to different functions and levels of authority.*

Finally, in service of the protection of latency, a 10-year-old is provided opportunities to "fill the self," show off, display the self as well-run, its products as well-made. The 10-year-old's environment is meaningful by virtue of its opportunities for him or her to meet concrete needs. Central to this is a certain degree of "manipulability" at every level—physical, social, psychological; that is, a given set of consequences can be relied upon for a given set of behaviors. Inconsistent parents (who may, e.g., shield their children from the consequences of their behaviors in one instance and make them suffer the consequences of the same behaviors in the next instance) are actually letting down their children by their *failure* to be manipulable. The implications of this for treatment of the sociopath are: *A therapeutic environment for persons diagnosed sociopathic provides opportunities for effectance at concrete levels of self-enhancement; persons are engaged at the level of their needs and the* external *circumstances relative to meeting them, rather than at the level of their feelings and the* internal *circumstances that lead to them; the emphasis is on outsight not insight.*

But the natural facilitation of development from latency to adolescence seems to involve not only the protection of the former, but eventually the active promoting of the latter. The epistemological evolution from Stage 2 to Stage 3 amounts to the gradual "bringing inside" of the other's point of view; the other's point of view goes from being something that one merely takes into account in order to pursue satisfactorily the self's objectives, to being a part *of* the self (often as unwelcome but undispatchable intruder during the transition, and eventually as a natural part of who the self is). We can see this evolution in longitudinal and cross-sectional studies, typically between latency and adolescence, but we do not yet know enough about what facilitates it. *A chief implication of this whole chapter for the treatment of sociopathy is that a better understanding of the natural facilitation of development from latency to adolescence, and an extracting of its formal, systematic features, would serve as an excellent resource for the better design of environments therapeutic to persons whose ages and bodies suggest adulthood but whose psychologies suggest they have never been adolescent.*

One source of this facilitation seems certainly to be the peer culture, and particularly those special relationships which differ from the latency character of doing/exchanging/comparing/competing/compromising and signal instead the first bloom of co-constructing, co-experiencing interpersonalism. Whether these be Sullivan's chum relationships (1953) or the more unilateral fascination with someone deemed especially admirable, such relationships, by virtue of the individual's *identification* with the other, are facilitators of a kind of trick nature plays upon the second epistemology, for it must seem at first as if no other view has "really" gotten inside. But the other-who-is-just-like-the-self is a "transitional object," both part of the old epistemology and part of the new. In taking the other into account one is simultaneously continuing the embeddedness in a single point of view (since the other's point of view is the same as one's own, a feature of identification) *and* bringing another's point of view into the process of constructing the self's point of view. Working from the direction that this is someone one considers very *like* oneself, and whom one *wants* to *continue* considering like oneself, one responds to one's inevitable discoveries of slight differences between the two views in ways quite different from making the other into the antagonistic holder of competing points of view. On the contrary, perhaps one tries to *restore* one's sense of an identity between the two views by finding some way to bring the views back into line. Such radical "behavior" can lead to a whole different epistemology!

Environments likely to promote the possibilities of such relationships would seem to be therapeutic to the development of persons diagnosed as sociopathic. *Such environments would need to be committed to a Stage 3 ideology of inclusiveness but simultaneously willing and able to survive the rigors of admitting persons whose* initial *form of connection to and participation in the community will be self-interested.* This feature of naturally therapeutic adolescent milieux is probably replicated in certain street-oriented religious and political communities (or even certain prison communities) that recognize the people who come to them have often never had relationships of trust or mutuality, have "bad attitudes," are "just here to rip us off," and cannot, immediately anyway, "get with the program." As Vaillant writes:

> The paths out of sociopathy are like the paths out of drug addiction and adolescence. These are usually quite independent of formal therapy

and are derived from peer identifications. Membership in altruistic but revolutionary movements like Black Panthers, in self-help groups like Alcoholics Anonymous and Synanon, or even marriage to a person as needy as themselves are all more useful than intensive psychotherapy (1975, p. 183).

CONCLUSION

As Cleckley said, these persons we diagnose as sociopathic do *not* make the ordinary meaning of human experience. But when we look at the meaning they *do* make—when we look at the form of their cognitive, social-cognitive, and affective experiencing—what we find revealed behind the "mask of sanity" is not the picture of insanity but that of a child. We find a child, sometimes even a quite bright child, of eight, nine, or ten, who has outgrown the illogical, fantasy-embedded, impulse-driven world of early childhood, but who has not yet grown into the abstract thinking, interpersonally mutual, and intrapersonally subjective state common to adolescence. We find a child, captive of concrete thinking, with an orientation to others as short-term supplies to the self, embedded in its own goals and purposes, unable to coordinate more than a single point of view internally or interpersonally.

We find a child, but in distressed circumstances of a particular sort, for every child is not a sociopath. (Indeed, as we have said, every adult who operates out of the second epistemology is not necessarily a sociopath.) We find a child, with the body and age of an adolescent or adult, living unprotected from the extraordinary vulnerabilities of his ordinary mental limitations. No 10-year-old is equipped to handle either the freedoms or responsibilities of adult life. Most of those who are made to and can find no substitute family to take them in end up either dead or the exploited prey of others. Some few, like plucky orphans of the street, manage to avoid either fate by summoning the capacities they do have, however constrained, to produce finely honed survival skills. Such skills and behaviors may be aberrant products of a mental organization continuously confronted with challenges beyond its capacity *but nonetheless, as best it can, meeting that challenge.* The person diagnosed sociopathic is like this plucky, orphan child. As destructive as his behavior is to himself and those around him, he is without malicious intent, and there is even, in this behavior, a certain admirable achievement, given the limitations with which he must deal.

Foremost among these limitations is the lack of support for development *beyond* his preadolescent state. I am speaking here of the psychologically intricate, yet altogether ordinary, features of those familial, social-institutional, and peer group contexts which regularly foster development into adolescence. We take such contexts for granted, as we do the availability of oxygen, but when either is in short supply the effects are dramatically toxic. We do not know as much as we could about the naturally therapeutic contexts which support development at every age (Kegan, 1982), and odd as it may sound, a largely untapped source of wisdom for better treating sociopathy may be those contexts that ordinarily surround children between the ages of 12 and 16. For what is most hopeful about the formulation of sociopathy advanced here is that what we are looking at is a disturbance in *the ordinary process of growth and development*, the powerful, reliable, and constant force of life itself. Because something is delayed does not mean it can never arrive at all.

REFERENCES

Basseches, M. (1984). *Dialectical thinking and adult development*. Norwood, NJ: Ablex.

Blakeney, R., & Blakeney, C. (1977). Knowing better: delinquent girls and the 2–3 transition. Unpublished paper, Harvard University, Cambridge, MA.

Broughton, J. (1978). The development of concepts of self, mind, reality and knowledge. In W. Damon (Ed.), *Social cognition*. San Francisco: Jossey-Bass.

Cleckley, H. (1941). *Mask of sanity*. St. Louis: C. V. Mosby.

Elkind, D. (1974). Egocentrism in children and adolescents. In *Children and adolescents*. New York: Oxford University Press.

Erikson, E. (1950). *Childhood and society*. New York: Norton.

Fodor, E. (1973). Moral development and parent behavior antecedents in adolescent psychopaths. *Journal of Genetic Psychology, 122*, 37–43.

Fowler, J. (1981). *Stages in faith*. New York: Harper & Row.

Frank, S., & Quinlan, D. (1976). Ego development and adjustment patterns in adolescence. *Journal of Abnormal Psychology, 85*, 505–510.

Gardner, H. (1982). *Artful scribbles*. New York: Basic Books.

Gilligan, C. (1978). *In a different voice*. Cambridge: Harvard University Press.

Gold, S. (1980). Relations between level and ego development and adjustment patterns in adolescence. *Journal of Personality Assessment, 44*(6), 630–638.

Hickey, J. (1972). The effects of guided moral discussion upon youthful offenders' level of moral judgment. Doctoral dissertation, Boston University School of Education, Boston, MA.

Hudgins, W., & Prentice, N. (1973). Moral judgment in delinquent and nondelinquent adolescents and their mothers. *Journal of Abnormal Psychology, 82*, 145–152.

Jennings, W.,Kilkenny, R., & Kohlberg,L. (1983). Moral-development theory and practice for youthful and adult offenders. In Wm. S. Laufer & J. M. Day, (Eds.) *Personality theory, moral development & cultural behavior.* Lexington, MA: Lexington Books.

Jurkovic, G., & Prentice, N. (1977). Relation of moral and cognitive development to dimensions of juvenile delinquency. *Journal of Abnormal Psychology, 86,* 414–420.

Kegan, R. (1979). The evolving self: a process conception for ego psychology. *Counseling Psychologist, 8*(2), 5–34.

Kegan, R. (1982). *The evolving self.* Cambridge: Harvard University Press.

Kegan, R. (1985). The loss of Pete's dragon: transformation in the development of the self during the years five to seven. In R. Leahy (Ed.), *The development of the self.* New York: Academic Press.

Kohlberg, L. (1958). The development of modes of moral thinking and choice in the years ten to sixteen. Doctoral dissertation. University of Chicago, Chicago, IL.

Kohlberg, L. (1981). *The philosophy of moral development.* New York: Harper & Row.

Kohlberg, L. (1984). *The psychology of moral development.* New York: Harper & Row.

Kohlberg, L. & Freundlich, D. (1973). Moral reasoning and delinquency. Unpublished paper, Harvard University, Laboratory of Human Development, Cambridge, MA.

Kohlberg, L. & Gilligan, C. (1972). The adolescent as a philosopher. In J. Kagan & R. Coles (Eds.), *Twelve to sixteen.* New York: Norton.

Lickona, T. (Ed.) (1976). *Moral development and behavior.* New York: Holt Rinehart and Winston.

Loevinger, J. (1976). *Ego development.* San Francisco: Jossey-Bass.

Noam, G. (1984). Self, morality, and biography: Studies in clinical-developmental psychology. Doctoral dissertation, Harvard University, Cambridge, MA.

Noam, G., Hauser, S. , Santostefano, S., Garrison, W., Jacobson, A., Powers, S., & Mead, M. (1984). Ego development and psychopathology. *Child Development, 55,* 184–194.

Parks, S. (1986). *The critical years.* New York: Harper & Row. In press.

Parsons, M. (1983). Baldwin and aesthetic development. In J. M. Broughton & D. J. Freeman-Moir (Eds.), *The foundations of cognitive developmental psychology.* Norwood, N.J.: Ablex Press.

Perry, W. G. (1970). *Forms of intellectual and ethical development in the college years.* New York: Holt, Rinehart and Winston.

Piaget, J. (1937). *The construction of reality in the child.* New York: Basic Books.

Schachtel, E. (1959). *Metamorphosis.* New York: Basic Books.

Selman, R. (1980). *The growth of interpersonal understanding.* New York: Academic Press.

Sullivan, H. (1953). *The interpersonal theory of psychiatry.* New York: Norton.

Vaillant, G. (1975). Sociopathy as a human process. *Archives of General Psychiatry, 32,* 178–183.

Vaillant, G. (1977). *Adaptation to Life.* Boston: Little, Brown.

Vincent, L., & Vincent, K. (1979). Ego development and psychopathology. *Psychological Report, 44,* 408–410.

Werner, H. (1940). *Comparative psychology of mental development.* New York: International Universities Press.

4

Social Crises and Psychopathy:
Toward a Sociology
of the Psychopath

José Sánchez

As early as 1835, James C. Pritchard recognized that, among other factors, industrialization, along with its many consequences, was an important cause of psychopathy ("moral insanity"). In spite of the interest of Pritchard and some of his contemporaries in sociological factors, the psychopath became primarily a psychiatric concern. Consequently, little empirical research or theoretical work which deals with the social structural determinants of psychopathy can be found in the literature.

Much of the work which claims to examine the social causes of psychopathy has to some extent neglected macroscopic social factors and socio-historical events as basic precipitants of this problem. Instead, such factors as the broken home, parental rejection, violence in the family, parental loss, reduced capacity for role-taking in interaction, etc., have occupied the discussion. Some writers, however, have sought explanations in economic individualism and industrialization, but such factors are presented as abstract principles, the origin of which can be found in the rise of modern capitalism and in the industrial revolution.

I am grateful to Professors Joseph Bensman, Edward Sagarin and William McCord for their helpful comments and suggestions, and to Ms. Gwen McClarren for her asistance in the editing and typing of this chapter.

These social changes have themselves had consequences, economic and political, which historically have had varying effects on individuals. The task then becomes one of locating various points in history at which industrialism and/or capitalism have become most capable of producing psychopaths.

This chapter represents a modest attempt to refocus sociological attention on this problem and to propose an initial framework with which to study it.

SOCIOLOGY AND PSYCHOPATHY

What is sociology's approach to psychopathy? In describing the "sociological imagination," C. Wright Mills discussed the impact of specific structures on individuals. Mills demonstrated the interconnectedness between individuals and their society, and provided the approach to be taken in this chapter:

> The sociological imagination enables us to grasp history and biography and the relation between the two within society. That is its task and its promise. To recognize this task, this promise, is the mark of the classic social analyst (Mills, 1959, p. 6).

> When a society is industrialized, a peasant becomes a worker; a feudal lord is liquidated or becomes a business man. When classes rise or fall, a man is employed or unemployed; when the rate of investment goes up or down, a man takes a new heart or goes broke. When wars happen, an insurance man becomes a rocket launcher; a store clerk, a radar man; a wife lives alone; a child grows up without a father. Neither the life of an individual nor the history of a society can be understood without understanding both (p. 3).

The social analyst must then attempt to define the specific ways in which social trends are experienced within the lives of individuals. Along these lines, he will ask how the presence or absence of psychopathy is made possible within given historical social structures. He might also ask whether psychopathy is a necessary feature of all social structures, and what the social factors are that determine increases and decreases in the incidence of psychopathy in society. Thus the sociologist must do more than simply show that specific child-rearing practices are harmful or produce psychopathy. He must study the socio-historical trends which influence the selection of such practices from the vast array of techniques that are culturally available to parents.

After posing the problem in such terms, the sociologist employs the method of comparative, dynamic, and/or static analysis. He will be interested in the effects of a particular social structure, at a given point in time and over time, on the production of psychopaths; in how the incidence of psychopathy varies with the emergence and disappearance of certain historical social structures; and in how it varies across societies. The sociologist will seek to discover the ways in which social structures differ in producing psychopaths.

PSYCHOPATHY AND LEGITIMACY

It is claimed that the psychopath has not internalized authority; he has an underdeveloped superego. He is amoral. The psychopath has not internalized the moral content of his community. Rather, he has internalized only those elements which will insure the attainment of immediate pleasures at little or no pain. This sometimes differentiates him from the psychotic or neurotic. In psychoanalytic terms, the psychopath develops an ego from the id, but full development of the superego occurs inadequately and sometimes not at all.

The ideal-type of the "normal person" achieves a balance among moral demands, instinctual demands, and the demands made by his environment during the course of his life. The "normal" person, like the psychopath, stops himself from fantasies and behavior defined as improper because these may harm his self-presentation or cause him physical pain. Like the psychopath, the normal person may, out of desperation, engage in acts which violate his deepest moral commitments. But the "normal" person also adheres to sets of values, norms, and beliefs, all made legitimate by exposure to and identification with their exponents. He may even resort to criminal acts in order to earn punishment he feels was deserved for an earlier or imaginary offense. This *internalization of the authority* guarantees the present and projected future validity of its precepts.

There is a formal requirement in every social order that everyone cooperate to some degree with all others. Limits are set in every social structure which dictate the degree of conformity that is acceptable. In America, many individuals who have been labeled "neurotic" are said to suffer from extreme conformity. Thus, too much or too little adherence to social norms may arouse public reaction and sanction.

The product of this tacit agreement among individuals is a *legitimate order*. A legitimate order guarantees, and is guaranteed by, the respect, internalization, and diffusion of social norms and values.

Legitimation and internalization may operate in relative interdependence. They signify a point of relation among personality, social structure, and culture.

The classic psychopath does not internalize external authority; he feels no guilt in violating its rulings but professes adherence to them *when it is useful*. His conformity is situational and superficial; he betrays his "principles" at the slightest opportunity.

Individuals, groups, and governments claim their legitimacy on the basis of personal charisma, tradition, or law. Whatever the grounds, however, such claims are usually challenged by some segments or, in extreme cases, by significant minorities of a particular society. During times of crisis, the faith that people place in the prevailing systems of legitimacy of society's institutions declines, thereby weakening central social values, norms and authority structures.

When institutional orders undergo change, some classes improve their positions while others suffer; some governmental systems are attacked and others may rise, and people's perceptions of their world undergo transformation. The tacit agreement holding society together is fractured and further weakened as its traditional form gives way to a new, promised, order.

Legitimacy Crises

> . . . the existence of a legitimacy crisis is . . . widely claimed. This crisis is essentially perceptual, but also has behavioral symptoms and structural roots. It may be attributed to the conditions of a modern mass society, to a particular economic system (e.g. "late capitalist"), or to the impact of specific events, leaders and controversies (Friedrichs, 1980, p. 550).

Friedrichs distinguishes the 1960s and 1970s from the more stable decade of the 1950s. He may be overstating the case, since there were groups during the 1950s whose most explicit goals included the rejection of American values. However, these groups were less active and more apathetic than the revolutionary groups of the 1960s, who used the streets as a theater for acting out their dissenting scenarios. Recent polls, statements from United States political leaders, rising violent crime rates, political corruption, and voter apathy all point to a growing disbelief in institutional authority.

A demystification of established political, academic, religious and familial authority has helped to neutralize the absolute moral imperatives and values often cynically propounded by the heads of these institutions. Cynicism has become part of American culture. In measuring public attitudes between 1965 and 1980, a "diffuse public cynicism," a "moral malaise," and "mistrust of political leaders" can be found. They represent, in part, a product of the perceived failure of American ideals, as incorporated in the criticism that American ideals have been used by authority figures to mask greed, exploitation, and opportunism. "Polls conducted in the last two years of the 1970s reveal strikingly high levels of distrust, lack of confidence and delegitimation" (Friedrichs, 1980, p. 542). These attitudes are not characteristic of only one social class, although some socioeconomic strata experience greater deprivation and increasing frustrations, but cut across that American class hierarchy.

Riots and social protest, voter apathy, violence and crime, and high-level institutional corruption are behavioral manifestations of a crisis of confidence and of rising expectations that were not fulfilled. "Anomie" and "alienation" became part of the academic jargon that was to describe the American social structure (Bell, 1976; Blumberg, 1967; Horvat, 1979; Lane, 1979; Rosenberg and Silverstein, 1969). Others, such as Paul Tillich, spoke of a "sacred void," which depicts an increasingly rational, impersonal, and godless society—a relative loss of moral commitment. Attitude surveys, as noted earlier, bear out these claims.

Legitimacy and Internalization: The Moral Content of Socialization

Legitimation is a structural consequence of the internalization of institutional authority by individuals. Whether the basis for legitimacy is rational-legal, charismatic, or traditional, the individual is expected to internalize the authority of a society's institutions. Freud (1933, 1961) noted that the formation of conscience involves the internalization of external authority, and emphasized the importance of identification in the formation of the superego. Thus, "by means of identification [a person] takes the *unattackable authority* into himself. The authority now turns into his superego and enters into possession of all aggressiveness which [a person] would have liked to exercise against it" (1961, p. 76). The result of such internalization through identification is a moral individual — one who adheres to authority *even in its physical absence*.

During times of crisis, however, the claims of heads of social institutions come under organized scrutiny and attack. Consequently, the content of what individuals will accept and internalize becomes transformed. The moral content of existing modes of socialization is compromised.

Institutional spokesmen respond to these challenges with attempts to make their rhetoric more coherent and/or acceptable to the populace, in the form of either legitimate compromises or "double-talk." If this fails, they may create new ideologies which call for greater institutional control over people or even political repression. Scapegoats may be designated to take the blame for the authorities' misdoings. These are responses, however, and they occur after the disenchantment with or failure to achieve promised goals. Should society's prophets be unable to reestablish traditional modes of legitimacy, individuals will find it hard to "go home again," since doubts about the consistency of the order will have been raised. The new legitimate order will have to live with this doubt, as it has been diffused through the culture.

During crises of confidence the images of the structure of society are transformed, either by the dissenters or by attempts of institutional leaders to redefine their positions. As a consequence, new social structures emerge which place new demands on individuals. The individual is then compelled to accept these new demands. In times of stability, deviation often evokes negative sanctions that keep most people in society within the margin of the acceptable. However, during crises of confidence the margins become blurred and deviation from previous standards may become acceptable, if not exemplary, behavior. The morality espoused by the establishment is scrutinized and questioned by dissenters; its promoters are closely observed to determine the measure of their commitment to the moral precepts they so fervently advocate. The mass media often benefit "street politicians" as they hungrily seek sensation. As a consequence, atypical views and behavior are widely broadcast, perhaps fomenting large-scale ambivalence regarding authority.

The moral content of socialization is further defined by its ambivalence as parents show their lack of confidence in the institutional values they once held dear. Their openly hypocritical behavior seems to be saying, "Do as I say, not as I do." As noted by Charles A. Reich (1970), the crisis of confidence which came to full force during the 1960s did not aim to destroy the basic American values of American society, but was produced by the perceived "phoniness" of adults who preached one thing and actually believed another. While this is probably true of most younger generations throughout history, what made 1960 youth different from the youth of the 1950s, 1970s, and 1980s is their openly revolutionary stance against institutionalized parental authority. Erving Goffman (1959) analyzed what David Riesman and his associates (1950) called the "other-directed" character structure of the post-Second World War middle-class American. Following this, Goffman described the individual who presents himself in accordance with a particular definition of the situation he wishes to create. Goffman (like Freud or Marx) brought into focus the duality of human nature and of human beings. But, more than this, his work represented a critique of American society. He anticipated a perspective which would later be modified and applied in vulgarized form by the counterculture of the 1960s to describe their parents and other adults. Anyone over 30 just could not be trusted.

The "credibility gaps" experienced by many Americans during the '60s and '70s conditioned the content of what was transmitted to their offspring through socialization. Much of the doubt, pessimism, ambivalence, cynicism, and anomie of parents was undoubtedly internalized by their offspring.

OUR TROUBLED TIMES

Since the days of Marx, the critique of modern society has aimed its guns at the alienation, depersonalization, and isolation seen under modern capitalism. Some looked back at a time when people lived in communities where primary relationships reigned, at a time when the purely human qualities of individuals were permitted full expression. Others envisioned a future society in which all humans would have equal opportunity for self-actualization. In either case, the society according to which these critics evaluated their own did not yet exist, in all probability never did, and probably never would. Nevertheless, the experience of time and the countless commentaries of the last hundred years make it very difficult to ignore the fact that human unhappiness persists, and that major societal trends may have been at the root of this pervasive unhappiness.

Allen Wheelis (1958), a practicing psychiatrist, observed the character of middle-class Americans and incisively described the emergent character configuration of these individuals. He wrote:

> The cultural horizons have receded; the diverse modes of distant cities seep in through each television antenna. Exposure to alien mores causes one to examine his native mores. And as soon as mores are examined they are seen to be relative; their claim to absolute validity evaporates, the superego is thus deprived of that support that had been provided by the unquestioning acceptance of an unopposed pattern of life . . . the decline of religious belief has sharply diminished this support (pp. 101–102).

The conscience of individuals is a distillation of the past and based, in part, on tradition. Individuals, through socialization, accept social morals without questioning their validity. These serve as guides to living by defining what is right and wrong, derive their authority from the very fact that they exist, and are inculcated into individuals. For Wheelis such conditions of unquestioned acceptance are becoming more rare, as the traditional recedes in favor of the modern. In traditional society the superego was the basic source of control against the potentially antisocial impulses of human beings. In modern society the ego has taken the upper hand as the agency of control. Increasing rates of cultural change may be at the root of this phenomenon.

> Nowadays no character that is fixed can remain adjusted . . . to be of fixed character and also receptive to the environing culture generates a mounting tension — a circumstance in which psychiatrists become acquainted with a large number of patients. To remain open to a changing culture and also adaptive to it implies the capacity for characterological change. For there is no longer such a thing as an average predictable environment. The only thing that can be predicted with certainty is continued change (Wheelis, 1958, pp. 137–138).

> The development which runs from mores and institutions to values to goals to action and to identity has been undermined at its source. The confusion of values, the lack of goals, and the problem of identity are reflections of this trouble at the source (p. 22).

Even within the dynamic of technological change these conditions impact with quickening blows on institutions, and constantly shorten the
life span of traditional ways. Institutions have no authority except that
they exist, and when the technological process makes their continued
existence incompatible with the industrial arts, their death by attrition
is underway (p. 201).

Wheelis here addresses the relationship of social structure to personality. He makes it clear that accelerated societal/cultural change
leads to fragmentation of the ego, if not an erosion of the superego
and of the sense of identity of individuals. Such trends point to the
emergence of a particular type of modal character structure, one which
lacks any semblance of a stable superego.

Hans Gerth and C. Wright Mills (1953) speak along the same lines.
They refer to the existence of *crises of conscience* at many points and
places in world history. Using a perspective derived in part from George
Herbert Mead (1934), they note that societal change often has the effect of decomposing the authority of the generalized other. As new ap-
praisals are made of old authorities, new generalized others emerge
and are then internalized by individuals in society. The perceptual
changes regarding the nature of the generalized other may result simply
from maturational processes operating on specific individuals, but very
often these changes are society-wide. In such cases, Gerth and Mills
comment,

> If . . . the norms of society are smashed, new significant and authori-
> tative others may emerge who define new values and loyalties, and there
> is a crisis in every person's conscience as his authoritarian others change
> (p. 98).

Political, economic, and social crises are the springs of such crises
of conscience which, according to Gerth and Mills, are widespread in
contemporary society. They add that

> In modern society insecurity tends to be experienced not as a personal
> mishap or misfortune nor as . . . due to supernatural forces nor even
> to natural forces. And men, full of the tension of insecure positions cor-
> rectly blame social factors for personal defeat. . . . It is under such con-
> ditions that belief in traditional social and political values may be shat-
> tered (p. 462).

The resulting confusion regarding acceptable guides to action, and the frequency with which such confusion occurs, produces unstable series of values, beliefs and morals to be internalized by the psyches of individuals. Confusion regarding collective values leaves individuals with the feeling that in some ways they would be better off relying on purely personal advantages. Lacking a collective frame of reference, society is perceived as a war of all against all in which institutions and their authority cannot be counted on for the protection of each from all, and vice-versa.

It is this very sentiment that is conveyed by Goffman, who, in most of his writings, focused his attention on the interpersonal experience of middle-class Americans while ignoring master social trends. In his early work, he described society as an information game, in which individuals constantly, consciously or unconsciously, attempt to manage the impressions that they give to others in the quest for self-enhancement. Everyone has something to hide; everyone is a conspirator in creating individual and collective fronts by means of public performances. The boundary between appearance and reality is blurred, while each person tries to put down and/or use another before being put down or abused himself. What is most striking about this depiction of the person in modern society is that he seems to be little more than a player of roles: an "other-directed" creature evaluating his own worth according to the feelings and judgments of others; a creature lacking a stable inner core. In modern society the ego has taken upon itself the task of satisfying ever-present and ever more powerful desires, thereby establishing itself as a powerful provider of pleasure for the body and psyche. In such a situation the role of social ethics is diminished and impression management is placed at the disposal of the deepest, and sometimes the worst, of our impulses.

Bernard Rosenberg (1972) discusses the declining legitimacy of American and other modern societies:

> The pervasive crises of confidence, not yet as grave as that which afflicted seventeenth century England or Imperial Rome in its senescence, is still very real and variously acute in every part of the world. Wherever we look the crisis is manifest (p. 38).

> . . . the richest, in many respects, the freest, technologically most advanced people on earth are also more unstable than anyone predicted (p. 39–40). . . .

Distrust and suspicion, nowadays called credibility gaps, are incompatible with social order (p. 41).

Rosenberg echoes the concerns of Wheelis and of Gerth and Mills in noting that when the confidence of individuals in their own institutions falters, authority is eroded and institutional orders are perceived as vulnerable. No form of coercion or institutionally sanctioned violence against the nonconformist will be able to reestablish legitimate authority, though it may often produce some surface conformity.

Crises of confidence color the nature of socialization practices that condition personality formation, as well as the kinds of pathologies most likely to be found during the particular historical periods in which they occur.

> Parents project their images of what is right and wrong in making demands on the child. If the child goes unrebuked, and unaware of his limits, identification will be badly inhibited. His biological drives are likely to dominate him while, with an underdeveloped superego, he is unable to defer their gratification. This psychic equipment puts him in a collision course with his society. . . . Not the overblown superego, the heavy conscience, the weight and terror of guilt but its opposite, a weak or nonexistent superego, the normlessness and deregulation that Emile Durkheim was to baptize anomie . . . is central in modern society (Rosenberg, 1972, pp. 76–77, 78).

> Modern urban-industrial life, having fragmented our social allegiances, loyalties and commitments, also has shattered our capacity to live by the tenents of cooperative morality. The consequent deregulation and demoralization have little to do with class and much to do with modernity (Rosenberg and Silverstein, 1969, p. 165).

Rosenberg and Silverstein offer a theory of moral anomie, which they claim is becoming an integral part of modern society at all of its levels. The proliferation of such currents has produced individuals which are similar to Robert J. Lifton's "Protean Man" (1968), a personality type which lacks a stable superego. Individuals of this type, described to some extent by each of the aforegoing authors, resemble the psychopath. Robert Lindner (1956) saw the signs that a transformation of the character of American youth was taking place. To Lindner, young people were in a state of mutiny against civilization itself. He found it to be characteristic that psychopathic personalities tend to rise to the top of social movements. The opportunity to challenge societal values, and not the "cause" underlying such movements, is a source of sterile sensation for psychopaths. It is likely that after the excitement of a movement dies down, so will their participation in the newly established order. They then move their operations into "normal" society.

Michael Glenn (1967) noted that during the 1960s the psychopath was becoming the hero of our age. Like Norman Mailer (1958) before him, Glenn saw the greater presence of this type of individual among society's members. Both Mailer and Glenn emphasized *the relative adaptability of such a character structure* to the contradictions inherent in modern American society.

This line of thinking is pursued by Alan Harrington in his *Psychopaths . . .* (1974), who wrote that

> It is not so much that individuals who may be diagnosed as at least part-psychopaths have risen to eminence and leadership in our country . . . , but that the psychopath ideal of acting out all desires has become routinely accepted, possibly as supreme—even among people who are not psychopaths (p. 45).

> In a Godless universe, the anxiety-free psychopathic style may be the antidote to mass suicide (p. 46).

Hervey Cleckley (1976), like Harrington, noted the low proclivity of the psychopath to commit suicide. In a world where the threat of total nuclear destruction, institutional crisis, growing discrimination and the victim's realization of it, and rapid social/cultural change are ever-present the psychopath emerges as a most adaptable personality type. The costs of such anxiety-free living are very high, however: lack of feelings and emotions, lack of concern for others, and increased narcissism. Harrington ends his book by stretching the imagination and offering psychopathy as a solution to mankind's problems. He enters the realm of the absurd when he proposes that a religion of humanity, based on psychopathic "principles," be erected. Nonetheless, his sense of the effects of modern society on human beings echoes remarks by other, more careful, critics.

A more careful and precise critic of American society and student of the psychopath, Robert Smith (1978), suggests that psychopathy represents a logical extreme expression of values celebrated by American culture. If individuals want to move ahead in business or their careers, Smith claims,

> [p]erhaps an outwardly oriented marketing culture requires more façade construction and inauthenticity than those in which the "Mitsein" plays a more central and critical role (p. 139).

The achievement ethic of American society demands that individuals seek out self-satisfaction and economic success while, to some extent, suspending concern with the feelings of others. Late capitalism has placed a heavy burden of achievement and conspicuous consumption on Americans. In this environment the psychopath is often a most successful performer.

Smith (1973) is hopeful that a societal-wide solution may become possible, if only Americans would permit the core values of humanism to come to fruition. To the extent that America continues to ride the tracks of rationalization, bureaucratization, and secularization, psychopathy will be a collective product of those very same people who despise it, as well as of those who lead its institutions.

THE PROBLEM OF NARCISSISM

Psychiatrists and psychotherapists report treating an increasing number of patients with narcissistic character pathology. Although it may be argued that new professional interest in narcissism created this diagnosis and an increase in the volume of literature on narcissism, Bader and Philipson (1980) conclude that these cases are actually more common today than in past years. Christopher Lasch (1978) cites the tremendous interest in leisure, self-awareness programs, sport, education, and self-help manuals as evidence of an increase in narcissistic character structures during the 1970s.

People with narcissistic personalities are unable to establish intimate relationships based simultaneously on mutuality and on the acceptance of another's autonomy. As parents, these narcissists are ambivalent towards their children's separation from them and respond aggressively to their attempts to become individuals. The family, as a crucial source of values and as a primary agency of socialization, carries much of the weight in creating personalities. But by no means has the family been the sole promoter of narcissism in America.

Mass society, which has increasingly suppressed individuality (or, at best, has permitted pseudo-individuality), and the threat of nuclear annihilation may also have provoked narcissistic responses to people's perceived aimlessness. These factors have narrowed the sphere over which individuals feel they have control in shaping their lives. The sphere of personal control has become confined to the intimate self, its more personal territories — and very little else. The middle and lower classes have experienced this as isolation. Such conditions have been exacerbated by increased rationality, secularism, and urbanization following the Second World War.

Narcissism has played an important role in defining the recent history of American society; persons with narcissistic personalities will thereby take an active part in shaping its future. It can be postulated that the resulting forms of social organization will continue to breed and select characteristics that fit well within the narcissistic character structure.

THE VIOLENT YOUTH OF THE EIGHTIES

Although evidence shows that narcissism has infiltrated the culture of all social classes, different social categories respond in different ways. The "baby boom" in the United States made America a young society in the 1960s. This demographic overload led to a breakdown in traditional channels of socialization represented by parents and other adults. The young turned to each other for guidance, as the peer group took over many functions of traditional socialization agencies. Thus emerged a strong youth culture with access to a large proportion of America's discretionary income. As their support for the household became less necessary, youths became an important market, spending much of their time segregated from adults, with more financial resources than young cohorts of past generations.

The tremendous buying potential of this group — and the market response — increased their wants, raised their aspirations, and created an atmosphere of frustrating, invidious comparison among lower-class youths. Increased wants combined with a lack of adult social controls led, according to Silberman (1980) and others, to the creation of a lethal criminogenic force — especially among those who lack the economic means for their satisfaction. Many youths who are economically deprived have turned to robbery, often of elderly victims, as a quick and easy way to generate income.

Today's juvenile robbers are opportunistic, violent, and disorganized. They lack the ability to plan and are incapable of specializing or professionalizing their activity. Silberman describes these individuals as insensitive, lacking any feeling about the consequences their behavior has on others.

> This absence of "affect," as psychiatrists call it, is the most frightening aspect of all. In the past juveniles who exploded in violence tended to feel considerable guilt or remorse afterwards; the new criminals have been so brutalized in their own upbringing that they seem incapable of viewing their victims as human beings, or of realizing that they have killed another person. . . . Increasingly, psychiatric reports on juveniles arrested for murder are filled with phrases such as "shows no feeling," "shows no remorse," "demonstrates no relationship" (p. 83).

Silberman stops short of calling such individuals psychopaths; however, the description above is similar to the concept of criminal psychopathic personality. These criminals, as they are described above, are as emotionally dead as the psychopath. If, in fact, they are "clinically psychopathic," we may be seeing the point at which the etiology of criminality intersects the etiology of psychopathy.

Most writers in the field of psychopathy have acknowledged its generalized nature. Psychopathy is distributed throughout the class structure of America society. Given the opportunities available to well-to-do psychopaths, the likelihood that they will engage in street criminal violence is extremely low. However, these individuals may continue to use white collar crime to pursue their desires. Such activities may demand guiltless and loveless, but charming and manipulative, personalities. Psychopaths who lack the economic means by which to satisfy their impulses may not think twice about engaging in armed robbery, and may injure or kill a victim who resists (or even one who is perceived as an object for bringing excitement or for breaking the monotony of everyday life).

If the writers discussed above are correct in their assessment of American culture, let us be prepared for a wave of criminal violence. This wave will not, as in the past, be produced by a growing absolute number of youth and young adults between ages 14 and 24; indeed the "baby boomers" are growing older. Rather, this author feels, the wave will be produced by an increasing number of individuals who are loveless and guiltless among the ranks of the poor.

On the one hand, increasing psychopathy among the more prosperous classes of American society will most likely create a social world in which expediency, impersonality, narcissistic manipulation, and corruption will continue to replace morality and sensitivity. On the other, the underclasses of our society will be a source of fear for us all. The future may be a bleak one on both counts.

CONCLUSION

Some students accept psychopathy as a type of mental illness; others view it as an alternative lifestyle and not a mental illness. The etiology of psychopathy remains a battleground even within the ranks of each position.

The battle, however, does not invalidate the concept. Rather, it serves to give it increased recognition as a facet of human life and, thus, a valid area for intellectual discussion. Psychopathy, in its more violent forms, presents a threat to human life. We yet lack the knowledge of its less aggressive forms. The non-criminal psychopath's talent for impression management, calculation, and charm, which he shares with all of us, makes it difficult to distinguish him from the rest of society.

Research on psychopathy has been limited to the study of aggressive, criminal, or delinquent psychopaths and to accounts of notable individuals in the fields of literature, politics, business, and the military. Investigative reporters, historians, biographers, and police have served as spotters of such people. In the meantime, we have been unable to identify those psychopaths who blend in so well with the rest of us. Our knowledge about psychopathy is not about them but rather about the farthest (usually lower-class) extremes of the continuum. Hervey Cleckley (1976) directly addressed the difficulty of separating the "superior" psychopath from the "superior" person.

> There is nothing odd or queer about him, and in every respect he tends to embody the concept of a well-adjusted, happy person. . . . He looks like the real thing. . . . More than the average person, he is likely to seem free from the minor distortions, peculiarities, and awkwardness so common even among the successful. (p. 364). . . . Everything about him is likely to suggest desirable and superior human qualities, a robust mental health (p. 365).

The effects of contemporary society on the character structure of individuals have been discussed by many writers, including Ellul (1964), Fromm (1941), Horney (1937), Lasch (1978), Riesman (1950), and Rosenberg (1972), as well as in earlier works by Durkheim, Marx, Weber, Nietzsche, and Freud.

These writers have emphasized the alienating and anomic effects of contemporary society brought about by technology, capitalism, stratification, narcissism, rationality, and value conflicts at structural levels. None, however, describes the psychopath as an emerging form. Yet, they do write about a society in which personal needs are given primacy over group needs, in which "love" has lost its meaning; expediency is emphasized over morality; appearance is given greater importance than "inner worth"; morality is no longer clearly defined. Such a world can serve as a fertile ground for the rise of the psychopathic personality.

Love-for-fellow-man has lost its importance over love for self. The omnipresent threat of nuclear holocaust, declining faith in authority figures (in the family, in government, and in the church), the Vietnam War, Watergate, alleged CIA and FBI involvement in the assassination of internal political and religio-political leaders—all have served to promote not only distrust in authority figures and their judgment over world matters, but also a certain insecurity about personal and social survival. In a society in which authority has begun to lose its legitimacy, and personal safety has become a more important issue than salvation, vocabularies of motives rise to express such conditions. Thus, the verbalizations "every man for himself" and "take care of number one first" gain a certain validity as guidelines for living and dramatize the decline of the superego.

Under the aforementioned conditions it seems likely that what the McCords (1964) and McCord (1982) define as the psychopath, "a guiltless and loveless" individual, may be emerging in increasing numbers. Rational man is evolving a new form: the psychopathic man. His coming is being heralded by Michael Glenn, Alan Harrington, Robert Lindner, Norman Mailer, and Robert Smith, among many. Some of these writers have at some points crossed into the realm of nonsense, panic or unrealistic utopianism; but all agree that psychopathy is more common today as an adaptation to modern society. The finding by the McCords (1956, 1964) and McCord and Sanchez (1983) that milieu therapy had "positive" effects on "psychopaths" supports this conclusion. A loving yet demanding environment differs greatly from the *gesselschaft* conditions which are becoming the norm and which have found their way into the family and into individual personalities.

Almost 30 years ago, the McCords recognized that psychopathy, more than any other mental disorder, threatened the serenity, safety and security of American society. At that time they claimed that psychopaths constituted only a small proportion of the American population.

It is unclear how such a small number of psychopaths could be such a great threat. Current knowledge, based on studies of "criminal" psychopaths, cloaks a larger number of which we are not aware, and of which some of us are probably a part. The assumption of such a large threat does not jibe with the belief among professionals that persons with antisocial personality are few in number.

Any real test of the theories of psychopathy must rest upon knowledge of the syndrome among the general population. Such knowledge is not yet available. Until such data become available, the degree to which psychopathy may be "normal" or "pathological" in a particular social structure cannot be known (see Durkheim, 1974). If the psychological and biological approaches to psychopathy are considered to be in their infancy, the sociological is still embryonic.

In conclusion, given the powerful world-historical processes of rationalization, bureaucratization, and secularization that direct the course of history in modern society, and the effects that such trends have upon the biographies and psyches of individuals, the increasing adaptability of a psychopathic style of life becomes obvious. The pace of these societal processes, which is usually slow, is accelerated by specific historical events such as the crises of confidence which occurred during the 1960s.

This chapter has dealt not so much with the evolution of such crises, or with the effects of these on the social structure, but with the ways in which these crises condition the character structures of individuals in society. In the revolutionary challenge of institutionally legitimate values, beliefs and morals, crises of confidence can erode authority even at deep levels of individual internalization. Although these crises of confidence are usually initiated by small, revolutionary segments, the challenges to institutionalized authority are diffused by an ever more powerful mass media. It is, thus, quite likely that adults during such times of crises, and the offspring whom they socialize, will be exposed to the ambivalence of conformity without commitment. The impact of such forces will vary according to social class, thereby eliciting different behavioral responses from the various strata in society. As such, the most deprived classes may have to resort to a kind of criminality which will be marked by detachment and viciousness. The more affluent, however, will also resort to viciousness and detachment in their treatment of others, but, in their case, in more sublime forms.

Exactly how different the character of Americans in the eighties is from that of past decades is not known, but research along these lines promises to sharpen the sociological profile of Americans and American society. The study of psychopathy should be exploited as both a model by which society can be studied and as a moral yardstick by which our current situation can be evaluated.

REFERENCES

Bader, M. & I. Philipson. (1980). Narcissism and family structure: A social-historical perspective, *Psychoanalysis and Contemporary Thought, 3, 3*, 299–328.

Bell, D. (1976). *The cultural contradictions of capitalism*. New York: Basic Books.

Blumberg, A. (1967). *Criminal justice*. Chicago, IL: Quadrangle.

Cleckley, H. (1976). *The mask of sanity* (5th Ed.) St. Louis: Mosby.

Durkheim, E. (1974). *Rules of sociological method*. New York: Free Press.

Ellul, J. (1964). *The technological society*. New York: Vintage Books.

Freud, S. (1976). New introductory lectures in psychoanalysis. In J. Strachey (Ed. and Trans.) *The standard edition, 22*, New York, Norton. (Original work published 1933.)

Freud, S. (1976). Civilization and its discontents. In J. Strachey (Ed. and Trans.) *The standard edition*. New York: Norton. *21*, pp. 59–145. (Original work published in 1930.)

Friedrichs, D. (1980). The legitimacy crisis in the United States: A conceptual analysis. *Social Problems, 27, 5*, 540–555.

Fromm, E. (1941). *Escape from freedom*. New York: Avon Books.

Gerth, H. & Mills, C. W. (1953). *Character and social structure: The psychology of social institutions*. New York: Harcourt, Brace Jovanovich.

Glenn, M. (1967, September 14). Press of Freedom. *Village Voice*.

Goffman, E. (1959). *The presentation of self in everyday life*. New York: Doubleday.

Harrington, A. (1974). *Psychopaths* . . . . New York: Simon and Schuster.

Horney, K. (1937). *The neurotic personality of our time*. New York: Norton.

Horowitz, I. (1967). The norm of illegitimacy — Ten years later. In B. Denitch (Ed.). *Legitimation of regimes — International frameworks for analysis*. Beverly Hills, CA: Sage.

Horvat, B. (1979). The delegitimation of old and the legitimation of new social relations in late capitalist societies. In B. Denitch, op cit.

Lasch, C. (1978). *The culture of narcissism: American life in an age of diminishing expectations*. New York: Norton.

Lifton, R. (1968, Winter). Protean man. *Partisan Review*, 13–27.

Lindner, R. (1956). *Must you conform?* New York: Rinehart and Company.

Mailer, N. (1958). The white negro. *Voices of dissent*. New York: Grove Press.

McCord, W. (1982). *The psychopath and milieu therapy*. New York: Academic Press.

McCord, W. & McCord, J. (1956). *Psychopathy and delinquency*. New York: Grune and Stratton.

_____. (1964). *The psychopath: An essay on the criminal mind*. New York: Van Nostrand Reinhold.

McCord, W. & Sanchez, J. (1983, April). The treatment of deviant children: A twenty-five year fear follow-up study. *Crime and Delinquency, 29*, 238–253.

Mead, G. (1934). *Mind, self and society*. Chicago, IL: Chicago University Press.

Mills, C. (1959). *The sociological imagination*. New York: Oxford University Press.

Reich, C. (1970). *The greening of America*. New York: Bantam Books.

Riesman, D. (1950). *The lonely crowd*. New Haven, CT: Yale University Press.

Rosenberg, B. (1972). *The province of sociology: Freedom and constraint*. New York: Thomas Y. Crowell Company.

Rosenberg, B. & Silverstein H. (1969). *Varieties of delinquent experience*. MA: Xerox Corporation.

Silberman, C. (1980). *Criminal violence, criminal justice*. New York: Vintage Books.

Smith, R. (1973). Some thoughts on psychopathy. *Psychotherapy: Theory, Research and Practice, 10*, 354–358.

_____. (1978). *The psychopath in society*. New York: Academic Press.

Wheelis, A. (1958). *The quest for identity*. New York: Norton.

5

Ego Dysfunction in Psychopathic Psychiatric Inpatients

Darwin Dorr & Peggy K. Woodhall

In this chapter we advance the proposition that psychiatric patients manifesting a psychopathic[1] character embody certain specific and severe deficiencies in ego structure. Cleckley maintained throughout his career that the psychopath, though not psychotic, manifested a major mental illness. His attempt to understand and explain psychopathy led him to postulate a "semantic aphasia," a psychological deficit possibly having a neurological substratum. Semantic aphasia is an extensive and deep loss of understanding of meaningful language, a loss that may not at first be evident to the casual observer because the dysfunction may be disguised by intact superficial functions. Thus viewed, the psychopath is not exactly hypocritical but rather oblivious to the true meaning of language. To quote Cleckley (1976):

> Let us assume tentatively that the psychopath is, in this sense, semantically disordered. We have said that his outer functional aspect masks or disguises something quite different within, concealing behind a perfect mimicry of normal emotion, fine intelligence, and social responsibility, a grossly disabled and irresponsible personality (p. 385).

---

[1]As this volume was prepared to honor the memory of Dr. Hervey Cleckley, we use his term "psychopath" throughout.

Although Cleckley revised *The Mask of Sanity* several times, he did little to expand his hypothesis, perferring to limit his speculation and admit his ignorance of the cause or essential psychological feature of this major mental illness. In a personal communication shortly before his death, Cleckley emphasized to the first author that he knew little of the causes of psychopathy, although he remained convinced that there was a biochemical anomaly, and he was little confident of any successful treatment.

It may be important to remind the reader that Cleckley was not merely "physiologizing"when he postulated that there may be a central neurological deficit (lesion at or about the supramarginal gyrus). After graduating with his B.S. degree from the University of Georgia majoring in mathematics and science, he took a Rhodes Scholarship at Cambridge for two years, receiving another B.A. in the school of physiology. He also pursued advance training in neuroanatomy in Paris before obtaining his M.D. at the University of Georgia. He was a Diplomate in neurology as well as psychiatry. He also completed a medical internship and a surgical residency before entering the field of psychiatry.

Further, Cleckley had a profound sensitivity for and knowledge of classical literature. The reader is reminded that Hervey Cleckley wrote the poetry in the beginning of *The Mask of Sanity*. However, he was not trained formally or informally in psychology or psychoanalysis, nor in the research and scholarly methods of these fields. It is not surprising then that Cleckley approached his subject with his sharpest tools, a knowledge of physiology and brilliance in literary description. Yet, while biological and social forces are crucial to an understanding of the psychopath, they do not lie at a psychological level of analysis. There are relatively few researches on the essential psychological deficit in the psychopath. All levels of analysis will be necessary to further our understanding of the psychopath, but it seems that since Cleckley posited that the psychopath suffers from a "mental" (psychological?) disease, we should attempt to determine the psychological nature of this mental illness. In this volume there are several analyses that might be described as mental or psychological rather than biological or social. Our chapter represents one attempt to address this subject.

If we choose a psychological level of analysis, we must select from a large array of paradigms: cognitive, behavioral, psychometric, social-psychological, etc. A psychodynamic approach initially seems implausible because Cleckley was so antagonistic to psychoanalysis as a theory of personality or as a treatment approach, particularly when used with the psychopath. Yet we may extend our knowledge of psychopathy by examining our phenomenon through a variety of lenses. Psychoanalytic study has afforded deep understanding of other major forms of psychopathology. Thus, it seems reasonable to attempt further analytic studies of the form of psychopathology known as psychopathy.

There has been a small number of psychodynamic investigations of psychopathic character, including those of Reich (1949) and Bender (1947). Bender argued that the main deficiency of the psychopath is an inability to form relationships, to identify empathically, and to share in the experiences of others. In her view, the developmental process in psychopaths appears to be fixated at an early age. Reich understood the psychopath's acting-out to be a defense. In recent years, Kernberg has written that the psychopath manifests a lower level borderline personality structure (1967). However, Kernberg and his associates, to our knowledge, have not extended this analysis.

If one attempts an elementary psychodynamic assessment of psychopaths, it is obvious that they suffer from "to much id" and "too little superego." Rarely does one read that the psychopath manifests an ego deficiency. However, of psychopathy Blatt and Shichman have written that *"the problem appears to be not an expression of superego deficit but an impairment of the development of basic ego functions"* (1981, p. 333, italics added). Actually, even if the "essential" psychological deficit of the psychopath were in superego, the major researchers/therapists in ego psychology maintain that we still must turn to ego in order to study superego. Bellak, Hurvich, and Gediman (1973) state, "We, typically, cannot observe superego functioning directly: we only observe its effects in ego functioning" (p. 37).

If we accept Blatt and Shichman's assertion that psychopaths manifest an ego deficiency, it seems reasonable to employ methodologies that have been developed to examine ego functions. This line of reasoning led us to choose the method of Ego Functions Analysis developed by Bellak and his colleagues (Bellak et al., 1973; Bellak and Goldsmith, 1984).

Ego Function Analysis (EFA) is a modern extension of classical psychoanalytic theory influenced, especially, by Hartmann (1958), Mahler (1963), and Jacobson (1964). The central and most significant element of ego analysis is the concept of the "conflict-free portion of ego"—the proposition that major elements of ego develop independently of conflict and its resolution, and that these ego functions play a major role in allowing or even facilitating the organism to adapt to its environment and to grow toward a higher level of actualization.

Bellak et al. employed the ego functions concept implied by Hartmann (1958) and extended by writers such as Beres (1956), Arlow and Brenner (1964), and Weiner (1966). They selected 12 ego functions and developed a procedure for assessing subelements of these functions. A manual provides detailed description of each ego function and each subdimension. After examining the patient or subject, the clinician makes a rating on a 7-point scale (each point is referred to as a stop), with the option of making half-point ratings, e.g., one may rate 4.5 if unable to rate 4 or 5. High ratings reflect health. EFA provides extensive behavioral descriptions for each stop along the 7-point scale, affording greater rater reliability. For reporting purposes Bellak et al. convert the rating scale to 13 points with $1 = 1, 1.5 = 2, 2 = 3, 2.5 = 4,$ . . . , $7 = 13$. To comply with this convention we also employed this conversion. After all subdimensions of the ego function are rated, the examiner then makes a global rating of the level of ego functioning based on a clinical integration of the subratings. EFA ratings can also be graphically depicted to facilitate analysis.

Although ego function analysis has been employed in a large variety of personality and psychotherapeutic studies (Bellak and Goldsmith, 1984), there has been no attempt to use this methodology with psychopaths, hospitalized or nonhospitalized. (Bellak, personal communication, 1985). Hence our study represents a first step in using EFA methodology in the study of psychopaths. Our primary objective was to determine if EFA could be used to demonstrate specific ego weaknesses in psychopaths.

METHOD

Ratings

The 20 patients comprising the sample have been involved in a long-term clinical study by the second author, who has extensive clinical experience and familiarity with each patient as well as his/her family. In addition to her intimate knowledge of past history and daily clinical involvement while the patient was in hospital, she has continued to follow each patient's posthospital course via personal and phone contact, letters, discussion with the family, and communication with other knowledgable sources, such as referring professionals, lawyers, and police. The EFA ratings were done by the second author and reviewed and rechecked by the first author. It was not possible to compute meaningful interrater reliabilities because no one knew these particular patients as well as the rater, thus low interrater rs may reflect ignorance in the checkers more than unreliability of the criterion ratings. Other studies of the reliability of ratings (Bellak et al., 1973; Dahl, 1984) suggest that experienced clinicians can achieve a rather high level of agreement.

Each subject was assigned a "stop" rating (7-point scale with option of half point ratings) on each subscale and then a global rating was made for each of the ego function scales based on clinical judgment of the subscale scores. Following the convention of Bellak et al. these scores on the 7-point scales were converted to a 13-point scale and are reported as such. Occasionally in the text we refer to a stop score (7-point scale) because each of the 7 stops is accompanied by anchoring descriptions which are convenient to allude to in discussion.

Subjects

The patients ranged in age from 15 to 33 at the time of their first admission to Highland Hospital. Of the 20, 18 were men. Ten subjects had been hospitalized previously at other facilities prior to admission to Highland. All subjects were known substance abusers. At discharge, four subjects had a primary diagnosis of antisocial personality disorder; nine carried a secondary diagnosis of antisocial personality disorder; four carried a diagnosis of substance abuse/drug dependence; two carried a primary diagnosis of unsocialized aggressive reaction to adolescence; and one was diagnosed group delinquent reaction to adolescence. Length of stay at Highland Hospital ranged from eight to 615 days, with the average length of stay being 219 days.

Most of these patients came from middle- to upper-middle-class families. Two subjects were adopted. At admission, four were married and two of these were separated from their spouses. At the time of admission, none was a member of single-parent families. Two subjects were only children and five were oldest children; seven were middle children; and six were the youngest children. At least eight subjects had other members of their immediate families who had antisocial traits.

Of the 20 subjects, six were tried on medication during their hospital stay. One subject responded well to antidepressant medication; another was withdrawn from narcotics with Methadone successfully. Two patients were tried on Lithium with no positive effect. Loxitane, used briefly after admission, was helpful for one patient; Mellaril was useful in calming threatening behavior in one patient. At times, with most patients in the study, major tranquilizers were used on a p.r.n. basis to control violent acting-out.

Each of the 20 subjects had been involved in criminal activity prior to admission and 13 had been in jail. The most common transgression was multiple drug abuse and the sale of drugs for profit. Other offenses included grand theft, burglary, assault with a deadly weapon, driving under the influence of drugs and alcohol, forgery, breaking and entering, grand larceny, lewd or threatening calls to females, carrying concealed weapons, and theft of firearms. Antisocial behavior continued during these subjects' hospitalizations. We observed abuse of illicit drugs, abuse of other patients' medications, absconding from hospital grounds, theft of a hospital vehicle, sexual acting-out with other patients, and threatening of patients/staff.

Three of the subjects were below the age of 18 (aged 15, 16, and 17) and technically cannot be diagnosed as psychopathic (antisocial) by DSM-III. However, in each case, the history and contemporary clinical picture were so clearly psychopathic that they were included in the study.

Compliance with the DSM-III Criteria

In accordance with the criteria set forth by DSM-III, most of the subjects were exhibiting many antisocial features by the age of 15. Sixteen subjects had been truant for at least five days a year for two years. Twelve had been suspended or expelled from school for misbehavior. Fourteen had been referred to juvenile court because of their behavior. Fourteen had run away from their parental home. Nineteen had been found to be persistent liars. Nine had been sexually active in casual relationships on a regular basis. Nineteen had been involved in regular alcohol and/or substance abuse. Seventeen had been known to steal. Nine had committed offenses related to vandalism. Seventeen had low school achievement relative to their capability. Seventeen had been regular rule-breakers at home and at school. Ten were known to initiate fights at school, with peer groups, or at home.

None of the subjects was able to sustain regular work/school behavior. Three of the four married or separated subjects were irresponsible parents/spouses in the home. Four subjects met the criteria in relation to inability to sustain relationships. It should be noted that other subjects had never been able to form a meaningful relationship with others and therefore could not be rated in the strict sense of this criteria. Thirteen subjects showed evidence of irritability or aggressiveness which was evidenced by initiation of or participation in fights. Thirteen were also known to be unable to repay debts and to default on other financial obligations. All subjects were unable to plan ahead, were said to be chronic liars, and were reckless.

All but one of the subjects had a continuous history of antisocial behavior. None was engaged in this kind of behavior as a result of severe mental retardation, schizophrenia, or manic episodes. All subjects were rated positively on the DSM-III criteria C, D, and E even if they had not reached the age of 18. In summary, we were confident that our subjects were, indeed, psychopaths.

RESULTS OF EFA

In presenting the EFA of our 20 psychopathic patients, we will briefly describe each dimension, each subdimension and its scale, and summarize our averaged ratings. The results are summarized in Table 1; each averaged rating is also included in parenthesis after the headings of each subdimension.

Our data are preliminary and must be interpreted with caution. We do not yet have ratings on comparison groups within Highland Hospital. However, we believed that interpretation of our ratings might be enhanced if we used as a reference (not control) group the findings of Bellak et al. (1973), based on their extensive and methodologically sophisticated study of 50 schizophrenics, 25 neurotics, and 25 normals.

We do not have reliability data because our rating methodology differed from that of Bellak et al. (e.g., our one rater was intimately and extensively familiar with the patients versus Bellak et al.'s method of making ratings based only on a single interview but with good inter-

TABLE 1
Summary of Mean EFA Ratings

Function	(a)	(b)	(c)	(d)	Global (13)
I. Reality Testing	7.40	5.60	5.84	NA	6.70
II. Judgment	4.04	3.10	2.96	NA	3.84
III. Reality Sense	11.96	12.24	6.80	7.00	9.90
IV. Regulation	4.20	3.76	NA	NA	4.24
V. Object Relations	5.80	5.50	4.44	5.70	5.40
VI. Thought Processes	10.20	7.40	10.30	NA	8.80
VII. ARISE	5.50	5.70	NA	NA	5.76
VIII. Defensive Functions	6.16	7.30	NA	NA	6.90
IX. Stimulus Barrier	8.16	8.04	NA	NA	8.20
X. Autonomous Functions	10.04	8.30	NA	NA	7.84
XI. Synthetic Integrative Functions	5.56	5.76	NA	NA	5.84
XII. Mastery Competence	6.00	9.64			

rater reliability data; also, it is unclear if the two populations are demographically equivalent). Consequently, we believed it unwise to calculate inferential statistical ratios. We have included in Table 2 and Figure 1 our results, together with those of Bellak et al. To examine the methodology used by Bellak et al., the reader is referred to their 1973 volume.

TABLE 2
Mean Ratings of this Study and of
Bellak, Hurvich and Gediman

	Dorr & Woodhall	Bellak, Hurvich and Gediman		
	Psychopath (20)	Schizophrenic (50)	Neurotic (25)	Normal (25)
Ego Function				
Reality Testing	6.70	6.76	8.44	9.78
Judgment	3.84	6.30	7.44	9.12
Reality Sense	9.90	5.60	7.00	9.40
Regulation	4.24	5.72	6.68	8.30
Object Relations	5.40	5.08	6.76	8.76
Thought Processes	8.80	6.20	8.26	9.78
ARISE	5.76	6.16	7.78	8.32
Defensive Functions	6.90	4.86	6.94	8.66
Stimulus Barrier	8.20	6.70	7.82	9.12
Autonomous Functions	7.84	5.84	7.68	9.32
Synthetic Functions	5.84	5.22	6.84	9.28

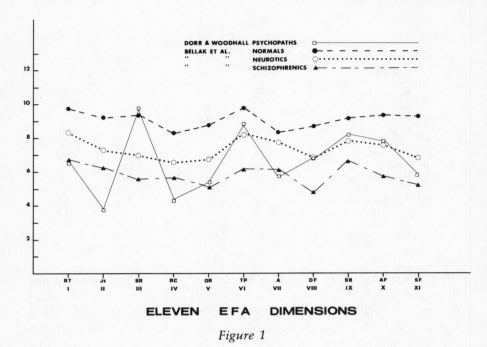

Figure 1

I. REALITY TESTING

One of the most commonly discussed ego functions, reality testing, refers to the continuous assessment, sifting, weighing, and judging the amorphous mass of stimuli bombarding our consciousness. Obviously, to examine reality testing one must accept the premise that there is some sort of reality.

Freud repeatedly addressed the concept of reality testing, focusing on fantasy activities and reality thinking and on the importance of distinguishing between the two. Erikson (1962) described reality testing as phenomenal experience perceived with a minimum of idiosyncratic distortion.

There are three elements to this dimension: (a) distinction between inner and outer reality; (b) accuracy of perception of external events including orientation to time and place; and (c) accuracy of perception of internal events, including reflective awareness of accuracy/distortions of inner reality.

I. Reality Testing (a): Distinction Between Inner and Outer Stimuli (7.40)

The average rating for our 20 psychopathic patients on the first reality testing subscale was 7.40. None of our subjects evidenced hallucinations or even illusions (at least when sober), but there was a clear and obvious tendency to project inner states onto external reality. What was "out there" and what was "in me" were often confused. Reality was often twisted to conform to wants and needs. For example, when many of our patients wanted to watch a certain television program, they would simply change the channel of the television in the patient lounge. If challenged about this behavior, they would typically say: "Well, everyone looked bored to me!" When one patient was asked to evaluate his appearance (longer-than-shoulder-length hair, torn jeans, earring, bandana around head, sloppy T-shirt, and sneakers) to assess what an employer might think of him at an interview, he refused to acknowledge his appearance, saying: "I look fine to me. People ought to be able to see me for what I truly am—look at the real me." This kind of refusal to look beyond wants and needs to what is obviously real was typical in many interchanges with these patients.

Thus, it was difficult to give many ratings above the 5th stop (confusion about inner and outer states occurs mainly upon awakening or going to sleep). The distortions were generally too pronounced.

I. Reality Testing (b): Accuracy of External Events, Time, Place (5.60)

None of our subjects exhibited extreme disorientation or confusion in their perceptions. On the other hand, it was not possible to declare that any of them suffered only relatively "minor" perceptual inaccuracies and/or that the difficulties with orientation were minor or sporadic. In most cases reality was readily distorted to conform to strong need states (stop 4) and in the majority of cases there were significant distortions and misinterpretations of reality, especially when intoxicated by alcohol or drugs.

Patients often seemed to exhibit selective perception of reality. When confronted about antisocial behaviors, such as lying, intimidating others, or blatantly manipulative behavior, our patients seemed to have little or no recall of the situation as staff members viewed it. The actual confusion or distortion of situations was minor but remarkable in light of their continuous hypervigilance in other situations.

All patients abused alcohol and drugs to extreme. Most criminal activity occurred while under the influence. One patient, while being followed by the police for a traffic offense, began firing a handgun at the police car in hopes of eluding arrest. Another attempted an armed robbery while drunk and began a high-speed chase through a large metropolitan area to elude arrest. Several patients submitted to extensive, somewhat disfiguring, nonprofessional tattooing while drunk or high on drugs.

I. Reality Testing (c): Awareness of Accuracy of Perception of Internal Events (5.84)

Twelve of our subjects showed the beginnings of a subjective sense of their own errors in perception, but generally this was discovered or acknowledged after the fact and often with therapeutic coercion. The remainder of our patients were able to recover from distortions when not in the situation that precipitated them. This subgroup had a moderate degree of awareness of feelings coming from within the self.

No one in the group truly lacked an awareness of the craziness of some perceptions, and conversely none could be judged as resilient, able to recover to a state of objectivity more or less naturally, or generally aware of inner feelings.

After relatively dramatic outbursts of anger, some subjects denied the wealth of emotion present until urged by the staff to examine the problem. In one such situation, a male patient launched a verbal attack on a clinician (P.W.), with many derogatory remarks, impassioned anger, and restrained physical aggression. When the subject was asked about this extreme outburst, he denied feeling anger toward the clinician: "I was just upset that you found out about me taking the pills." Later, the subject was able to verbalize some recognition of the anger he had felt toward the clinician: "You never let me get away with anything! You and my wife always tell the truth! It makes me feel terrible!"

I. Reality Testing Global Score (6.70)

Our patients were somewhat better at distinguishing between inner and outer reality than they were on the other two reality subdimensions but their global ratings were low.

Visual inspection of Table 2 and Figure 1 reveals that the judged level of reality testing of our psychopaths was virtually identical to the schizophrenics in the Bellak et al.'s reference group. Clearly they were far below normals and neurotics. Although other ratings must be done on other samples, these results provide us with some clues regarding the nature of the psychopath's mental illness. Because psychopaths can usually distinguish between inner and outer reality, the casual or even informed observer does not usually view them as "crazy." Yet further analysis reveals major distortions of reality, distortions that result in a functional level not unlike that of the schizophrenic. Perhaps an especially good example of deficient reality testing can be illustrated by the action of one subject, who truly believed his neighbor would not report the theft of her vehicle at knifepoint because his parents were "good people."

II. JUDGMENT

According to Bellak et al., good judgment depends on good reality testing. If one of the components of reality testing is not adequate, judgment will likely be affected. While judgment and reality testing seem so intimately related, Bellak et al. assessed these functions separately because anticipation and appropriateness, major elements of this conceptualization, play such a major part in judgment. The developers of the EFA argue that judgment is dependent on reality testing but extends beyond it.

There are three subscales: (a) anticipation of consequences; (b) extent to which manifest behavior reflects the awareness of its likely consequences and the extent to which behavior expressing maladaptive judgment is repeated; and (c) appropriateness of behavior.

II. Judgment (a): Anticipation of Likely Consequences (4.04)

Eleven of our subjects had a clear history of inappropriate judgment involving at least moderate danger to life and limb. Their awareness of consequences was very defective. For example, one patient used to practice an unusual form of "chicken." He would "play in traffic" to see if he could "outrun" on-coming cars on foot! Another regularly ventured to one of the most dangerous communities in America (Harlem) to buy and sell drugs, never acknowledging the danger until he was beaten and knifed.

Several of the remaining subjects had a somewhat better capacity to anticipate consequences, but this awareness fluctuated from one situation to another. For example, one patient risked his life in burglary, but was known as a responsible worker and good student, liked and respected by many adults.

No one could be judged to make "only occasional" errors in appraising their own and others' intended behavior. In behavioral terms, their signal anxiety was defective.

II. Judgment (b): Pattern of Behavior Reflects Awareness of Consequences (3.10)

The behavior of most of our subjects appeared to be relatively unaffected by life's consequences. The majority of them took unnecessary risks to the degree that self and/or others were endangered. They generally had histories reflecting poor awareness of consequences. For example, one patient was convinced that he would never get caught during his burglaries. Even when he was out on bond, after being charged with 10 counts of breaking and entering and grand larceny, he continued his criminal activities. When new warrants were issued by the judge and his bond was revoked, he still felt he could "get off" in spite of the ire he kindled in the trial judge. Another patient, although married, repeatedly established romantic liaisons with young teenaged female patients. He was cognizant that 1) this behavior would result in punishment at the hospital and 2) his wife would have to be told of his loss of privileges. But he continued to risk his marital relationship in this frivolous manner.

II. Judgment (c): Appropriateness of Behavior and Emotional Adjustment to Relevant Aspects of External Reality (2.96)

Seven patients were judged to be extremely inappropriate, socially and otherwise. For example, one of our patients was granted emergency leave of absence to attend his father's funeral. Upon returning to hospital, he was asked how he had handled death of his father and his time away from the hospital. He responded, "I had a great time! I got to see all my friends — especially my girlfriend! It was great!" Another patient engaged in obvious sex-play (mutual masturbation) in a crowded front lounge in the hospital while staff were present. Most patients were devious, destructive, dishonest, and often not even moderately appropriate in close interpersonal relationships.

II. *Judgment Global Rating* (3.84)

It is not surprising that our group received very low ratings on the judgment dimension. Indeed, clinical observation reveals that most of our psychopaths had poorer judgment than most of the schizophrenics under our care. Comparison to the Bellak et al. ratings confirms this. Our average ratings fell well below their schizophrenics' ratings.

III. SENSE OF REALITY OF THE WORLD AND OF THE SELF

This concept is central to experiencing oneself and the world. Although sense of reality is related to reality testing, it differs in that sense of reality refers to an awareness of inner states, whereas accurate appraisal of inner states is more relevant to reality testing. Although explanations of this dimension often appear to be rather esoteric, the face valid definition of "sense of reality" is fairly simple. Persons at one end of this dimension experience extreme derealization, depersonalization, grossly distorted identity, and fusion with others. Persons at the highest or healthiest end are very stable, even under great stress, have no disturbances in their reality sense and have a distinct self vis-à-vis others.

This scale has four dimensions: (a) the extent to which external events are experienced as real and as being embedded in a familiar context; (b) the extent to which the body (or parts of it) and its functioning and one's behavior are experienced as familiar and unobtrusive and as belonging to (or emanating from) the self; (c) the degree to which the person has developed individuality, uniqueness, a sense of self, a stable body image, and self-esteem; and (d) the extent to which the ego boundaries are clearly demarcated between the self and the outside world.

III. *Reality Sense (a): Experiencing External Events as Real* (11.96)

Our patients had very high ratings on this dimension. Derealization occurred only with extreme environmental alteration. There were no trances, fugues, or other dreamlike states. Indeed, many of these patients had "the right stuff." In this way they are highly reality-bound and may have a capacity to stay reality-bound, even in the face of fearful consequences. Only one case was rated relatively low, and this man had especially poor reality testing scores on the Rorschach.

III. Reality Sense (b): Realness of Body (12.24)

Again, on this dimension our psychopaths obtained high scores. We observed few disturbances in sense of reality of the self, the body, or the body-image. Their sense of body and behavior patterns were experienced as familiar and belonging to themselves.

III. Reality Sense (c): Individuality, Uniqueness, Sense of Self, Stable Body-Image, and Self-Esteem (6.80)

This dimension necessarily introduces the use of a reality standard external to the subject. When assessment is removed from the purely subjective, we found most of our patients to be fragmented, unintegrated, and unstable. They had seemingly insatiable quests for symbols of "success," e.g., "sex, drugs, and rock 'n' roll." Their personalities were stereotypic and phony. There was a clear "as if" quality present, and, despite protestations that they were "all man" or "all woman," they often appeared to be acting or role-playing.

One subject was, from all appearances, *the* "macho man." He was attractive, muscular, blonde, and always "in control." He wore the best of clothes (revealingly tight at times), gold chains, and a dazzling smile. He projected to the outside world the image of a man who could handle anything. On the other hand, he felt the need to use at least four preparations on his hair with every shampoo; he used many facial creams; and he had to have a special soap with which to cleanse his body. None of these was medically necessary, but suggested that he might have some problems with self-image.

III. Reality Sense (d): Demarcation Between Self and External World (7.00)

Because the psychopath is so unlikely to view others as separate from the self, it was rather difficult to rate our subjects on this dimension, and it was difficult to rate them highly. We could not usually say that their sense of self faltered or was threatened when they received negative feedback (a low rating), because most of the patients had such a narcissistic sense of omnipotence that they had great difficulty acknowledging that anyone else was important enough to deserve to be listened to in the first place, especially when the feedback was negative! To be wounded by negative feedback requires seeing others as separate from the self and as important in their own right.

On the other hand, we could usually not judge that there was a "moderately good sense of inner reality, continuity, and internalized self-representations" because these terms imply a degree of maturity or individuation not particularly characteristic of these people.

We rated most of our patients toward the middle of this scale, perhaps out of conservatism. As these scales were not originally developed to measure the omnipotence of personality-disordered individuals, we found them to be sometimes inadequate to our purposes. In our view, our patients manifested severe deficiencies in ego boundaries that demarcate the self from the world, but they more or less encroached upon others rather than were encroached upon or fused with.

III. Reality Sense Global Rating (9.90)

When we rated sense of reality based on the patient's subjective appraisal, they obtained high scores, higher than normal. However, when an external gauge or standard was introduced to assess reality sense, we found that their sense of reality was often seriously distorted. Despite the relatively lower ratings on subscales (c) and (d), the global ratings on sense of reality appeared to be about the same as the normals in the Bellak et al. study. Again, this is consistent with the casual observation that they do not appear "crazy." But assessment of other functions leads us to suspect that the "realness" of the psychopath should be questioned.

IV. REGULATION OF DRIVES AND AFFECTS

This scale assesses a person's ability to tolerate anxiety, depression, disappointment, frustration, and the necessity of postponing satisfaction. It refers to modulation of the expression of inner wishes, emotional strivings, and urges. The ego must ultimately serve the aims of the id, but to protect the total self it must do so in a regulated fashion.

The adapted person uses thinking and other psychological apparatus to stay impulsivity and harness psychic energy so that it can be used to achieve longer-range goals. We are not speaking here of superego constraints. It is probably best to think of this ego function in terms of its capacity to aid the organism to adapt and to adjust.

There are two dimensions to regulation: (a) directness of impulse expression, and (b) effectiveness of delay and control mechanisms.

IV. Regulation (a): Directness of Impulse Expression (4.20)

Most of our psychopaths were very impulsive. For example, when one patient was returned to hospital after a brief A.W.O.L., he was extremely intoxicated. He was threatening and abusive toward the staff and patients. When he was placed in a seclusion room to control his outburst and to provide him with a place to "sleep off" the alcohol, he became enraged—totally destroying the room. He tore off the lighting fixture and some molding, dislodged the flooring, broke out the plexiglass window in the door, and used these objects to beat innumerable divots in the solid core door. For several hours, it was impossible to contain or interact with him. Finally he began to cry uncontrollably.

IV. Regulation (b): Effectiveness of Delay and Control Mechanisms (3.76)

Dimension (b) tends to focus on the psychological regulatory structure more than on the direct expression, although obviously both are reflected in behavior. Most of our subjects had much difficulty controlling sexual, aggressive, or other urges. External controls were often necessary to inhibit expression of urges.

No patient was found to have "reasonably good controls."

IV. Regulation and Control Global Rating (4.24)

Overall, our patients were rated very low on regulation and control. Our averaged ratings even fell below the Bellak et al.'s ratings of schizophrenics. Our patients' frustration tolerance was very limited. Drives were generally not harnessed to further the goal of adaptation.

V. OBJECT RELATIONS

An object representation is a mental representation of a person (self or other) having one or more perceptual components, such as visual, tactile, olfactory, etc., and being imbued or cathected with emotions and feeling. In recent years this ego function has been studied as much or more than any other owing to the remarkable growth of modern object relations theory, led by such persons as Hartmann (1939, 1958), Kris (1951), Kernberg (1967), Rinsley (1978), Masterson (1971), and Mahler (1972).

As an ego functions dimension, object relations refers to the ability to form friendly and loving bonds with others with relatively little hostility, and to sustain relationships over time in a reasonably healthy way. Some persons are so wooden or primitive that others are more or less literally "objects." The internalized representations of most persons may be periodically disturbed by hostility and poorly controlled sexuality, but in the majority of cases the internalized representation is maintained relatively undisturbed and unchanged, except by changes in external circumstances or internal growth or trauma.

There are four subelements to the object relations dimension: (a) degree and kind of relatedness to others; (b) primitivity-maturity of object relations; (c) extent to which the person perceives and responds to others as independent entities rather than as extensions of himself; and (d) extent to which the person can maintain object constancy.

V. Object Relations (a): Relatedness to Others, Degree of Closeness (5.80)

Most of our patients were severely narcissistic. Since others were generally seen as self-extensions to gratify their immediate needs, healthy and mature love relationships were virtually impossible. Most relationships were "cool" and distant. Rarely was there a genuine attachment to others, unless the other was a source of need gratification. Most were described as "loners."

Several patients were rated slightly higher on this dimension because we could discern more "advanced" forms of sadism, sophisticated "game playing," and even sustained interpersonal love relationships including marriage, although those relationships were usually riddled with strife. None of the patients reflected flexibility in relations with significant others. None was judged to show disturbed interactions with only a few people, nor was there a maintenance of optimal closeness-distance.

One patient had little or no attachment to her family though she relied on them for her support. She stole from her parents' wallets and purses. She stole her father's gun collection to sell to support a drug habit. She forged checks in the amount of $1,500.00 on her father's checking accounts.

Another was married and had an infant son at the time of his admission. He was unfaithful to his wife prior to admission and became romantically involved during his hospital stay with several young teenage girls. He viewed his parents as being "at his service" for money or requests, but showed little affection for them except in the most superficial of ways.

V. Object Relations (b): Present Relationships Influenced Adaptively or Maladaptively by Older Ones (5.50)

In no case could we judge that transference and repetitions of early patterns of relating were the "exception." These distortions were routinely "the rule." Most patients were immature and narcissistic. They saw other people as things that could be used to attain their own ends. In most cases our patients expected to be gratified ("fed") by others and became irate when this didn't happen. Their internalized representations of others were simplistic and primitive and this persistent distortion of others routinely led to problems in interpersonal relationships.

V. Object Relations (c): Perception of Others as Independent Entities — Not Extensions of Self (4.44)

Half of our patients fell at "stop 2." People's feelings, motives and beliefs were usually understood in terms of the direct impact on the self. They derived pleasure from exercising "power" over others. It was extremely difficult for most of our patients to understand the feelings and emotions of others, much less empathize with them.

The more "advanced" patients could "tune in" to others in order to achieve some selfish end. This usually amounted to using flattery or to preying on someone else's weak spots in order to gain control or to get out of a jam. None of our patients received ratings over stop 4.

V. Object Relations (d): Object Constancy (5.70)

When internalized representations of others are primitive and strongly distorted by their own needs, it is difficult to even speak of true object constancy. Our psychopaths hardly had rich, accurate, internalized representations of others that endured through the thick and thin of conflicts, separations, and frustration. An internalized representation of their physician as a benevolent power who gives privileges changes instantly when the physician refuses a demand. Good guy became bastard in an instant.

Five of our patients received a scale rating of 7. Other people could be responded to in their own right if the situation were not too highly charged. None of the patients could be rated higher. Half received scale ratings of 5 (representations of others not too well internalized).

V. Object Relations Global Rating (5.40)

Our averaged ratings were about equivalent to Bellak et al.'s schizophrenics. We found object representations and object relationships to be immature, easily distorted, and strongly influenced by their own need status. They were narcissistic and egocentric. Although their object representations were not as disturbed as those of psychotic schizophrenics, they were considerably more primitive than the neurotics.

VI. THOUGHT PROCESSES

Thinking is a major factor in helping us adapt. It frees us from the immediate situation and allows us to delay motor discharge. Freud described thinking as a type of experimental action that uses small amounts of energy to modify the direction of behavior. Thus, the importance of trial and error is minimized.

There are three subdivisions of the overall thought processes dimension: (a) degree of adaptiveness in memory, concentration, and attention; (b) ability to conceptualize; and (c) extent to which language and communication reflect primary or secondary process thinking.

III. Thought Processes (a): Adaptiveness in Memory, Concentration, and Attention (10.20)

This subdimension assesses the degree of freedom from encumbrance of the pure cognitive functions. In most cases we found little distortion of cognitive functions even under stress. These patients didn't forget, stutter, or have other thought signs of "foggy" sensorium. Indeed, they tended to be able to think clearly even when under emotional strain, such as being arrested.

Facing arrest after a chase through town, one patient was able to get rid of the gun he had used to fire upon the police before they could pull over the car. Perhaps because he was so glib, even under pressure, he was able to convince the police he never even had a gun!

When finally arrested, several patients were able to convince police or other law enforcement officials that they were in need of psychiatric care rather than incarceration. This kind of focused attention and planning was not unusual at times of great stress even when patients were intoxicated or under the influence of drugs.

VI. Thought Processes (b): Conceptualization and Abstraction-concreteness (7.40)

Because most of our patients were rather concrete it was difficult to rate them over stop 5. We found it hard to say that there was satisfactory use of conceptualization, flexibility in willingness to entertain new ideas, etc. More typically our patients were concrete or overly ideational. Occasionally they showed some manifestations of flexibility, particularly during therapeutic sessions, but once they reentered their usual environment their simplistic and narrow cognitive tendencies reemerged.

VI. Thought Processes (c): Language (10.30)

Most of our patients received high ratings on this dimension. Because they were generally fairly cool and not inclined to be disturbed or disrupted by anxiety, there were few signs of loose or disorganized speech, blocking, imprecise substitutions, and malapropisms, or "peculiar" ways of saying things. These patients were usually fairly articulate, even under stress. Three patients were especially gifted at articulating long accounts of their midadventures. Their glibness would leave the novice clinician confused and "off-base"—never realizing how adept these fellows were at misdirecting the interaction.

VI. *Thought Processes Global Rating* (8.80)

As was the case with the Reality Sense scale, we experienced a rating problem here. The EFA scales were originally developed for use with schizophrenics and normals, not character-disordered persons. Perhaps here Cleckley's concept of "semantic aphasia" is especially relevant. According to Cleckley, overt speech disorder is not technically demonstrable in the psychopath. The speech disorder is *concealed* by an outer surface of intact function. The Thought Processes scale tends to tap overt signs of disruption in language. Apparently the psychopath can, in the absence of much anxiety, and with cavalier disregard for the emotional significance and consequences of his attitude and behavior, think and speak quite clearly in circumstances when the average person would stammer and stumble about. Because we were unsure of the applicability of this EFA scale with our psychopaths we deferred making any comparison to the reference groups.

VII. ARISE

ARISE (Adaptive Regression In Service of the Ego) is a concept that grew out of Freud's speculations regarding wit and comedy. It was expanded considerably by Kris (1952), who introduced the term "regression in service of the ego," and by Varendonck's (1921) speculations regarding daydreams. Bellak became interested in this concept as it related to the concept of projection (Bellak 1944), and this interest led to his work with the T.A.T. and C.A.T. and Rorschach projections.

A major reason to examine ARISE as an ego function is that ego tends to exclude itself from service. When this is extreme we may see inability to rest, insomnia, and an inability to perform creative tasks. Controlled regression allows ego to rest and permits less rational forces to come to the fore, thus increasing the likelihood that alterations, and perhaps more creative solutions to ego's problems (adaptation), will become available to ego's powers.

ARISE refers to the ability of the ego to initiate a partial, temporary, and controlled lowering of its own functions to further its major aim, which is adaptation. There is an oscillation of this process—controlled regression followed by reintegration, which may be at a higher level. At the bottom of ARISE scale we find uncontrolled pathological regression. At the top we find "controlled regression that affords rest for the ego, rejuvenation, and application of the regressive material to creative problem solving."

There are two dimensions to the ARISE scale: (a) degree of relaxation of perceptual and conceptual acuity with corresponding increase in awareness of previously preconscious and unconscious contents and the extent to which these "regressions" disrupt adaptation or are uncontrolled; and (b) extent of controlled use of primary process thinking in the induction of new configurations.

VII. ARISE (a): Dimension of Aware Relaxation to Uncontrolled Regression (5.50)

We found it rather difficult to rate our subjects on this scale. They were usually not severely regressed, as a schizophrenic in psychosis might be. Yet, when they did regress, especially in rage or sexual acting-out, they were hardly aware or able to use the regressive material in an adaptive or creative way. The results of the regression were usually split-off. They were very regressed in terms of psychic organization, but over this core of primitivity they wore an "as if" cloak of maturity. Such persons cannot really regress healthily because regression implies the growth or development to some higher level of maturity in the first place. Yet, because of their primitivity and because of their phony cloak of maturity and their concreteness, it was difficult for them to even access fantasy material, much less use it. Most of our subjects were rated in the middle of the range largely by default, because they didn't fit the ends of the continuum. Further, the middle anchor point contains the phrase that "there may be virtual absence of regressive phenomena." While these subjects were regressed, the kind of regressive phenomena described in the scale was generally not present.

VII. ARISE (b): Use of Regression for Adaptation and Creativity (5.70)

We also had difficulty applying this subscale to our psychopaths. They hardly were inclined to profit from their regressive experiences because they were so unlikely to benefit from any experience. Further, their tendency to be concrete—divorced from fantasy—made it difficult for them to vacate their hardworking egos to sojourn through the primitive forest of their unconscious, emerging with new fruits of insight.

VII. ARISE Global Rating (5.76)

In summary, we found it necessary to give rather low ratings on ARISE because there was usually little adaptive value to the frequent regression of these patients. Our average rating fell between Bellak et al.'s schizophrenics and neurotics. The potential to use primary process material generated in the regression was very limited because the ego's safety net was poorly developed.

VIII. DEFENSIVE FUNCTIONING

Classical psychoanalysis has dealt extensively with defenses. There is little doubt that a healthy individual must have a sound armamentarium of defenses and that "higher level" defenses afford greater adaptation. The defenses (mechanisms and processes) operate within an organization that is one element of overall ego organization. Defenses fall on a continuum ranging from pathological to adaptive. Repression has generally been viewed as a mature, healthy defense so long as it is not extreme or prevents constructive psychological work toward maturity. Interestingly, Schupper and Calogeras (1971) pointed out that in recent years repression is losing ground to regression as a defense. Regressive acting-out has replaced the tight gloom of repression in our narcissistic culture (Lasch, 1978).

There are two major dimensions to this ego function: (a) extent to which defense mechanisms have maladaptively affected ideation, behavior, and adaptive level of other ego functions; and (b) success or failure of defenses.

VIII. Defensive Functioning
(a): Interference with Adaptation (6.16)

Our patients did not adapt well to society. Although not without intellectual assets and talents, they all had been hospitalized in a mental institution and many had been in jail. Although we were rating defenses, this scale also forces us to rate another dimension, adaptation.

If we accept Reich's argument that character anomalies may act as a defense, then we may argue that psychopathic behavior may be a defense and that this defense is generally maladaptive, at least in our sample. In addition to acting-out, our patients used a variety of other rather primitive defenses, such as denial, splitting, projection, avoidance, and quasi delusions, all defenses that did not contribute—indeed that hindered—healthy adaptation to society at large.

VIII. *Defensive Functioning (b): Success or Failure* (7.30)

A small variance reflected our difficulty in applying this particular subscale to our population. The painful anxiety of the neurotic and the "pan anxiety" of the schizophrenic were not known to our patients, either because they were not capable of experiencing much anxiety, as some authors argue, or because their character defenses (Reich, 1949) were too strong. Reich pointed out that the meaning of the character defense is in its protection of the ego from internal and external dangers (e.g., among other things, anxiety).

We rarely found that our patients experienced anxiety only to a moderate degree and had "some tolerance" for it, because this implies a degree of health and resiliency not usually seen in them. Many patients were irritable or jumpy, and they dealt with this by acting out. Stop 3 (frequent breakthroughs of anxiety) did not seem very appropriate either. Hence, we rated most patients at stop 4 on the basis of reasoning that most of the anxiety was bound in the acting-out symptoms.

VIII. *Defensive Functioning Global Rating* (6.90)

Our ratings were similar to the reference group neurotics.

We encountered some difficulty in applying this scale to our psychopaths because ratings depended on a theoretical supposition, i.e., we assume that the psychopath's acting-out is a defense. If this is true, then we could conclude that the acting-out is effective in protecting the patient from anxiety but is highly maladaptive vis-à-vis the demands of the world.

Clinically, we can merely conclude that the defensive structure of the psychopath is primitive and the defenses, although often effective in protecting the organism from anxiety, are highly maladaptive.

IX. STIMULUS BARRIER

Freud's concept of *Reizschutz* (protective shield) was the antecedent of the concept of stimulus barrier. In part, Freud's concept grew out of or was related to his belief in the Nirvana principle — the belief that the organism strives to keep stimulation to a minimum. Freud wrote that the nervous system sought to reduce stimulation — or the precep-tion of stimulation.

Casual observation easily instructs us that some persons are psycho-logically thin-skinned, overstimulated, nervous, irritable, and jumpy. Everything seems to "get on their nerves." Others are "thick-skinned," often oblivious to the cacophony of irritants that bombard modern man. Further, although there is a defensive function to this "thick-skinnedness," it is not exactly a defense mechanism. Likely there is a physiological substrata that interacts directly with mothering style, mod-eling, and life history, including trauma.

There are two dimensions to the Stimulus Barrier scale: (a) threshold for, sensitivity to, or registration of external and internal stimuli im-pinging upon various sensory modalities; and (b) degree of adaptation, organization, and integration of responses to various levels of sensory stimulation.

IX. *Stimulus Barrier (a): Stimulus Threshold* (8.16)

We found that it may be necessary to expand or modify this scale for use with character-disordered persons. No one would be surprised that the psychopaths in our sample were rather "thick-skinned." One, in fact, proved to be more "thick-skinned" than seemed possible. Under extreme pressures of repeated offenses of breaking and entering, ar-rests on multiple felony charges, and confrontation from family mem-bers, he was able to function at work and at school adequately. At work, he was considered a valued employee — always prompt, efficient, and reliable. None of these major stresses had a bearing on his abil-ity to function well in some areas in his life.

Other patients were notably unruffled by the stresses of their arrests and imminent court appearances. In the face of challenges to their casual manner, they observed that family, friends, and staff were merely overreacting to minor difficulties.

Although our patients' stimulus barriers were rather high, stop 6 refers to an "automatic fluctuation in thresholds to stimuli . . . "; "good screening mechanisms to permit *adequate* input and avoid sensory overload" (italics ours). It is likely that some highly adapted psychopaths may achieve high scores on this dimension, as it implies flexibility or optimal screening. Our psychopaths were not flexible, however. They simply shut out stimulation. They ran away from anything aversive.

IX. *Stimulus Barrier (b): Adaptation, Organization and Integration to Various Levels of Sensory Stimulation* (8.04)

Stop level 3 on this subdimension generally describes a rather thin-skinned "neurotic" type of person. None of our patients could be rated as such. Yet neither were they flexible, able to "ride the waves," adapting well to most or all sensory impingements (level 5). This, in a way, is "stimulus barrier," but it is not *adaptive*.

This is why we had some difficulty rating our patients on Stimulus Barrier. Regarding the ability to withstand the racket of rock music, loud noise, endless parties, constant change, scrapes with the police, etc. they seemed, at times, to be nearly impervious to overstimulation. Indeed, classically they seemed to seek high stimulation. Other times it seemed that they would run from the slightest aggravation because they seemed so unable to handle the stimulus input. We could not say that there was flexible, adaptive adjustment.

IX. *Stimulus Barrier Global Rating* (8.20)

To summarize, we gave moderately high ratings on this dimension, as our patients were generally rather thick-skinned. Our averaged rating was slightly higher than Bellak et al.'s neurotics. However, our patients were usually not adaptive or flexible.

X. AUTONOMOUS FUNCTIONING

The concept of autonomous functioning primarily grows out of Hartmann's concept of the conflict-free portion of ego, the idea that regions of intellect develop independently from conflict resolution. According to Hartmann, primary functions that develop conflict-free are perception, intention, object comprehension, thinking, and language. These do not depend on conflict for their genesis or development. Secondary functions or secondary autonomous functions are habit patterns, complex attitudes, learned complex skills, work routines, hobbies, and interests. Perhaps one may simplify these functions as "normal psychology." Certainly psychologists, including those with minimal familiarity with or even hostility towards psychoanalytic propositions, readily study, understand, and manipulate these "autonomous functions." Because of their central importance to adaptation, Bellak et al. include them as a dimension of ego functioning.

The Autonomous Functioning scale has two subdimensions: (a) the degree of interference with primary autonomy (perception, intentionality, concentration, attention, memory, hearing, vision, speech, language, productivity, motor development, and expression); and (b) degree of impairment of secondary autonomy. This refers to disturbances in habit patterns, learned complex skills, work routines, and interests.

X. Autonomous Functioning (a): Impairment of Primary Autonomous Functions (10.04)

Unlike the depressive, the severe neurotic, or decompensated schizophrenic, psychopaths exhibited few signs of impairment of primary functions. Their sensorium was largely clear and unaffected by their emotional problems. They did not stutter, block, or forget names.

X. Autonomous Functioning (b): Interference With Secondary Autonomous Functions (8.30)

We encountered some difficulty with this scale. At issue is the definition of secondary autonomous functions. One may argue that our patients exhibited a low level of secondary autonomous functions if these are defined as steady work habits, complex job related talents, and healthy habit patterns. Yet one may argue that pulling off an armed robbery, conning a State Trooper into letting you out of a scrape, cracking a safe, or fencing your mother's silver—especially if done with relative ease, good resistance to intrusion, and diabolically clever flexibility—all represent high level of secondary autonomous functioning!

X. *Autonomous Functioning Global Rating* (7.84)

The primary autonomous functions were not particularly disturbed but the assessment of secondary autonomous functions was somewhat of a problem owing to some question about the meaning of this concept with the psychopath. Initial comparison to the reference group suggests that our global ratings are not dissimilar to the neurotics and the reference group.

XI. SYNTHETIC-INTEGRATIVE FUNCTIONS

The life of all persons is characterized by inconsistencies and contradictions within the psyche and between the psyche and the environment. Psychologically healthy persons struggle to synthesize inconsistency and contradiction in order to gain greater maturity and wholeness. Synthesis is not homogeneity but rather a unity or connection. Nunberg (1960) described synthesis as an assimilation of alien elements from within the self and from the broader environment. There is a mediating and reconciling of oppositional elements. According to Nunberg, the origin of synthesis is eros, the ultimate source of binding and productive power.

According to Bellak et al., synthesis represents a reconciliation of conflicting demands of id, super ego, and the environment, as well as contradictions within the ego. Ratings of level of this ego function consider reconciliation of conflictual issues and reconciliation of nonconflictual issues.

There are two subelements to the Synthetic-Integrative dimension: (a) reconciliation of discrepant or potentially contradictory attributes, values, affects, behavior, and self-representations; and (b) active relating together of intrapsychic and behavioral events that may or may not be conflict-ridden.

XI. *Synthetic-Integrative Functioning*
(a): Reconciliation of Conflict Areas (5.56)

The majority of our patients were rated at stop 3 because there appeared to be "significant indications of unintegrated ego functioning." Generally there were no consistent life goals and divergent career plans. Many of them exhibited elements of stop 2 (saying that they oppose violence while the overall description seemed too primitive.) While many patients were rated at stop 3, we did not generally observe that they were "puzzled by apparent contradictions and ambiguities." More commonly conflictual discrepancies were denied or split-off.

XI. Synthetic-Integrative Functioning (b): Active Relating Together of Conflictual and Nonconflictual Issues (5.76)

Many of our patients were able to mount a drive to organize different areas of their experiences and behavior, but these efforts were usually short-lived. More typically organizational efforts were fragmented and results were sparse. They lived from day to day. Some patients were able to achieve moderate success in purposefully planning and implementing personal projects.

XI. Synthetic-Integrative Functioning Global Rating (5.84)

Overall, our patients were rated approximately the same as the 50 schizophrenics in the reference group.

XII. MASTERY-COMPETENCE

Bellek et al. introduced this dimension as an ego function because of its relevance to psychotherapy and to overall adaptation. They argued that Freud dealt, at least indirectly, with this function when he introduced the mastery instinct, linking it to sadism. Others (Hartmann, 1958; White, 1963) have argued that the instinct or need to master is not primarily motivated by sadistic or aggressive conflicts and, instead, that there is a primary pleasure resulting from mastery, whatever the arena may be.

In EFA the subject's objective level of mastery is assessed, followed by his/her subjective appraisal. High discrepancy in either direction reflects conflict, but because of the nature of the scales, a global rating is not possible.

XII. Mastery-Competence (a): Objective Level of Performance (6.00)

The competence level of our patients was mediocre. They mastered through manipulation or they waited for "luck." They used others to achieve their ends rather than developing their own competencies.

XII. Mastery-Competence (a): Subjective Level of Performance (9.64)

As would be expected, most of our patients believed that they achieved a high level of environmental mastery. They generally believed that they were very bright, talented, accomplished and skillful. They were pleased with their achievements and with the level of industry that went into the achievement.

In short, they seriously distorted their actual level of competence in an upper direction. Their narcissism, primitive denial and splitting were especially effective in protecting them from the pain of self-knowledge and objective self-appraisal.

SUMMARY

In this chapter we presented the argument that psychopaths manifest specific deficiencies in ego structure and that these deficiencies result in functional deficits that can be measured using Ego Functions Analysis. Twenty psychopathic psychiatric inpatients were studied extensively and assessed on 12 dimensions of ego functioning. While no control group was available, we used the analysis of Bellak et al. as a reference to further understanding of our results. We found that: 1) it was possible, in most cases, to use Ego Functions Analysis with this population; and 2) assessment of our sample provided preliminary evidence that psychopaths manifest especially severe deficiencies in six ego functions: Reality Testing, Judgment, Regulation and Control of Drives and Affects, Object Relations, Adaptive Regression in Service of Ego, and Synthetic Functions.

Further, we found that our psychopaths were similar to normals (in the reference group) with regard to their capacity to experience external events as real and with regard to their sense of bodily reality. They generally had good memory, concentration, attention, and language function. They had a high barrier against external, aversive stimulation.

If the variability among our ego ratings is an accurate representation of psychopaths in general, it is not surprising that clinicians and laypersons have been confused about who these people are and what can be expected of them. In some ways they clearly resemble normal people and can thus "pass" as reasonably normal or sane. Yet we found them to be extremely primitive in other ways, even more primitive than frankly schizophrenic patients. In some ways their thinking was sane and reasonable but in others it was psychotically inefficient and/or convoluted.

METHODOLOGICAL ISSUES

The reader is asked to view our study as preliminary and exploratory. Clearly there are methodological issues that must be attended to in future replications. Some of these are: calculation of interrater reliability, validity studies with additional criteria, and assessment of additional samples of psychopathic psychiatric inpatients to provide a test of replicability. Additionally, to extend the meaning of our analysis, we would need to undertake replications with additional samples of other kinds of psychopaths (e.g., nonhospitalized psychopaths, prison populations, higher functioning psychopaths, successful psychopaths, etc.). Further, it would be helpful to compare our ratings of psychopaths with other patients at our hospital. Presumably, any measurement bias that exists in our "shop" would extend to our other patient groups as well. Hopefully, at the least we might balance measurement error, thereby making it possible to meaningfully examine specific differences in ego functions across our various patient groups.

The inferences we draw from the study of our sample must of course be limited as we focus only on hospitalized psychopaths. The ego structure and ego strength of nonhospitalized, highly functioning psychopaths, such as the ones described by Person in Chapter 12, will of course differ from ours. We would expect the ego strength of our hospitalized psychopaths to be low, as it takes a large amount of dysfunction to be hospitalized in a psychiatric setting in these times. Yet, we observed qualitative differences among various ego functions that led us to believe that we were not merely measuring global pathology.

Other research questions that we might examine are:

1) What is the range of level of ego functioning in psychopaths? Is their lowest to highest level of functioning greater than that of other patients? This would seem to be a reasonable hypothesis to examine, because clinically psychopaths seem to function at such a high level at certain times and yet can regress to a remarkably low level at other times.

2) What changes (if any) take place in ego functions as a result

of treatment and what changes (if any) take place as a result of different kinds of treatment? For example, one might argue that a highly confrontive reality-based cognitive approach that pounds away at the matter of ego boundaries might result in a half-step or more improvement after a period of treatment.

3) How do our hospitalized psychopaths compare to other patient groups? Because Highland Hospital is a referral hospital treating highly treatment resistant patients who have been relatively untouched by previous therapies, we would expect the majority of our patients to manifest severe ego deficiencies. However, we must ask exactly what specific weaknesses appear in what kinds of patients and what therapies seem to help what ego functions.

CONCLUSIONS

In this study we sought to learn if EFA can be used to describe specific ego deficiencies in psychopathic patients. Although we experienced certain problems in applying some of the scales, we generally found it possible to use EFA with the psychopath. Further, we believe that we have demonstrated Blatt and Shichman's (1981) assertion that the problem in psychopathy appears to be "an impairment of the development of basic ego functions" (p. 333). Hitherto no one to our knowledge has attempted a systematic description of ego dysfunction in psychopaths using EFA. Thus, our major contribution lies in making this first step. At the least, our results would suggest that it would be fruitful to continue to use EFA, and perhaps related methods, to more systematically study the psychological deficit in the psychopath.

REFERENCES

Arlow, J. & Brenner, C. (1964). *Psychoanalytic concepts and the structural theory.* New York: International Universities Press.

Bellak, L. (1944). The concept of projection: An experimental investigation and study of the concept. *Psychiatry, 7,* 353–370.

Bellak, L. & Goldsmith, L. (Eds.). (1984). *The broad scope of ego function assessment.* New York: Wiley.

Bellak, L., Hurvich, M., & Gediman, H. (1973). *Ego functions in schizophrenics, neurotics, and normals.* New York: Wiley.

Bender, L. (1947). Psychopathic behavior disorders in children. In R. M. Lindner & R. V. Seliger (Eds.), *Handbook of correctional psychology* (pp. 360–377). New York: Philosophical Library.

Beres, D. (1956). Ego deviation and the concept of schizophrenia. In R. Eissler et al. (Eds.), *The psychoanalytic study of the child: Vol. XI.* (pp. 164–235). New York: International Universities Press.

Blatt, S. & Shichman, S. (1981). Antisocial behavior and personality organization. In S. Tuttnam, C. Kaye, & M. Zimmerman (Eds.), *Object and self: A developmental approach: Essays in honor of Edith Jacobson* (pp. 325–367). New York: International Universities Press.

Cleckley, H. (1976). *The mask of sanity* (5th ed.). St. Louis: Mosby.

Dahl, A. (1984). A study of agreement among raters of Bellak's ego function assessment test. In L. Bellack & L. A. Goldsmith (Eds.), *The broad scope of ego function assessment* (pp. 160–166). New York: Wiley.

Erikson, E. (1962). Reality and actuality. *Journal of the American Psychoanalytic Association, 10,* 451–474.

Hartmann, H. (1958). *Ego psychology and the problem of adaptation.* (D. Rapaport, Trans.), New York: International Universities Press. (Original work published 1939).

Hartmann, H. (1964). Comments on the psychoanalytic theory of the ego. In *Essays on ego psychology* (pp. 113–141). New York: International Universities Press. (Original work published 1950).

Hendrick, I. (1934). *Facts and theories of psychoanalysis* (2nd ed.). New York: Knopf.

Jacobson, E. (1964). *The self and the object world.* New York: International Universities Press.

Kernberg, O. F. (1967). Borderline personality organization. *Journal of the American Psychoanalytical Association, 15,* 641–685.

Kris, E. (1951). The development of ego psychology. *Samiksa, 5.*

Kris, E. (1952). *Psychoanalytic explorations in art.* New York: International Universities Press. (Original work published 1936).

Lasch, C. (1978). *The culture of narcissism.* New York: Norton.

Mahler, M. (1963). Thoughts about development and individuation. In *The psychoanalytic study of the child, Vol. XVIII* (pp. 307–324). New York: International Universities Press.

Mahler, M. (1972). On the first three subphases of the separation-individuation process. *International Journal of Psycho-Analysis, 53,* 333–338.

Masterson, J. (1971). Treatment of the adolescent with borderline syndrome: A problem in separation-individuation. *Bulletin of the Menninger Clinic, 35,* 5–18.

Nunberg, H. (1960). *The practice and theory of psychoanalysis.* New York: International Universities Press. (Original work published 1930).

Reich, W. (1949). *Character analysis* (3rd ed.). New York: Orgone Institute.

Rinsley, D. (1978). Borderline psychopathology: A review of aetiology, dynamics and treatment. *International Review of Psycho-Analysis, 5,* 45–54.

Schupper, F. & Calogeras, R. (1971). Psycho-cultural shifts in ego defenses. *American Image, 28,* 1.

Varendonck, J. (1921). *The psychology of daydreams.* London: Allen and Unwin.

Weiner, I. (1966). *Psychodiagnosis in schizophrenia.* New York: Wiley.

White, R. (1963). Ego and reality in psychoanalytic theory. (Monograph 11). *Psychological issues, 3,* 1–210.

6

Human Aggression:
A Biological Perspective

Gerald L. Brown &
Frederick K. Goodwin

Human aggressive behavior has been studied from various perspectives, but direct study of possible central nervous system (CNS) contributions has been relatively recent. One of the stimuli for recent biochemical studies has been a renewal of interest in the relationship between aggression and suicide. Aggression and suicide have been considered to be integrally related by some authors, the most well-known quote probably being that of Freud, "We have long known, it is true, that no neurotic harbours thoughts of suicide which he has not turned back upon himself from murderous impulses against others, but we have never been able to explain what interplay of forces can carry such a purpose through to execution" (1953). More recently, the studies of Asberg and colleagues (Asberg, Thoren, and Traskman, 1976; Asberg, Traskman, and Thoren, 1976) and Brown et al. (1979a, 1982) have stimulated considerable further work on the aggression/impulsivity/suicide relationship from the point of view of CNS biochemistry.

ANIMAL MODELS—AGGRESSIVE BEHAVIORS

The literature of the biological study of aggression in animals is quite extensive. According to Moyer (1968, 1971, 1976), representations of aggressive behavior include seven categories: predatory, intermale, fear-induced, irritable, territorial, maternal, and instrumental. Reis (1974) grouped aggressive behaviors into two major categories: predatory and affective. Certain CNS neurotransmitters, i.e., serotonin (5HT), gamma-amino-butyric acid (GABA) and dopamine (DA) (neurotransmitters that are largely inhibitory to the CNS), and norepinephrine (NE) (a neurotransmitter that is largely excitatory), as well as others, such as acetylcholine, are associated with aggressive behavior in animals (West, 1977). Other biochemical compounds (CNS/peripheral) have also sometimes been associated with aggressive behaviors in animals (Angel, Deluca, and Murphree, 1976; Orenberg et al., 1975; Sheard, 1979). Further, various pharmacological compounds that induce changes in the CNS, particularly the neurotransmitters, have also been shown to alter aggressive behavior in animals and humans (Leventhal, 1984; Luchins, 1983; Neppe, 1982; Sheard, 1971, 1975).

Although not all studies have been consistent, a large body of data indicates that depletion of CNS 5HT can lead to aggressive behaviors, e.g., mouse-killing by rats (Grant, Coscina, Grossman, and Freedman, 1973) and the reversal of this behavior by repletion of 5HT (Kulkarni, 1968). Depletion may be the result of lesions (Grant et al., 1973), compounds that inhibit the CNS synthesis of 5HT (Koe and Weissman, 1966; Miller et al., 1970; Sanders-Bush, Bushing and Sulser, 1972), specific neurotoxins (Kantak, Hegstrand, and Eichelman, 1981), or dietary restrictions (Kantak, Hegstrand, and Eichelman, 1980). Some studies indicate that treatment with parachlorophenylalanine (PCPA), a tryptophan (TP) hydroxylase inhibitor (Koe and Weissman, 1966; Jequier, Lovenberg, and Sjoerdsma, 1967), can reduce the septal rage syndrome in rats with septal lesions (Dominguez, and Longo, 1969; Sofia, 1969), but have minimal behavioral effects in normal rats (Tenen, 1967). Thus, the prior condition of the animal is important (i.e., possibly different drug effects in pathological vs. normal humans). Some studies further indicate that not only a decrease in inhibitory neurotransmitter metabolism, e.g., 5HT, but also an increase in excitatory neurotransmitter metabolism, e.g., NE (Eichelman, Thoa, and Perez-Cruet, 1972; Thoa et al., 1972), DA (Eichelman, Thoa, and Ng, 1972; Geyer and Segal, 1974) and AcH (Eichelman and Thoa, 1973) may be related to aggressive behavior, such that relative balances may be very important. Excellent reviews of the animal literature have been provided by Eichelman (1979) and Valzelli (1981).

It is much more problematic to discuss animal counterparts for suicidal behavior than for aggressive behavior, since suicide may appear to involve higher levels of cognitive and, apparently, intentional mental processes than some aggressive behaviors. Though cognition and intention surely play important roles in many instances of suicidal behavior, it would be an assumption to ascribe cognition and intention primary etiological roles. Whether a behavior is self-destructive or "suicidal" can be as difficult to discriminate in animals as in humans. Certain advantages accrue in looking at self-destructive behaviors in animals, in that one might come to see otherwise overlooked evolutionary and genetic contributions to the "proneness" for suicide in humans.

Certain kinds of animal behaviors that often lead to their demise from causes other than a "disease" or accident have been carefully reviewed (Crawley, Sutton, and Pickar, 1985). In earlier papers (Brown et al., 1979a, 1982a), we have alluded to the protest-despair model in primates as roughly analogous to the aggressive rage (protest), sometimes followed by depressive affect (despair), that can be seen in humans; furthermore, the "despair" in such animals can often be therapeutically modified by those medications effective in the treatment of human depressives (McKinney, Moran, and Kraemer, 1984). Not only does this primate model have an analogy in the "anaclitic depression" described by Spitz (1947; Spitz and Cobliner, 1965) in infants, which can lead to their death, but infants who have experienced such social deprivation have also been reported to show CNS changes related to the hypothalamic-pituitary axis and its regulation of hormones that influence glucose metabolism. These changes may or may not be entirely reversible with a restoration of the caretaker (Powell et al., 1967a,b).

Authors point perhaps more frequently to the obvious differences between man and animals than to some of their behavioral similarities. Most laboratory-controlled animal studies focus on a highly controlled "state." Human studies that are associated with cerebrospinal fluid (CSF) neurotransmitter metabolites and aggressive behavior have largely focused on "trait," although those studies that have distinguished "violent" vs. "nonviolent" suicide attempts relative to CSF neurotransmitter metabolites — 5-hydroxyindoleacetic acid (5HIAA), a major metabolite of 5HT; 3-methoxy-4-hydroxyphenylglycol (MHPG), a major metabolite of NE; and homovanillic acid (HVA), a major metabolite of DA — are not so easily categorized with regard to "state" or "trait," since in most of these studies behavioral history is not reported. As both suicide (Pokorny, 1983) and aggression (Robins, 1966, 1978) are best predicted by a history of similar behavior, one might wonder if those individuals who make a "violent" suicidal attempt are not generally more repetitively impulsive individuals in other behaviors. That suicide not associated with violence has not been consistently associated with decreased CSF 5HIAA might indicate that aggression/impulsivity is a more basic and primitive response than depression and suicide (45–85% of suicides are associated with depression as a syndrome or symptom) (Beskow, 1979). Animals bred for maximizing aggressive traits (Ciaranello, Lipsky, and Axelrod, 1974; Lamprecht et al., 1972), or those strains known to be aggressive (Angel et al., 1976; Southwick and Clark, 1968), would probably provide a better parallel for those patients reported below.

The other clinical studies reviewed herein either do not or only minimally focus on life histories; rather, they focus on a single observation or measure of a state or condition. The possible differences in CSF monoamine metabolite levels in depressives when comparing those whose depression was proximated by a significant life event vs. those without such a history have been reported by Roy et al. (in press). Perhaps the latter group represented a more endogenous group, in whom a relatively fixed biological alteration (lower CSF 5HIAA) either made them less prone to be influenced by specific life and/or environmental events or made them not "need" an additional environmental stress to result in clinical psychopathology.

Human behavior needs to be studied both as a "state" and as a "trait." A life history of impulsive behavior provides, on the one hand, a certain confidence that repetitive behaviors are less likely to be simply a reflection of the current situation or environment; on the other hand, there is a concern for the validity of history, particularly self-report, as opposed to the confidence one may have from direct observations or measures at the time of the behavior.

Another important difference between animal and human studies is the greater memory capacity in humans. A human, for example, may show less aroused, aggressive, and sometimes self-destructive behavior when exposed to a novel environment than is often the case for animals (Christmas and Maxwell, 1970). Possibly, with a greater store of memory and a greater cognitive capacity to search and utilize such a store, the human is able to make some association between the new environment and past experience to facilitate the adjustment process. Since the memory system of man is much more advanced than that of animals, one might hypothesize that memory of prior experience has the potential to contribute so greatly to behavior in man that innate biochemical characteristics have either a relatively insignificant role or a role "overwhelmed" by the social experience (and memory storage thereof), though the molecular characteristics of short-term and long-term memory are now being defined (Kandel, 1986). It is also conceivable that some individuals have such a predisposition or biological "readiness" for aggressive/impulsive behavior that, even without a relative lack of memory or learning capacity, they would be prone to impulsive, repetitive behaviors in an array of social situations and environments.

Humans have varying capacities to be influenced by previous experience. It would be important to determine if those relatively few individuals who have low CSF 5HIAA, but no pathological history of aggressive/impulsive/suicidal behaviors, do show certain unique traits, such as "sensation-seeking" (Zuckerman, 1983). In any case, muricidal behavior in rats with decreased CNS 5HT is attenuated by prior exposure to mice (Marks, O'Brien, and Paxinos, 1977). The influence of prior experience on one's "proneness" to "act on impulse" is surely variable in humans, and perhaps to a lesser degree in animals as well. Decrease in CNS 5HT in animals has also been associated with the inability to delay before acting (Sanger and Blackman, 1976), as well as release of inhibition of "punished behaviors" (Tye, Everitt, and Iverson, 1977; Tye, Iverson, and Green, 1979). One clinical analogy may be the relative incapacity of some aggressive/violent individuals and most impulsive individuals, by definition, to "delay gratification"; another may be the relative ineffectiveness of punishment (the relative lack of ability to learn from experience?) in many antisocial individuals, for whom incarceration often appears to serve more as a protective service to society than as a paradigm in which significant nonantisocial learning occurs. The animal data certainly would be consistent with the notion that, in general, CNS biochemistry may be more related to patterns of behavior than to psychiatric diagnoses, as has been discussed in an earlier review (Brown, Goodwin, and Bunney, 1982b). In large part, because of such animal data, we initiated a human study reported in 1979(a) and reported a replication in 1982(a).

TWO STUDIES OF HUMAN/AGGRESSIVE/
IMPULSIVE/SUICIDAL BEHAVIOR

The two independent studies were a joint effort between the National Naval Medical Center and the National Institutes of Mental Health, both in Bethesda, Maryland, involving inpatient, active-duty military men of normal intelligence; the first study was comprised of 26 subjects and the second 12 (more subjects were not available for the second study). For both studies, ages ranged from 17 to 32 years (mean $\pm$ SD = 22.1 ± 3.6 and 22.0 ± 5.2, respectively), and height from 68 to 73 inches (70.6 ± 1.4) for the second study. All were nonpaid volunteers from whom informed consent was obtained. Patients were excluded from both studies if medical disorders were present, if there was evidence of past or current primary affective disorder or schizophrenia, or if other than transient organic brain syndrome had ever been observed (according to DSM-II and DSM-III, respectively). Both studies were comprised of personality disorders.

An important clinical distinction between the two studies was that any presence or history of psychotic symptomatology was a basis for exclusion from the first study, whereas in some of the second group a history of Brief, Reactive Psychosis (DSM-III, 301.20) as a secondary diagnosis was present. Such a disturbance is often present in young military populations and confounds the differentiation between severe personality disorder and mild psychotic disorder (DSM-III) (Spitzer, Endicott, and Gibbon, 1977; Strange, 1974). Those personality disorder categories within both groups, along with descriptions of their clinical symptomatology have been further detailed elsewhere (Brown et al., 1979a,b, 1982a,b; Brown and Goodwin, 1984a). Clinical diagnoses and clinical history assessments were made independently of the biochemical investigations.

Further exclusion criteria were the ingestion of any drug, prescribed or illicit within 10 days of the lumbar puncture, and heavy use of alcohol (a score of more than 6 on the Michigan Alcoholism Screening Test) (Selzer, 1971; Zung and Charalampous, 1975). None of the patients had a history of heavy drug abuse, nor had any been prescribed a psychoactive drug except during transient symptomatic episodes. Methods to increase the likelihood of drug history veracity were described in previous studies (Brown et al., 1979a,b).

Material available for evaluating each patient included the full medical/psychiatric history, physical examination, and job performance assessments. Because a purpose of the study was evaluation of suitability for further military service, emphasis was given to a life history of aggression, particularly in response to authority. Most of the subjects were not returned to full active duty after the medical/psychiatric assessment. The categories of behavior used to determine a measure of aggression history, its scoring, its reliability, and its use in a normal, age-matched control group have been previously described (Brown et al., 1979a,b). The Buss-Durkee Inventory (BDI) for aggression (Buss, 1961; Buss and Durkee, 1957; Buss, Durkee, and Baer, 1957) and the Minnesota Multiphasic Personality Inventory (MMPI) (Lanyon, 1961; Welsh and Dahlstrom, 1956) were also available in the second study. Individual items of the psychopathic deviate (PD) scale of the MMPI approximate behaviors reflected in the history of aggression measure. A patient self-administered questionnaire containing subsections to score childhood behaviors and relationships, childhood school experience, childhood medical experience, similar items of adulthood behaviors and relationships, and similar items of adult medical experience was collected on all subjects; the questionnaire is further described by Brown et al. (in press).

CSF was obtained, as previously described (Brown et al., 1979a; Goodwin et al., 1973), between 8 a.m. and 9 a.m. after eight hours of bed rest and after postmidnight fasting. For 48 hours before the procedure, foods in the diet that might affect 5HT, NE, or DA metabolism or the assay itself were restricted by means of a low monoamine diet (Hoeldtke et al., 1972; Hoeldtke and Wurtman, 1974; Hollister et al., 1978; Muscettola, Wehr, and Goodwin, 1977; Sharpless, 1977; Taylor, 1979); coffee, tea, and cigarettes were also restricted. None of the patients was acutely symptomatic during this period. Details of specimen handling, assay methodology and statistical methods have been published elsewhere (Brown et al., 1979a, 1982).

Within the initial group of subjects, aggression scores showed a significant negative correlation with CSF 5HIAA, a significant positive correlation with MHPG and no correlation with HVA. The prediction formula obtained from multiple regression analysis indicated that 85% of the variance in aggression scores was accounted for by the combination of 5HIAA and MHPG. The major contribution came from 5HIAA, which alone accounted for 80% of the variance in aggression scores. When subjects with aggression scores above the median were compared with those below the median, 5HIAA levels of the more aggressive group were significantly lower, but there was no significant difference with regard to MHPG levels. Those subjects who had been given personality diagnoses more associated with behavioral impulsivity (antisocial, explosive, immature and hysterical) had a significantly higher mean aggression score, lower 5HIAA, and no difference in MHPG, when compared with the group with less impulsive personality disorders (passive-aggressive, passive-dependent, schizoid, obsessive-compulsive and inadequate).

Independent of both the aggression scores and the metabolite data, a Navy Medical Board judged 16 of the 26 subjects to be unsuitable for further military service. Compared with those who were not discharged, the discharged subjects had a significantly higher mean aggression score, lower 5HIAA, and higher MHPG. Of particular interest was the association among mean aggression score, a history of suicidal behavior, and CSF 5HT, NE, and DA metabolites in these subjects. The 11 subjects with a prior history of at least one suicide attempt had a significantly higher mean aggression score, a lower 5HIAA, and higher MHPG, than the 15 subjects with no history of suicide attempts; no significant associations were found with HVA.

In the second study, the PD ("psychopathic deviate") scores on the MMPI were negatively correlated with CSF 5HIAA (Figure 1); furthermore, a negative correlation between aggression history and 5HIAA was observed. Subjects with lower 5HIAA (by median split) showed higher aggression history scores than subjects with higher 5HIAA; also, the lower 5HIAA subjects scored significantly higher on the PD scale. Although lower 5HIAA subjects had higher BDI scores on both behavioral and total aggression, these differences were not significant; only the "irritability" score of the BDI showed a significant negative correlation with CSF 5HIAA, although all other categories, except "guilt," were negatively correlated (Brown and Goodwin, 1984a). PD scores, aggression history, and BDI scores were not significantly related to MHPG or HVA. None of the relationships between age and height and metabolite data was significant, although the expected negative correlation was observed for height.

In the initial study, a history of suicidal behavior was associated with life histories characterized by higher levels of aggression and both behavior patterns were associated with decreased CSF 5HIAA. The second study reexamines the relationship between aggression and suicide,

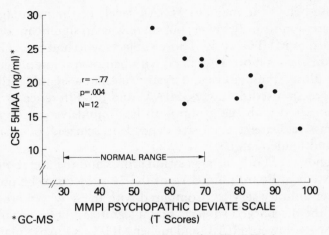

Figure 1. Psychopathy and CSF 5HIAA

as well as the relationships of both behavior patterns to neurotransmitter metabolites. Significantly higher aggression history scores were
found among those subjects with suicidal history vs. those without such
history in both studies (see Figure 2). The trivariate relationship between mean aggression scores, suicidal history, and CSF 5HIAA is
readily apparent (see Figure 3). A relationship between a history of

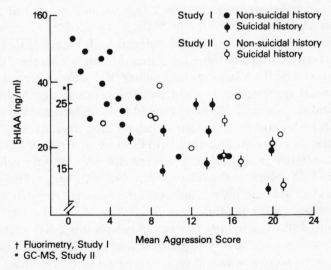

Figure 2. Aggression, Suicidal History, and CSF 5HIAA

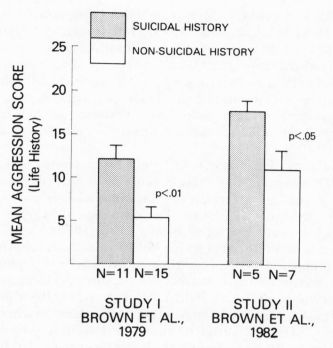

Figure 3. Suicidal History and Aggression

suicide attempts and CSF 5HIAA was confirmed; those with such history had significantly lower 5HIAA than those without such history in both studies. No relationships between suicidal behaviors and CSF MHPG or HVA were observed.

Aggression history correlated significantly with BDI scores for total aggression, behavioral aggression, and hostility, and with the PD scale of the MMPI as well. The PD scale score did not correlate significantly with the BDI scores for total aggression or behavioral aggression but did with the score for hostility.

LITERATURE REVIEW

Since the initial studies linking biologically, aggression and suicide, there have been five additional studies published relating aggressive/impulsive behavior, suicidal behavior, and CSF 5HIAA (see Table 1) (Bioulac et al., 1978, 1980; Lidberg et al., 1984, 1985; Linnoila et al., 1983). Studies of CSF MHPG and HVA have yielded inconsistent results. Those of Bioulac et al. (1978, 1980) from France reported decreased CSF 5HIAA turnover (via the probenecid method) in 47, XYY institutionalized criminals. Though the history of aggression was not quantified in these reports, descriptions of aggressive behaviors were provided; they included mental retardation, personality disorder, temper outbursts, instability, perversity, fits of hysterics, alcoholism, arson, vagrancy, death threats, burglary, torture of animals, assaults, and fights.

Linnoila and associates (1983) studied incarcerated murderers in Finland. It was noted that those personality disorder diagnoses associated particularly with impulsivity, i.e., antisocial and explosive, had the lowest levels of CSF 5HIAA. These more specific clinical findings replicated the earlier work of Brown et al. (1979a,b). Lower CSF 5HIAA was also associated with a history of suicidal behavior in the Finnish group. Lidberg and associates in Sweden (1984) reported three suicidal individuals who killed their own children; all three individuals had quite low levels of CSF 5HIAA. More recently Lidberg and associates (1985) have reported a larger group of murderers in whom suicide was related to lower CSF 5HIAA; however, only those who murdered sexual partners (and were not alcoholics) had lower levels of CSF 5HIAA when contrasted to nonemotional or nonviolent murderers (e.g., a murderer who had killed a number of patients in a nursing home because of a belief in euthanasia).

Although one must be quite cautious in deriving hypotheses from individual case reports, they can be clinically instructive. Brown, Linnoila, and Goodwin (1985) studied an individual who made four suicidal attempts between the ages of eight and 22 and then killed his lover; he had a quite low level of CSF 5HIAA compared to normal controls studied under the same conditions. Kreusi and associates (1985) described an adolescent with a low level of CSF 5HIAA whose antisocial behavior was largely that of burglaries to obtain "sweets"; this report is consistent with studies (Fernstrom, 1982; Fernstrom and Wurtman, 1971, 1972) that show the effect of carbohydrate ingestion in raising the level of CNS 5HT. Virkkunen (1982, 1983; Virkkunen and Huttunen, 1982) has also described Finnish murderers with abnormal glucose metabolism. That depression, suicide, and homicide can be closely linked in the same individual has been recently supported by Rosenblum and Bennet (1986). Another individual who was acutely suicidal, then murdered his wife, demonstrated (in part through serially administered MMPIs) how a person with overly controlled hostility might erupt into suicidal and/or homicidal behavior (Arnold, Fleming, and Bell, 1979). In another case report, a clear history of lifelong periodic aggressivity/impulsivity in a 47 XYY male was documented (Camen and Mullen, 1979). He was eventually convicted as an arsonist. Imprisoned young male arsonists have also been shown to have lower levels of CSF 5HIAA (Virkkunen et al., 1985). All of these studies taken together tend to lend credence to the idea that some form of impulsivity, disinhibition, or dyscontrol, rather than antisocial acts in and of themselves, is the behavioral variable linked to CSF 5HIAA.

Following the initial of Asberg, Thoren, and Traskman (1976; Asberg, Traskman, and Thoren, 1976), nine additional studies have assessed the relationship between CSF 5HIAA and violent vs. nonviolent suicidal behavior (Table 2) (Banki and Arato, 1983a, 1983b; Banki et al., 1984; Oreland et al., 1981; Roy et al., 1985; Roy-Byrne et al., 1983; Traskman et al., 1981; Van Praag, 1982, 1983). CSF MHPG and HVA have yielded inconsistent results. Five of seven groups of patients with lower CSF 5HIAA also had a history of a violent suicidal attempt, whereas, four of seven groups had lower (but less so) CSF 5HIAA if they had had a history of suicidal behavior by nonviolent means. Two studies showed no relationship between low CSF 5HIAA in those with histories of violent or nonviolent suicidal attempts (Roy et al., 1985; Roy-Byrne et al., 1983). In general, the distinction between violent and nonviolent suicide has been that of the use of guns, knives, and hanging for the former and minor cuts and overdoses for the latter. Among those studies in Table 1 the diagnoses are primarily that of personality disorders, whereas among those in Table 2 the diagnoses are major affective disorders and schizophrenia.

Another nine studies (Table 3) (Agren, 1980, 1983; Banki, Molnar, and Vojnik, 1981; Berrettini et al., 1985; Leckman et al., 1981; Montgomery and Montgomery, 1982; Ninan et al., 1984; Palaniappan, 1983; Vestergaard et al., 1978) have also reported observations of suicidal behavior and CSF 5HIAA, MHPG, and HVA, in which neither the violent or nonviolent nature of the suicide, nor any life history of the subject's aggressivity/impulsivity was reported. Again, among these studies CSF MHPG and HVA have yielded inconsistent results. In these studies, seven of nine have reported a lower level of CSF 5HIAA associated with suicidal behavior. These studies have looked primarily at

TABLE 1

Aggressive/Impulsive Behavior, Suicidal Behavior and CSF 5HIAA

		CSF 5HIAA	
Study	Diagnosis	Aggressive/Impulsive Behavior	Suicidal Behavior
1. Brown et al., 1979b	Personality Disorders (military)	↓	↓
2. Bioulac et al., 1978, 80	Personality Disorders XYY (prisoners)	↓[a]	?
3. Brown et al., 1982	Borderline Disorders (military)	↓	↓
4. Linnoila et al., 1983	Personality Disorders (prisoners)	↓	↓
5. Lidberg et al., 1984	Murderers of own children (forensic)	↓[b]	↓
6. Lidberg et al., 1985	Murderers—depression anxiety, Personality Disorders (forensic)	↓[b,c]	↓

a = post-probenecid; b = not necessarily a history of aggressivity/impulsivity
c = only if victims were sexual partners and subjects were not alcoholics
1 of 4 studies in which CSF HVA was examined found it lower in more aggressive subjects;
1 of 3 studies in which CSF MHPG was examined found it higher in more aggressive subjects
↓ = decrease; ? = not reported (see study for details)

Branchey et al., 1984 (alcoholics)—↓ plasma tryptophan/neutral amino acids in more aggressive subjects

patients with major affective disorders. Of particular interest is that a relationship between suicidal behavior and CSF 5HIAA has not been observed in any of five studies in Tables 2 and 3 in which bipolar affective illness has been studied.

The subjects in all previously cited CSF 5HIAA-aggression-suicide studies have been either European or American, but one study in this last group (Palaniappan et al., 1983) reports decreased CSF 5HIAA in depressive Indian patients with a history of suicidal behavior (though no biochemical findings were related specifically to subtypes of depression). The fact that a similar behavioral-biochemical association has been found from such diverse social, cultural, and national backgrounds could be evidence for a biological contribution in some aggressive/impulsive behaviors that is more basic than environmental and/or social variables.

Although relatively little has been published that pertains to the behavioral interactions of aggression/impulsivity, suicide, and 5HIAA in alcoholics, several studies are of interest. Early studies (Major et al., 1977; Takahaski et al., 1974) showed no differences in CSF 5HIAA between alcoholics and controls during abstinent states; however, one of these groups of investigators later showed that CSF 5HIAA decreased with the interval of time between acute inebriation and a period of "drying out" (Ballenger et al., 1979). More recently, Branchey et al. (1984) have shown the ratio of plasma TP to neutral amino acid to be lower in alcoholics, particularly those with a history of aggressive/impulsive behaviors and suicidal behaviors. This ratio is important in that it is directly related to the amount of TP, the dietary precursor of 5HT, that is transported across the blood-brain barrier for the CNS synthesis of 5HT (Gessa et al., 1974). Furthermore, this group showed a statistically significant relationship between aggressive behavior and suicidal behavior, similar to that reported in the two studies by Brown et al. (1979a, 1982a).

More studies related to CNS neurotransmitters need to be done in

TABLE 2
Violent and Non-Violent Suicidal Behavior and CSF 5HIAA

		CSF 5HIAA	
Study	Diagnosis	Violent Suicide	Nonviolent Suicide
1. Asberg et al., 1976a,b	Unipolar depression	↓↓	NS
2. Oreland et al. 1981; Traskman et al., 1981	Depression and controls (anxiety; personality disorders)	↓↓	↓
3. Van Praag, 1982	Depression	↓↓	↓
4. Van Praag, 1983	Schizophrenia	↓↓	↓
5. Roy-Byrne et al., 1983	Unipolar depression	NS[a]	NS
	Bipolar depression	NS	NS
6. Banki and Arato, 1983a,b; Banki et al., 1984	Depression, schizophrenia, alcoholism, adjustment disorder	↓	NS
7. Roy et al., 1985	Schizophrenia	NS	NS

a = non-significantly lower in unipolar depressives
1 of 3 studies in which CSF HVA was examined found it lower in violent attempts; CSF MHPG was examined in 2 studies and was lower in neither
↓ = decrease; ↓↓ = greater decrease; NS = nonsignificant change (see study for details)

TABLE 3
Suicidal Behavior and CSF Amine Metabolites

Study	Diagnosis	CSF Amine Metabolites		
		5HIAA	HVA	MHPG
1. Vestergard et al., 1978	Unipolar depression Bipolar depression	NS	—	—
2. Agren, 1980	Unipolar depression	↓	NS	↓
	Bipolar depression	NS	NS	NS
3. Leckman et al., 1981	Affective and schizophrenic psychoses	↓[a]	NS	NS
4. Banki et al., 1981	Major depression	↓	NS	—
5. Montgomery et al., 1982	Depression and Personality Disorder	↓	↓	—
6. Agren, 1983	Unipolar depression	↓	NS	↓
	Bipolar depression	NS	NS	NS
7. Palaniappan et al., 1983	Depression	↓	↓	NS
8. Ninan et al., 1984	Schizophrenia	↓	—	—
9. Berrettini et al., 1985	Euthymic bipolar depression	NS	NS	—

a = suicidal ideation
↓ = decrease; NS = nonsignificant change; __ = not measured (see study for details)

alcoholics, but the studies thus far reported suggest the hypothesis that some alcoholics may drink excessively in an attempt to treat themselves for depressive, aggressive, and suicidal affects. Although alcohol is often considered a precipitant of violence, the use of alcohol proximate to a violent act (Arnold, Fleming, and Bell, 1979; Camen and Mullen, 1979) could also be an attempt at self-medication. Furthermore, whether alcohol precipitates aggression or has an inhibitory effect may depend on its "dose" (Cherek, Steinberg, and Vines, 1984). That aggressive acts may be more often associated with repeated alcohol withdrawal (Ballenger and Post, 1978; Post et al., 1983), rather than precipitated by alcohol, is of special interest in view of a model of pathological aggression and other behaviors developed by Post (1983) in the induction of kindling seizure activity in animals.

Bioulac et al. (1978, 1980) reported the administration of 1-5-hydroxytryptophan (1-5HTP) for five months. Although the CSF 5HIAA level at baseline was raised substantially, the 1-5HTP treatment showed only equivocal advantages over neuroleptic treatment in the area of fights and temper tantrums and equivocally increased side-effects of hyperactivity and euphoria (one patient was discontinued from treatment because he became manic). The use of a 5HT precursor or a 5HT reuptake blocker alone may not produce a sustained increase in CNS 5HT levels; a combination of the two is more likely to lead to the desired pharmacological effect (Fuller, 1982). Lithium has been administered to prisoners in a short-term controlled study (Sheard, 1971, 1975), as well as in an extended study (Tupin et al., 1973). In both there were significant therapeutic responses; lithium has been shown specifically to raise CSF 5HIAA in humans (Berrettini et al., 1985; Fyro et al., 1975) and CNS 5HT in animals (Mandell and Knapp, 1977; Sheard and Aghajanian, 1970). Plasma pharmacokinetic studies of identical single oral doses of TP revealed a significantly lower fasting and a slower absorption of TP in prisoners (characterized as "predominantly having personality disorders") compared with controls, although diet and activity were not controlled. Within the prison group, prisoners characterized as depressed vs. nondepressed on the basis of MMPI scores had significantly lower fasting TP levels (Domino, 1976; Domino and Krause, 1974).

The central question appears to be whether both aggression and 5HT play a necessary but not sufficient role in suicide. An affect of aggressive rage may be critical for the development of depression and, in some instances, suicide; thus, aggression would be a more primitive affective response to the environment than depression. One might construct a model in which certain basic biological characteristics, such as the level of CNS excitation-inhibition in neuroanatomical areas (influenced by internal and external biological stimuli), are thought to interact with the laying down of short-term memory, the transformation of short-term memory to long-term memory, and the retrieval of the latter, all together forming a system from which behavior originates (Brown and Goodwin, 1984b). That aggressivity/impulsivity may be more basic than suicidal behavior appears consistent with the fact that aggression is found at all ages in all species (and probably in all individuals) (Arnold, Fleming, and Bell, 1979), but significant depression and suicide are not. Furthermore, since a small number of "normal" subjects, i.e., those who do not report a history of either aggressive/impulsive behavior or suicidal behavior, have also been shown to have a lower CSF 5HIAA (Ballenger, Post, and Goodwin, 1983) than other normals, one would question whether the former group might be different in some way other than CSF 5HIAA. For example, normals show a significant negative correlation between a measure of sensation-seeking and CSF NE (Ballenger et al., 1984). One wonders what kind of "compensating" mechanisms — biological, psychological, or social — might be coming into play?

Since we have considerable new data regarding the possible biological contributions to aggressive/impulsive and suicidal behavior, it would now seem important to reassess some of the nonbiological questions that might be further studied. For example, if a certain propensity for aggressive/impulsive/suicidal behavior exists in certain individuals "waiting for the right kind of environmental stress," what new clinical studies might be done to assess the families and childhood of such individuals?

Brown and associates (in press) have recently reported that the levels of childhood problems (particularly conduct problems and those childhood problems reported by adults with "minimal brain dysfunction") were significantly negatively related to the levels of CSF 5HIAA found in young adult males; Stoff (in press) has also recently reported a decrease in platelet tritiated (3H) imipramine binding in children with aggressive, impulsive behavior when compared to pediatric controls. These studies tend to buttress the argument that CSF 5HIAA is related to human aggressive/impulsive behavior as a trait variable.

In summary, there have now been a substantial number of scientific reports indicating that central nervous system serotonin may be altered in aggressive/impulsive and suicidal behaviors in humans; these reports constitute one of the most highly replicated findings in biological psychiatry. Alteration of brain serotonin was associated with animal aggression before work which suggested a relationship to suicidal behavior in humans. These relationships might suggest that suicidal behavior is a special kind of self-destructive behavior in humans. If we are to further our understanding of the bases of aggressive behavior in humans, we must be careful not to exclude contributions from any discipline, and we must further strive to differentiate etiological and contributory factors, as well as their interactions, as they lead to the final expression of behavior.

REFERENCES

Agren, H. (1983). Life at risk: Markers of suicidality in depression. *Psychiatric Developments, 1*, 87–104.

Agren, H. (1980). Symptom patterns in unipolar and bipolar depression correlating with monoamine metabolites in the cerebrospinal fluid. II. Suicide. *Psychiatry Research, 3*, 225–236.

Angel, C., Deluca, D., & Murphree, O. (1976). Probenecid induced accumulation of cyclic nucleotides, 5-hydroxyindoleacetic acid, and homovanillic acid in cisternal spinal fluid of genetically nervous dogs. *Biological Psychiatry, 11*, 743–753.

Arnold, L., Fleming, R., & Bell, B. (1979). The man who became angry once: A study of overcontrolled hostility. *Canadian Journal of Psychiatry, 24*, 762–766.

Asberg, M., Thoren, P., & Traskman, L. (1976a). "Serotonin depression"—biochemical subgroup within the affective disorders? *Science, 191*, 478–480.

Asberg, M., Traskman, L., & Thoren, P. (1976b). 5-HIAA in the cerebrospinal fluid: A biochemical suicide predictor? *Archives of General Psychiatry, 33*, 1193–1197.

Banki, C. & Arato, M. (1983a). Amine metabolites and neuroendocrine responses related to depression and suicide. *Journal of Affective Disorders, 5*, 223–232.

Banki, C. & Arato, M. (1983b). Amine metabolites, neuroendocrine findings, and personality dimensions as correlates of suicidal behavior. *Psychiatry Research, 10*, 253–261.

Banki, C., Arato, M., Papp, Z., & Kurcz, M. (1984). Biochemical markers in suicidal patients. Investigations with cerebrospinal fluid amine metabolites and endocrine tests. *Journal of Affective Disorders, 6*, 341–350.

Banki, C., Molnar, G., & Vojnik, M. (1981). Cerebrospinal fluid amine metabolites, tryptophan and clinical parameters in depression, Part 2. *Journal of Affective Disorders, 3*, 91–99.

Ballenger, J., Goodwin, F., Major, L., & Brown, G. (1978). Alcohol and central serotonin metabolism in man. *Archives of General Psychiatry, 36*, 224–227.

Ballenger, J., & Post, R. (1978). Kindling as a model for alcohol withdrawal syndromes. *British Journal of Psychiatry, 133*, 1–14.

Ballenger, J., Post, R., & Goodwin, F. (1983). Neurochemistry of cerebrospinal fluid in normal individuals: Relationship between biological and psychological variables. In: Wood, J. (Ed), *Neurobiology of cerebrospinal fluid*. New York: Plenum. 143–155.

Ballenger, J., Post, R., Jimerson, D., Lake, C., Murphy, D., Zuckerman, M., & Cronin C. (1984). Biochemical correlates of personality traits in normals: an exploratory study. *Personality Individual Differences*, 1–11.

Berrettini, W., Nurnberger, J. Jr., Scheinin, M., Seppala, T., Linnoila, M., Narrow, W., Simmons-Alling, S., & Gershon, E. (1985). Cerebrospinal fluid and plasma monoamines and their metabolites in euthymic bipolar patients. *Biological Psychiatry, 20*, 257–269.

Beskow, J. (1979). Suicide and mental disorder in Swedish men. *Acta Psychiatria, Scandinavia Supplement, 277*, 85–88.

Bioulac, B., Benezech, M., Renaud, B., Roche, D., Noel, B. (1978). Biogenic amines in 47, XYY syndrome. *Neuropsychopharmacology, 4*, 366–370.

Bioulac, B., Benezech, M., Renaud, B., Noel, B., & Roche, D. (1980). Serotoninergic dysfunction in the 47, XYY syndrome. *Biological Psychiatry, 15*, 917–923.

Branchey, L., Branchey, M., Shaw, S., & Lieber, S. (1984). Depression, suicide, and aggression in alcoholics and their relationship to plasma amino acids. *Psychiatry Research, 12*, 219–226.

Brown, G., Ballenger, J., Minichiello, M., & Goodwin, F. (1979a). Human aggression and its relationship to cerebrospinal fluid 5-hydroxyindoleacetic acid, 3-methoxy-4-hydroxyphenylglycol and homovanillic acid. In M. Sander (Ed), *Psychopharmacology of aggression*. New York: Raven Press, 131–148.

Brown, G., Ebert, M., Goyer, P., Jimerson, D., Klein, W., Bunney, W. Jr., & Goodwin, F. (1982a). Aggression, suicide, and serotonin: Relationships to CSF amine metabolites. *American Journal of Psychiatry, 139*, 741–746.

Brown, G., & Goodwin, F. (1984a). Diagnostic, clinical, and personality characteristics of aggressive men with low 5HIAA. *Clinical Neuropharmacology, 7*, 756–757.

Brown, G., & Goodwin, F. (1984b). Aggression, adolescence, and psychobiology. In C. Keith (Ed) *The aggressive adolescent: Clinical perspectives*. New York: The Free Press. pp. 63–95.

Brown, G., Goodwin, F., Ballenger, J., Goyer, P., & Major, L. (1979a). Aggression in humans correlates with cerebrospinal fluid amine metabolites. *Psychiatry Research, 1*, 131–139.

Brown, G., Goodwin, F., & Bunney, W. Jr. (1982b). Human aggression and suicide: their relationship to neuropsychiatric diagnoses and serotonin metabolism. In Ho, B., Usdin, E., Costa, E. (Eds) *Serotonin in biological psychiatry. Advances in biochemical psychopharmacology*, Vol. 34. New York: Raven Press. 287–307.

Brown, G., Linnoila, M., & Goodwin, F. (1985). Unpublished manuscript.

Brown, G., Kline W., Goyer, P., Minichiello, M., Kreusi, M., & Goodwin, F., (in press). Relationship of childhood characteristics to cerebrospinal fluid 5-hydroxyindoleacetic acid in aggressive adults. IV. World Congress of Biological Psychiatry.

Buss, A., Durkee, A., & Baer, M. (1957). The measurement of hostility in clinical situations. *Journal of Abnormal Psychology, 21*, 343–348.

Buss, A. & Durkee, A. (1957). An inventory for assessing different kinds of hostility. *Journal of Consulting Psychology, 21*, 343–348.

Buss, A. (1961). *The psychology of aggression*. New York: Wiley.

Camen, P. & Mullen, P. (1979). An XYY man. *British Journal of Psychiatry, 135*, 79–81.

Cherek, D., Steinberg, J., & Vines, R. (1984). Low doses of alcohol affect human aggressive responses. *Biology Psychiatry, 19*, 263–267.

Christmas, A. & Maxwell, D. (1970). A comparison of the effects of some benzodiazepines and other drugs on aggressive and exploratory behavior in mice and rats. *Neuropharmacology, 9*, 17–29.

Ciaranello, R., Lipsky, A., & Axelrod, J. (1974). Association between fighting behavior and catecholamine biosynthetic enzymes in two sublines of an inbred mouse strain. *Proceedings of National Academy of Science, 71*, 3006–3008.

Crawley, J., Sutton, M., & Pickar, D. (1985). Animal models of self-destructive behavior and suicide. In A. Roy (Ed.) *Self-destructive behavior*. Symposium conducted at Psychiatric Clinics of North America. Philadelphia: W. B. Saunders. *8*, (2), pp. 299–310.

Dominguez, M. & Longo, V. (1969). Taming effects of para-chlorophenylalanine on septal rats. *Physiological Behavior, 4*, 1031–1033.

Domino, E. (1976). Pharmacokinetics of oral tryptophan in drug-free psychiatric patients. In L. Gottschalk, S. Merlis, (Eds) *Pharmacokinetics of psychoactive drugs: Blood levels and clinical response*. New York: Wiley. 117–126.

Domino, E. & Krause, R. (1974). Plasma tryptophan tolerance curves in drug free normal controls, schizophrenic patients and prisoner volunteers. *Journal of Psychiatric Research, 10*, 247–261.

Eichelman, B. (1979). Role of biogenic amines in aggressive behavior. In Sandler, M.

(Ed.) *Psychopharmacology of aggression*. New York: Raven Press. pp. 61–83.

Eichelman, B., & Thoa, N. (1973). The aggressive monoamines. *Biological Psychiatry, 6*, 143–164.

Eichelman, B., Thoa, N., & Ng, K. (1972). Facilitated aggression in the rat following 6-hydroxydopamine administration. *Physiological Behavior, 8*, 1–3.

Eichelman, B., Thoa, N., & Perez-Cruet, J. (1972). Rubidium and cesium: Effects on aggression, adrenal enzymes, and amine turnover. *Fed. Proc., 31*, 289.

Fernstrom, J. (1982). Acute effects of tryptophan and single meals on serotonin synthesis in the rat brain. In B. Ho, E. Usdin, & E. Costa, (Eds) *Serotonin in biological psychiatry. Advances in biochemical psychopharmacology*. Vol. 34. New York: Raven Press. pp 85–106.

Fernstrom, J. & Wurtman, R. (1972). Brain serotonin content: Physiological regulation by plasma neutral amino acids. *Science, 178*, 414–416.

Fernstrom, J. & Wurtman, R. (1974). Brain serotonin content: Increase following ingestion of carbohydrate diet. *Science, 174*, 1023–1025.

Freud, S. (1976). Mourning and melancholia. In J. Strachey (Ed. and Trans.) *The standard edition*. New York: *14*, pp 239–258. Norton.

Fuller, R. (1982). Functional consequences of inhibiting serotonin uptake with fluoxetine in rats. In B. Ho, E. Usdin, E. Costa, (Eds), *Serotonin in biological psychiatry. Advances in biochemical psychopharmacology*, Vol. 34. New York: Raven Press. pp 219–228.

Fyro, B., Petterson, U., & Sedvall, G. (1975). The effect of lithium treatment on manic symptoms and levels of monoamine metabolites in cerebrospinal fluid of manic-depressive patients. *Psychopharmacologia, 44*, 99–103.

Gessa, G. L., Bigglio, G., Fadda, F., Corsini, C. V. & Tagliamonte, A. (1974). Effect of the oral administration of tryptophan-free amino acid mixtures on serum tryptophan, brain tryptophan, and serotonin metabolism. *Journal of Neurochemistry, 22*, 869–870.

Geyer, M. & Segal, D. (1974). Shock-induced aggression: Opposite effects of intraventricularly infused dopamine and norepinephrine. *Behavioral Biology, 10*, 99–104.

Goodwin, F., Post, R., Dunner, D., & Gordon, E. (1973). Cerebrospinal fluid amine metabolites in affective illness: The probenecid technique. *American Journal of Psychiatry, 130*, 73–79.

Grant, L., Coscina, D., Grossman, S., Freedman, D. (1973). Muricide after serotonin-depleting lesions of midbrain raphe nuclei. *Pharmacol Biochem Behav, 1*, 77–80.

Hoeldtke, R., Baliga, B., Issenberg, P., & Wurtman, R. (1972). Dihydroxyphenyl-alanine in rat food containing wheat and oats. *Science, 175*, 761–762.

Hoeldtke, R. & Wurtman, R. (1974). Cereal ingestion and catecholamine excretion. *Metabolism, 23*, 25–31.

Hollister, L., Davis, K., Overall, J., & Anderson, T. (1978). Excretion of MHPG in normal subjects. *Archives of General Psychiatry, 35*, 1410–1415.

Jequier, E., Lovenberg, W., & Sjoerdsma, A. (1967). Tryptophan hydroxylase inhibition: The mechanism by which p-chlorophenylalanine depletes rat brain serotonin. *Molecular Pharmacology, 3*, 274–278.

Kandel, E. (1986). Molecular basis of learning and memory. NIH Howard Hughes Memorial Lecture.

Kantak, K., Hegstrand, L., & Eichelman, B. (1981). Dietary tryptophan reversal of septal lesion and 5,7-DHT lesion elicited shock-induced fighting. *Psychopharmacology, 74*, 157–160.

Kantak, K., Hegstrand, L., & Eichelman, B. (1980). Dietary tryptophan modulation and aggressive behavior in mice. *Pharmacol Biochemical Behavior, 12,* 675–679.

Koe, B. & Weissman, A. (1966). P-chlorophenylalanine: A specific depletor of brain serotonin. *Journal of Pharmacology and Experimental Therapeutics, 154,* 499–516.

Kreusi, M., Linnoila, M., Rapoport, J., Brown, G., & Petersen, R. (1985). Carbohydrate craving, conduct disorder, and low 5HIAA. *Psychiatry Research, 16,* 83–86.

Kulkarni, A. (1968). Muricidal block produced by 5-hydroxytryptophan and various other drugs. *Life Science, 7,* 125–128.

Lamprecht, F., Eichelman, B., Thoa, N., Williams, R., & Kopin, I. (1972). Rat fighting behavior: Serum dopamine-B-hydroxylase and hypothalamic tyrosine hydroxylase. *Science, 177,* 1214–1215.

Lanyon, R. (1961). *A handbook of MMPI group profiles.* Minneapolis: University of Minnesota Press.

Leckman, J., Charney, D., Nelson, C., Heninger, G., & Bowers, M., Jr. (1981). CSF tryptophan, 5HIAA and HVA in 132 psychiatric patients categorized by diagnosis and clinical state. *In* B. Angrist, G. Burrows, M. Lader, D. Lingjaerde, G. Sedvall, & D. Wheatley, (Eds) *Recent Advances in Neuropsychopharmacology.* New York: Pergamon Press. 289–297.

Leventhal, B. (1984). The neuropharmacology of violent and aggressive behavior. In Keith, C. (Ed.) *The aggressive adolescent: Clinical perspectives.* New York: The Free Press. 299–358.

Lidberg, L., Asberg, M., & Sunquist-Stensman, U. (1984). 5-Hydroxyindoleacetic acid levels in attempted suicides who have killed their children. *Lancet, II,* 928.

Lidberg, L., Tuck, J., Asberg, M., Scalia-Tomba, G., & Bertilsson, L. (1985). Homicide, suicide and CSF 5-HIAA. *Acta Psychiatric Scandinavian Supplement, 71,* 230–236.

Linnoila, M., Virkkunen, M., Scheinin, M., Nuutila, A., Rimon, R., & Goodwin, F. (1983). Low cerebrospinal fluid 5-hydroxyindoleactic acid concentration differentiates impulsive from nonimpulsive violent behavior. *Life Sciences, 33,* 2609–2614.

Luchins, D. (1983). Carbamazepine for the violent psychiatric patient. *Lancet, I,* 766.

Major, L., Ballenger, J., Goodwin, F., & Brown, G. (1977). Cerebrospinal fluid homovanillic acid in male alcoholics: Effects of disulfiram. *Biological Psychiatry, 12,* 635–642.

Mandell, A. & Knapp, S. (1977). Regulation of serotonin biosynthesis in brain—role of the high affinity uptake of tryptophan into serotonergic neurons. *Fed. Proc., 36,* 2142–2148.

Marks, P., O'Brien, M., & Paxinos, G. (1977). 5,7-DHT-induced muricide: Inhibition as a result of exposure of rats to mice. *Brain Research, 135,* 383–388.

McKinney, W., Moran, E., & Kraemer, G. (1984). Separation in nonhuman primates as a model for human depression: Neurobiological implications. In Post, R.M., Ballenger, J.C. (Eds.) *Neurobiology of mood disorders.* Baltimore: Williams & Wilkins. 393–406.

Miller, F., Cox, R. Jr., Snodgrass, W., & Maickel, R. (1970). Comparative effects of p-chloroamphetamine and p-chloro-N-methylamphetamine on rat brain norepinephrine serotonin and 5-hydroxyindole-3-acetic acid. *Biochemical Pharmacology, 19,* 435–442.

Montgomery S. & Montgomery, D. (1982). Pharmacological prevention of suicidal behavior. *Journal of Affective Disorders, 4,* 291–298.

Moyer, K. (1968). Kinds of aggression and their pathological basis. *Communications in Behavioral Biology (Part A), 2,* 65–87.

Moyer, K. (1971). The physiology of aggression and the implications for aggression control. In J. Singer (Ed.) *The control of aggression and violence: Cognitive and physiological factors.* New York: Academic Press. pp 61–92.

Moyer, K. (1976). *The psychobiology of aggression.* New York: Harper and Row.

Muscettola, G., Wehr, T., & Goodwin, F. (1977). Effect of diet on urinary MHPG excretion in depressed patients and normal control subjects. *American Journal of Psychiatry, 134,* 914–916.

Neppe, V. (1982). Carbamazepine in the psychiatric patient. *Lancet, II* 334.

Ninan, P., Van Kammen, D., Scheinin, M., Linnoila, M., Bunney, W. Jr., Goodwin, F. (1984). Cerebrospinal fluid 5-HIAA in suicidal schizophrenic patients. *American Journal of Psychiatry, 141,* 566–569.

Oreland, L., Weiberg, A., Asberg, M., Traskman, L., Sjostrand, L., Thoren, P., Bertilsson, L., & Tybring, G. (1981). Platelet MAO activity and monoamine metabolites in cerebrospinal fluid in depressed and suicidal patients and in healthy contols. *Psychiatry Research, 4,* 21–29.

Orenberg, E., Renson, J., Elliott, G., Barchas, J., & Kessler, S. (1975). Genetic determination of aggressive behavior and brain cyclic AMP. *Commun. Psychopharmacol., 1,* 99–107.

Palaniappan, V., Ramachandran, V., & Somasundaram, D. (1983). Suicidal ideation and biogenic amines in depression. *Indian Journal of Psychiatry, 25,* 286–292.

Pokorny, A. (1983). Prediction of suicide in psychiatric patients: Report of a prospective study. *Archives of General Psychiatry, 40,* 249–257.

Post, R., Ballenger, J., Putnam, F. & Bunney, W., Jr. (1983). Carbamazepine in alcohol withdrawal syndromes: Relationship to the kindling model. *Journal of Clinical Psychopharmacology, 3,* 204–205.

Post, R. (1983). Behavioral effects of kindling. In M. Parsonage, (Ed), *Advances in epileptology,* XIV Epilepsy International Symposium. New York: Raven Press. 173–180.

Powell, G., Brasel, J., & Blizzard, R. (1967a). Emotional deprivation and growth retardation simulating idiopathic hypopituitarism. *New England Journal of Medicine, 276,* 1271–1278.

Powell, G., Brasel, J., Raiti, S., & Blizzard, R. (1967b). Emotional deprivation and growth retardation simulating idiopathic hypopituitarism. II. Endocrinologic evaluation of the syndrome. *New England Journal of Medicine, 276,* 1279–1283.

Reis, O. (1974). Central neurotransmitters in aggression. *Research Publications, Association for Research in Nervous and Mental Disease, 52,* 119–148.

Robins, L. (1978). Sturdy childhood predictors of adult antisocial behavior: Replications from longitudinal studies. *Psychological Medicine, 8,* 611–622.

Robins, L. (1966). *Deviant children grown up: A sociological and psychiatric study of sociopathic personality.* Baltimore: Williams & Wilkins.

Rosenblum, M. & Bennett, B. (1986). Homicide and depression. *American Journal of Psychiatry, 143,* 367–370.

Roy-Byrne, P., Post, R., Rubinow, D., Linnoila, M., Savard, R., & Davis, D. (1983). CSF 5HIAA and personal and family history of suicide in affectively ill patients: A negative study. *Psychiatry Research, 10,* 263–274.

Roy, A., Ninan, P., Mazonson, A., Pickar, D., Van Kammen, D., Linnoila, M., & Paul, S. (1985). CSF monoamine metabolites in chronic schizophrenic patients who attempt suicide. *Psychological Medicine, 15,* 335–340.

Roy, A., Pickar, D., Linoila, M., Doran, A., & Paul, S. (in press). Cerebrospinal fluid monoamine and monoamine metabolite concentrations and the dexamethasone suppression test in depressive relationship to life events. *Archives of General Psychiatry*.

Sanders-Bush, E., Bushing, J., & Sulser, F. (1972). P-chloroamphetamine-inhibition of cerebral tryptophan hydroxylase. *Biochemical Pharmacology, 21*, 1501–1510.

Sanger, D., Blackman, D. (1976). Effects of chlordiazepoxide, ripazepam and d-amphetamine on conditioned acceleration timing behavior in rats. *Psychopharmacology, 48*, 209–215.

Selzer, M. (1971), The Michigan alcoholism screening test: The quest for a new diagnostic instrument. *American Journal of Psychiatry, 127*, 1653–1658.

Sharpless, N. (1977). Determination of 3-methoxy-4-hydroxyphenylglycol in urine and the effect of diet on its excretion. *Research & Communication Chemical Pathological Pharmacology, 18*, 257–273.

Sheard, M. (1971). Effect of lithium on human aggression. *Nature, 230*, 113–114.

Sheard, M. (1975). Lithium in the treatment of aggression. *Journal Nervous Mental Disease, 100*, 108–117.

Sheard, M. (1979). Testosterone and aggression. In Sandler, M. (Ed.) *Psychopharmacology of aggression*. New York: Raven Press. 111–130.

Sheard, M., Aghajanian, G. (1970). Neuronally activated metabolism of serotonin: Effect of lithium. *Life Science, 9*, 285–290.

Sofia, R. (1969). Structural relationship and potency of agents which selectively block mouse-killing (muricide). *Life Science, 8*, 1801–1210.

Southwick, C. & Clark, L. (1968). Interstrain differences in aggressive behavior and exploratory activity of inbred mice. *Communications in Behavioral Biology, 1A*, 49–59.

Spitz, R. (1947). Anaclitic depression: An inquiry into the genesis of psychiatric conditions in early childhood. II. In Greenacer, P., et al. (Eds.), *Psychoanalytic study of the child. 2.*, 313–342.

Spitz, R. & Cobliner, W. (1965). *The first year of life: A psychoanalytic study of normal and deviant development of object relations*. New York: International Universities Press.

Spitzer, R., Endicott, J., Gibbon, M. (1979). Crossing the border into borderline personality and borderline schizophrenia. *Archives of General Psychiatry, 36*, 17–24.

Stoff, D. (in press). ^{3}H-imipramine binding in children with conduct disorders compared to pediatric controls. Paper presented at the IV World Congress Biological Psychiatry.

Strange, R. (1974). Personality disorders in the military service. In Lion, J. (Ed.), *Personality Disorders — Diagnosis and Management*. Baltimore: Williams & Wilkins. 267–281.

Takahaski, S., Yamane, H., Kondo, H., & Tani, N. (1974). CSF monoamine metabolites in alcoholism, a comparative study with depression. *Folia Psychiatric Neurologica Japan, 28*, 347–354.

Taylor, M. (1979). Dietary modifications of amphetamine stereotyped behavior: The action of tryptophan, methionine, and lysine. *Psychopharmacology, 61*, 81–83.

Tenen, S. (1967). The effects of p-chlorophenylalanine, a serotonin depletor, on avoidance acquisition, pain sensitivity, and related behavior in the rat. *Psychopharmacologia, 10*, 204–219.

Thoa, N., Eichelman, B., Richardson, J., & Jacobowitz, D. (1972). 6-Hydroxydopa depletion of brain norepinephrine and the facilitation of aggressive behavior. *Science, 178*, 75–77.

Traskman, L., Asberg, M., Bertilsson, L., & Sjostrand, L. (1981). Monoamine metabolites in CSF and suicidal behavior. *Archives of General Psychiatry, 38*, 631–636.

Tupin, J., Smith, D., Classon, T., Kim, L., Nugent, A., & Groupe, A. (1973). The long-term use of lithium in aggressive prisoners. *Comprehensive Psychiatry, 14,* 311–317.

Tye, N., Everitt, B., Iversen, S. (1977). 5-Hydroxytryptamine and punishment, *Nature, 268,* 741–743.

Tye, N., Iversen, S., Green, A. (1979). The effects of benzodiazepines and serotonergic manipulations on punished responding. *Neuropharmacology, 18,* 689–695.

Valzelli, L. (1981). *Psychobiology of aggression and violence.* New York: Raven Press.

Van Praag, H. (1983). CSF 5-HIAA and suicide in non-depressed schizophrenics. *Lancet, II,* 977–978.

Van Praag, H. (1982). Depression, suicide and metabolism of serotonin in the brain. *Journal of Affective Disease, 4,* 275–290.

Vestergaard, P., Sorensen, T., Hoppe, E., Rafaelson, O., Yates, C., & Nicolaou, N. (1978). Biogenic amine metabolites in cerebrospinal fluid of patients with affective disorders. *Acta Psychiatria Scandinavian (Supplement), 58,* 88–96.

Virkkunen, M. (1983). Insulin secretion during the glucose tolerance test in antisocial personality. *British Journal of Psychiatry, 142,* 598–604.

Virkkunen, M. (1982). Reactive hypoglycemic tendency among habitually violent offenders: A further study by means of the glucose tolerance test. *Neuropsychobiology, 8,* 35–40.

Virkkunen, M. & Huttunen, M. (1982). Evidence for abnormal glucose tolerance test among violent offenders. *Neuropsychobiology, 8,* 30–34.

Virkkunen, M., Nuutila, A., Goodwin, F., & Linnoila, M. (1985). CSF monoamine metabolites in male arsonists. Unpublished manuscript.

Welsh, G. & Dahlstrom, W. (Eds). (1956). *Basic readings on the MMPI in psychology and medicine.* Minneapolis: University of Minnesota Press.

West, L. (1977). Studies of aggression in animals and man. *Psychopharmacological Bulletin, 13,* 14–25.

Zuckerman, M. (1983). A biological theory of sensation seeking. In Zuckerman, M. (Ed.), *Biological Bases of Sensation Seeking, Impulsivity, and Anxiety.* Hillsdale, NJ: Erlbaum. 37–76.

Zung, B., Charalampous, K. (1975). Item analysis of the Michigan Alcoholism Screening Test. *Journal of Studies in Alcohol, 36,* 127–132.

II

Treatment Approaches

7

Behavioral and Cognitive Treatment of Criminal and Delinquent Behavior

William D. Barley

This chapter surveys the use of behavioral and cognitive interventions for antisocial and delinquent behavior. I will review pertinent characteristics of juvenile delinquents and adult antisocial personalities; the relationship of cognitive to behavioral approaches and vice-versa; practical, social, legal, and ethical issues raised by the implementation of behavioral interventions; surveys of cognitive and behavioral interventions and their effects on target behaviors; and integration of behavioral and psychodynamic approaches to the treatment of delinquent and antisocial patients. I will not review basic detailed information about behavioral and cognitive treatment techniques. For this introductory material the reader is referred to Rimm and Masters (1979).

Reid (1981) has noted that antisocial personalities are found not only in prisons or in socially underprivileged settings, but also practically anywhere in society where antisocial traits have survival value, including business and political circles. However, the approaches surveyed and discussed here have generally been applied to the behaviors of "unsuccessful" antisocial patients or prisoners and not to the behaviors of the so-called successful entrepreneurial antisocial personalities

I want to thank Darwin Dorr (who did invaluable editing) and Kimberly Storrs (who prepared the manuscript) for their help with this chapter.

159

described elsewhere (see Chapter 12). These interventions have been applied to groups and individuals variously labeled as antisocial, criminal, delinquent, predelinquent, and so on, without careful differentiation into diagnostic categories (Templeman and Wollersheim, 1979). The cognitive and behavioral literature avoids the definitional Gordian knot by focusing on the behaviors themselves, not on their etiology or psychiatric diagnosis.

Delinquent behavior in juveniles has huge costs, including wasted lives, disrupted families, and societal resources expended to repair the damage. Further, juvenile delinquents often go on to become adult antisocial personalities; in fact, number, frequency, and seriousness of childhood and juvenile antisocial problems are often cited as the most important forerunners of serious adult antisocial problems (Reid, 1981; Templeman and Wollersheim, 1979). Consequently, cognitive and behavioral efforts to remediate juvenile delinquency are of utmost importance.

A distinction has been made between primary and secondary antisocial personality (or sociopathy or psychopathy) which emphasizes the emotional unresponsiveness in anxiety-producing situations, lack of ability to experience guilt feelings and absence of conscience, and resulting untreatability of the primary group (Fagan and Lira, 1980; Templeman and Wollersheim, 1979). However, Reid (1981) noted that more recent research and clinical experience shows that "true" antisocial personalities experience at least state anxiety. Yochelson and Samenow (1976, 1977) indicated that antisocial personalities, whom they term "criminals," may seem impervious to stress but are actually extremely fearful, more fearful than noncriminals, and that, because criminals actually do hold some things morally inviolate, they also have the experience of conscience. (Yochelson and Samenow also maintained that features of criminals' thinking allow them to eliminate these troublesome experiences for long periods, however.) Research suggests that primary antisocial personalities can be distinguished from others exhibiting antisocial behavior by a lessened sensitivity to physical punishment and threats of punishment, that they are more likely to learn avoidance tasks when the consequences involve obtaining or losing tangible rewards, that there must be well-specified and immediate relationships between behaviors and consequences, that verbal feedback will sometimes modify at least their overt behavior, and that they may learn better during high intensity stimulation, possibly because they then attend and concentrate better (Rimm and Masters, 1979; Templeman and Wollersheim, 1979). Reid (1981) stated that the traditional intrapsychic motivation to change may not be necessary for the success of some treatment approaches to antisocial behavior.

In fact, several of the cognitive and behavioral interventions discussed here have been applied in reaction to the ineffectiveness of more traditional approaches (Gross and Brigham, 1980; Temple and Wollersheim, 1979; Yochelson & Samenow, 1976, 1977). Cleckley (1976) was very discouraged about psychiatry's power to alter the behavior of these people. However, his concept of pathological thought in the psychopath foreshadowed some aspects of cognitive therapy, and he held out hope for the efficacy of consistent consequation of "irresponsible and destructive conduct" (p. 445).

COGNITIVE AND BEHAVIORAL TREATMENT

Current cognitive therapy is ultimately based on cognitive or field theories of earlier workers such as Tolman and Lewin. It focuses on cognitive processes as mediators of behavior and emotion and posits that disordered behavior and emotion are largely consequences of various cognitive deficiencies. It relies chiefly on speech as the vehicle for identifying and remediating these deficiencies.

Behavioral interventions (often referred to as behavior therapy and behavior modification) have their basis in stimulus-response (operant), stimulus-stimulus (respondent), and vicarious or modeling theories of learning. Their focus is on behavior, not on any presumed mediator of behavior. Processes governing behavior and emotion are held to be environmental, and cognitions are viewed largely as representations of the environment. Disordered behavior and emotion may result from faulty learning, and the goal of treatment is modification of pathological relationships between behaviors and stimuli that elicit them or consequences that follow them. The means of behavioral change is usually nonverbal, i.e., the behavior itself (Ledwidge, 1978, 1979; Mahoney and Kazdin, 1979; Marzillier, 1980).

These approaches seem to be moving toward *rapprochement*, and many argue that clinical practice often requires combining cognitive and behavioral approaches, that the basic theoretical and practical differences between the two approaches are less than meet the eye, and, most importantly, that the relationship between cognition and behavior is reciprocal: Changing cognition alters behavior, and vice-versa (Foa and Foa, 1983; Mahoney and Kazdin, 1979; Marzillier, 1980; Templeman and Wollersheim, 1979). Both cognitive and behavioral interventions can be differentiated from more traditional psychodynamic ones along several dimensions having to do with assumptions about the nature of psychological problems and their treatment.

COGNITIVE AND COGNITIVE-BEHAVIORAL INTERVENTIONS WITH ADULTS AND ADOLESCENTS

Rational-Emotive Therapy

Ellis' rational-emotive therapy (or RET) is the original member of a large family of cognitive therapies (Ellis and Grieger, 1977; Rimm and Masters, 1979). It has come to include adjunctive behavioral techniques. The literature of rational-emotive therapy is not very specific about the mechanics of programming this therapy for antisocial or delinquent patients. What is generally presented is a molecular view of the technique of the therapy itself without a molar view of the context in which such therapy would occur with antisocial or delinquent patients (Ellis, 1962, 1977, 1980; Watkins, 1980).

The focus is on elements of "irrational" thinking and the dysfunctional attitudes that result. The means is intensive intellectual disputation. Ellis (1962) noted that the psychotherapist attempting this kind of intervention must be "unusually sane and non-blaming" and must "vigorously maintain a challenging, circuit-breaking attitude" (p. 298).

Evidence for effectiveness of rational-emotive therapy with antisocial or delinquent symptoms is limited. Ellis (1962) reported treatment of a 25-year-old male who had engaged in antisocial behavior since the age of 14, and who had been convicted once and institutionalized for a year. Two-year follow-up showed that the patient was finishing college and doing well there. Ellis stated that he had developed RET based partially on his experiences in treating persons with delinquency and antisocial problems, and he alluded to RET having been used with "several other individuals with severe character disorders and symptoms of acute antisocial behavior" (p. 298) with good results. Watkins (1977) described RET with five patients with antisocial impulsivity (a pedophile, an auto thief, an obscene phone caller, a voyeur, and an impulsive buyer). These patients were seen in group treatment, and

Watkins reported that within a few weeks to a few months the patients said that they were able to control their impulsivity. Cox (1979) used rational-behavior therapy, a variant of RET, with 80 repeat criminal offenders with alcohol abuse problems. Of 15 paroled, two had relapsed sufficiently to have parole revoked by six-month follow-up; there was no control group. Thirty of 60 junior high school students referred for classroom disciplinary problems were treated with rational-behavior therapy by graduate students and showed significantly improved classroom behavior, classwork, and homework during treatment, compared to their 30 untreated counterparts (Zelie, Stone, and Lehr, 1980).

Yochelson and Samenow's Approach

A second major cognitive approach to antisocial problems is that of Yochelson and Samenow (1976, 1977). Their experience with "hardcore criminals" at St. Elizabeth's Hospital led to development of a treatment program based on a firm, directive stance toward "criminal thinking." Yochelson and Samenow identified 52 errors that pervade the thinking of antisocial personalities and severely delinquent adolescents, including general thinking patterns, more specific "automatic" thinking errors, and thinking patterns manifested most prominently during antisocial behavior.

The treatment is initially individual. If the patient (often a prisoner) decides to continue participation, he or she joins a group of three or four others. Patients are instructed to monitor their thinking every waking hour by means of a diary or journal. The contents and processes of thinking thus revealed are examined during treatment sessions without editing by the patient, and a new set of thinking processes is taught as a corrective. The treatment program ideally begins during confinement and continues daily for at least a year following release. During this first year after release from institutionalization the patient participates in daily three-hour sessions each weekday and is also expected to work at a full-time job and fulfill all other responsibilities. Following that first year outside the institution, treatment sessions may be continued, but they are less frequent.

Yochelson and Samenow noted that not all juvenile delinquents or antisocial personalities will benefit from this treatment, and the empirical evidence for its efficacy is limited. They have intensively studied a group of 240 mostly male "hard-core adult criminals," serious juvenile delinquents, adults and adolescents with less severe antisocial problems, and a few children considered at risk for future antisocial behavior. Thirteen of the 30 "hard-core adult criminals" who were in "a program for change" between 1970 and 1976 were found to be functioning responsibly in the community in terms of what Yochelson and Samenow considered to be strict outcome criteria (S. Samenow, personal communication, September 30, 1985).

Goodman (1983) described the application of this approach, in combination with reality therapy (Glasser, 1965), in a cottage at the Maine Youth Center, an institution for juvenile delinquents. Since the program had been operating, the boys' runaway rate and other important antisocial behavior had decreased; no control group was cited.

Cognitive-Behavioral Treatment Packages

Templeman and Wollersheim (1979) described an eclectic cognitive-behavioral treatment for antisocial patients. In logical support of their approach, they noted that treatment of antisocial patients relatively infrequently addresses problems such as excessive stimulation-seeking that may underlie antisocial behavior, that purely behavioral treatment of antisocial problems does not often lead to generalization of change outside institutions, and that such treatment often requires more control over the patient's environment than many clinicians possess.

Templeman and Wollersheim's treatment package includes suggestions for allying with the patient via "socialized hedonism" (Ellis, 1962) and for minimizing the stress of changing chronic antisocial behavior patterns via fixed role therapy (Kelly, 1955). They also suggested that antisocial patients be taught to think of their behaviors as problems to be solved and be given a systematic problem-solving method (Goldfried and Davison, 1976). Self-instruction training is suggested as a means of decreasing self-distraction and increasing self-control (Meichenbaum and Cameron, 1974). Templeman and Wollersheim offered their treatment as a prototype to be tested and modified, and they presented no empirical data to support its effectiveness as a treatment package.

Self-instructional training has been shown to increase appropriate self-verbalization by impulsive children and to increase decision-making time and decrease cognitive errors on psychometric tests compared to treatment and no-treatment control groups (Meichenbaum and Goodman, 1971). Controlled case studies (Bornstein and Quevillon, 1976; Kendall and Finch, 1976) of self-instruction training combined with other behavioral techniques supported the efficacy of this approach with children. Snyder and White (1979) used self-instruction training with institutionalized adolescents and obtained significant improvements in performance of daily living tasks and decreases in impulsive behaviors, which were maintained or augmented at two-month follow-up.

Burchard and Lane (1982) suggested that delinquent adolescents be taught other cognitive self-management skills, and much attention has been paid to self-control of adolescents' anger and aggression, in particular. Feindler and Fremouw (1983) and Varley (1984) cited several studies demonstrating that modifying what aggressive adolescents consciously think can help them control their angry behavior to some degree (for example, Camp, Blom, Herbert, and Van Doorninck, 1977; McCullough, Huntsinger, and Nay, 1977; Snyder and White, 1979).

Much of this work with cognitive and cognitive-behavioral self-control of adolescent anger and aggression has occurred under the umbrella of "stress inoculation" (Meichenbaum and Cameron, 1983), a treatment package for managing stress that can lead to maladaptive responses, including anger and aggression. Novaco (1976, 1977) developed the variant of stress inoculation used specifically for anger-induced aggression. Feindler and Fremouw (1983) described a stress-inoculation package of cognitive and behavioral methods successfully used with individuals and groups of adolescents to manage angry aggression. Some of these were tested as a package in controlled single-subject evaluations (Feindler, 1979) and a controlled group study (Feindler, Marriott, and Iwata, 1984) of aggressive and otherwise delinquent adolescents in a residential treatment facility and junior high school, respectively. Frequency and intensity of the target behaviors and (in the latter study) resulting expulsions were at least modestly reduced in most cases, compared to untreated controls, after 12 to 14 sessions and (in the latter study) at one-month follow-up. One very interesting element of the treatment package described by Feindler and Fremouw (1983) is the "barb" technique (Kaufmann and Wagner, 1972), the graduated presentation of provocations to the adolescent while prompts to "get ready" are faded out.

Conclusions

There are several types of cognitive therapy available for use with antisocial personalities and adolescent delinquents. One of these was developed solely for use with this population (Yochelson & Samenow, 1976, 1977). The eclectic treatment packages (Feindler and Fremouw, 1983; Templeman and Wollersheim, 1979) include less verbal and more behavioral interventions. These approaches have a great deal in common in terms of their emphasis on individual responsibility for antisocial actions, the need to self-monitor internal processes as well as actions, and their largely verbal means of inducing change. The eclectic packages particularly attend to internal processes besides broadly defined "thinking." Unfortunately, the empirical support for these forms of cognitive or cognitive-behavioral treatment is not extensive.

PROBLEMS AND ISSUES IN BEHAVIORAL INTERVENTIONS

The cognitive and cognitive-behavioral interventions discussed in the previous section can be conducted in one-to-one or group formats and do not present very unusual procedural difficulties for the patient or the treating professional. However, the nature of behavioral treatment and its often difficult context do give rise to important practical, ethical, legal, and social questions. This is especially but not solely true of operant behavioral interventions.

Target Behaviors

Behavioral treatment of juvenile delinquents and antisocial adults addresses a wide variety of target behaviors, including both directly delinquent and antisocial behaviors and desirable behaviors incompatible with them (for example, educational and living skills). Many target behaviors are not those that resulted in institutionalization or referral for treatment, and there is considerable concern that behavioral interventions serve the goals of institutions or other societal systems, rather than those of the individuals being treated. The problem has been cast in terms of treatment versus management or of therapeutic effectiveness versus administrative control. A frequent target of this criticism is prison token economies (Burchard and Lane, 1982; Franks, 1982; Kazdin, 1977; Rimm and Masters, 1979; Stumphauzer, 1981).

This is a practical as well as an ethical issue, since the treatment of target behaviors conducive to the establishment of administrative or societal control of antisocial or delinquent behavior is not necessarily consistent with acquisition of meaningful prosocial behavior that will generalize to real-life environments (Emery and Marholin, 1977; Moss and Rick, 1981a; Varley, 1984).

System-Level Change

A related criticism of behavioral treatment with these populations is that the focus is too frequently on the behavior of the individual only, and too infrequently on the system in which the individual behaves. Some consider system change necessary for behavior change to be meaningful and lasting (Emery and Marholin, 1977). Stumphauzer (1976b, 1981) has consistently urged that antisocial and delinquent behavior be analyzed and treated in the community and that more effort be devoted to prevention by addressing community systems that naturally encourage or inhibit these behaviors. He described an anti-shoplifting program as an example of this latter point (Stumphauzer, 1981).

Rights Issues

Social and legal challenges to behavioral treatment pertain largely to the application of operant procedures in institutional settings, and there has been much activity intended to safeguard the rights of those receiving such treatment, including institutionalized antisocial adults and delinquent adolescents. Budd and Baer (1976), Burchard and Lane (1982), Craighead, Kazdin, and Mahoney (1981), Franks (1982), Hedberg (1981), Kazdin (1977), Moss and Rick (1981a), and Schwitzgebel and Schwitzgebel (1980) have extensively reviewed efforts to safeguard the rights of persons, including criminals and delinquents, who receive behavioral treatment. Schwitzgebel and Schwitzgebel (1980) discussed the many practical obstacles to consistent implementation of mandated rights. Important legal concepts affecting behavioral treatment with these populations include the right to receive or refuse treatment, informed consent, individualized treatment, and the least restrictive alternative doctrine. These doctrines certainly present problems for behavioral interventions (Budd and Baer, 1976; Craighead et al., 1981;

Emery and Marholin, 1977; Kazdin, 1977; Schwitzgebel and Schwitzgebel, 1980), and there is some sentiment in the literature that rights
issues have doomed institutional operant conditioning programs (Franks,
1982). However, as Budd and Baer (1976) and Kazdin (1977, 1982)
have shown, there are legal and practical solutions to the reduced dis-
cretion of behavioral clinicians to determine the conditions of treatment.

Aversive Procedures

Unfortunately, the image of behavior therapy has been closely tied
to its formerly more frequent use of painful aversive treatment methods
(Franks, 1977). Stumphauzer (1981) noted that legal challenges and
lack of evidence for efficacy have greatly reduced the use of these procedures in recent years. Court decisions have limited the range of environmental events that can be contingently withheld from or imposed
upon institutionalized persons, including juvenile delinquents and adult
prisoners (Kazdin, 1977; Schwitzgebel and Schwitzgebel, 1980). Aversive procedures have some very undesirable side effects, including sus-
ceptibility to abuse, teaching of aggression via modeling, provocation
of angry and violent behavior, inadvertent reinforcement of undesirable behavior, temporary effectiveness, and failure to address social,
academic, vocational, self-care, and other important behavioral deficits
in delinquents and antisocial adults (Stumphauzer, 1981; Varley, 1984).
Nevertheless, there is general agreement that delinquent adolescents
and antisocial adults benefit from the immediate experience of some
kind of aversive consequences for their actions, and Templeman and
Wollersheim (1979) described research showing that antisocial adults
are more likely to respond to loss of tangible rewards than they are to
physical punishment.

Time-out, response-cost, and extinction are mildly aversive operant
conditioning procedures often used with these treatment populations.
Immediate withdrawal of the person from reinforcing situations via
time-out is quite effective (Rimm and Masters, 1979; Varley, 1984).
Linkenhoker (1974) described a variant of time-out involving having
a misbehaving adolescent think about and audiotape thoughts about
alternative behaviors that would be preferable to that which resulted
in the time-out; when the time-out is over, the taped material is evaluated by peers and staff members. Many effective operant conditioning programs involve response-cost, the loss of specified positive rein-

forcers as a result of undesirable target behaviors (Varley, 1984). Extinguishing or ignoring has sometimes been used with undesirable target behaviors in juvenile delinquents, but Varley (1984) has warned of some disadvantages of this procedure.

Mediated Treatment

Behavioral interventions are often not applied directly by trained behavioral clinicians. This frequently occurs in both institutional and community settings, where institutional staff members, probation officers, teachers, parents, and volunteers mediate the treatment. Behavioral clinicians often have only indirect control of the actual treatment and must first modify the behavior of those who interact with the juvenile delinquent or antisocial adult on a daily basis. If such personnel are not trained and supervised, behavioral treatment can deteriorate into harmful punishment, mechanical knowledge will fail at crucial times, and relationships between target behaviors and consequences will be inconsistent (Crabtree, 1982; Kazdin, 1977, 1982; Varley, 1984). Kazdin (1977, 1982) discussed methods of training token economy staff members and concluded that a combination of several approaches including direct reinforcement of staff performance has been especially useful. Unfortunately, the contingencies important to those persons who often actual carry out treatment programs are not usually under the control of the behavioral clinician (Burchard and Lane, 1982; Reppucci and Saunders, 1974). Behavioral interventions in the home, using parents as behavior change agents, are extremely difficult to carry out when the parents of juvenile delinquents have their own problems (Gross and Brigham, 1980). Fleischman (1979) found that compliance with treatment in low-income and/or single-parent families of delinquent adolescents was greatly improved by using "parenting salaries" at an average cost of $77.00 per family. O'Dell (1985) reviewed research on methods of training parents in child-management skills, including those taught to parents of delinquent adolescents.

Systemic Constraints

Institutional and other systemic constraints on application of behavioral interventions have been identified by Burchard and Lane (1980), Crabtree (1982), Franks (1982), Reppucci and Saunders (1974), and Stumphauzer (1981). These include governmental-political oversight, overlapping and conflicting spheres of authority and responsibility within the institution, dysfunctional institutional communication patterns, interdisciplinary rivalries, and practical problems attendant to shift changes, weekend coverage, and temporary patient absences from the treatment setting. There is also a general resistance to change among administrators and staff members who work directly with patients, residents, inmates, probationers, and other subjects of the treatment effort. Further, behavioral clinicians are under strong pressure, systemic and personal, to conform to the values of the setting in which they work, so that they can maintain their treatment programs in that setting. Finally, procuring the necessary time, money and personnel to carry out behavioral interventions can be very difficult, and public funding as a source of support is never certain.

TOKEN ECONOMIES AND SYSTEMS

A commonly used behavioral intervention for problems of juvenile delinquency and adult antisocial behavior is operant conditioning, behavior change based on control of events that elicit and follow target behaviors. The most common form of operant intervention in institutional, other residential, and school settings is the token economy or smaller-scale token system in which immediate consequation occurs by means of tangible symbols that can later be exchanged for reinforcing events.

In Psychiatric Hospitals

Token economies and systems are still relatively rare in adolescent psychiatric settings treating delinquents. Moss and Rick (1981b) described a psychiatric hospital token economy for 12- to 18-year-old patients with records of incorrigibility, drug abuse, school problems, criminal acts, and various social deficits. Tokens (points) were earned for performance of a number of target behaviors, forfeited for specified undesirable behaviors, and spent for privileges and activities. The point system was shown to have specific effects on some target behaviors but not on others, and in one case room-restriction was found to be more powerful than token reinforcement. Follow-up data were not provided. House and Stambaugh (1979) designed an individual token system for a young delinquent boy, hospitalized on an adult inpatient psychiatric unit, who had a four-year history of severely delinquent behavior. His behavior improved during hospitalization, and his parents reported that gains were maintained at three- and 12-month follow-up.

Lawson, Greene, Richardson, McClure, and Padina (1971) reported an early token economy for adult offenders in a maximum security correctional hospital that produced at least short-term change in routine daily hospital activities among 41 "low-functioning" male patients. "Delinquent soldiers" with character and behavior disorders were treated on an army hospital psychiatric ward, their target behaviors were desirably affected in the hospital, and on follow-up they had considerable success completing their tours of duty compared to similarly diagnosed soldiers who either did not receive this treatment or did not complete it (Jones, Stayer, Wichlacz, Thomes, and Livingstone, 1977).

In Prisons

Token reinforcement programs have been used frequently in prisons, but many of these programs have not survived. Kazdin (1977), Rimm and Masters (1979), and Stumphauzer (1981) described several prison token economies, especially those at the Draper Correctional Center in Alabama, a maximum security facility for young adults with one or two felony convictions. Draper's token economies developed over time, with an initial emphasis on individualized programmed instruction and academic behaviors (McKee and Clements, 1971) and development of a "cell-block token economy" (Milan and McKee, 1976). Kazdin's comprehensive review (1977) described Draper as innovative in several ways. Inmates could leave the programs if they were dissatisfied with them, the programs did not rely on withholding of normally available reinforcers, many normally unavailable reinforcers were used to back up tokens, inmates had some say in establishing the programs' contingencies, and target behaviors went beyond compliance with prison rules to include more positive custodial behaviors and educational activities. Target behaviors changed desirably within the prison, but recidivism at 18-month follow-up was no better than for a no-treatment control group. Ayllon, Roberts, and Milan (1977) and Bassett, Blanchard, and Koshland (1975) also described token economies for imprisoned adults with a variety of target behaviors. These programs demonstrated the efficacy of token economies in altering in-prison target behaviors.

In contrast to these programs with records of at least short-term success, Kazdin (1977) cited the Special Treatment and Rehabilitative Training (START) Program conducted by the Federal Bureau of Prisons in Missouri as an example of controversial and ineffective use of operant principles in prisons. The START program moved problem prisoners to a special prison to alter their difficult behaviors so that they could then complete their sentences in their original institutions. It was a combination of prison-type contingencies with features of a token economy. It failed to achieve its rehabilitative goal, was terminated under legal pressure after two years, and was criticized severely for involuntary assignment of prisoners, reliance on normally available privileges as reinforcers, excessive focus on merely compliant target behavior, and use of aversive consequences (Kazdin, 1977). Some problems inherent in prison token reinforcement programs were illustrated by Bassett and Blanchard (1977), who described the deterioration into abuse that occurred in a prison token economy when its director took a several-month leave of absence, leaving the program without direct, on-site supervision.

In Residential Treatment of Adolescents

The Achievement Place or teaching-family model of adolescent residential treatment has used token reinforcement programs in many group homes around the country, as part of a broader group-home treatment program. Targets are behavioral deficits in social skills, self-care, and academic behavior thought to underlie the residents' predelinquent behavior. In contrast to token economies in institutions, teaching-family program target behaviors are more frequently community survival skills taught in a less-controlled environment. Residents' behavior during visits to their own homes is also targeted and consequated, and efforts are made to wean them from the token economy and transfer gains when they return to their homes. Several reviews of this experimental research have concluded that the Achievement Place program changes many target behaviors for the better in the group homes compared to non-teaching-family group homes, that there is some evidence of decreased recidivism among Achievement Place graduates compared to adolescents in institutional treatment or probation (but not in other group homes), and that the teaching-family homes may be less expensive than other group homes (Burchard and Lane, 1982;

Davidson and Seidman, 1974; Gross and Brigham, 1980; Kazdin, 1982; Kirigin, Braukmann, Atwater, and Wolf, 1982; Stumphauzer, 1976b).

Other residential token economies for adolescents have been investigated, some involving elements of the teaching-family program and others not. Their results are less encouraging, and one of them, the Crisis Care Center in Danville, Illinois, which used a progressive point system similar to that of Achievement Place, produced at best equal results following termination of treatment to those in a sample of matched controls (Davidson and Wolfred, 1977). Gross and Brigham (1980) and Burchard and Lane (1982) described mixed results regarding change in target behaviors during residence in these programs, and follow-up data were not as extensive. Burchard and Lane (1982) concluded that behavioral group homes for delinquent and predelinquent adolescents are probably more effective than institutional programs for most of these adolescents and are probably as effective as and less expensive than other community-based group homes.

Behavioral Employment Programs for Adolescents

Burchard and Lane (1982) reviewed two employment-related behavior modification programs (Mills and Walter, 1979; Shore and Massimo, 1979). The former involved severely delinquent juveniles, recruited and behaviorally trained local employers, provided behaviorally based prevocational training to the adolescents, placed the youth in jobs, and then faded out program supports. Some token reinforcement was involved. The latter reported 15-year follow-up data for a program for delinquent males that seemed to have used behavioral principles. Burchard and Lane (1982) noted impressive differences between treated and untreated participants in terms of reducing recidivism and enhancing employability, as well as academic achievement and marital stability in the Shore and Massimo study.

Issues in Token Reinforcement Programs

Delinquent adolescents and antisocial adults often have important skill and knowledge deficits, and these behavioral deficiencies are said by some to contribute to antisocial behavior. Token reinforcement systems can teach these skills and knowledge, but diagnosed "psychopaths," who comprise an unknown proportion of the adolescents and adults treated in these ways, seem to benefit most when positive reinforcement is very tangible and in some sense contiguous with the behaviors it consequates.

New, more desirable behaviors must often be shaped and particular care given to their nurturance and maintenance via various schedules of positive reinforcement. Varley (1984) suggested that adolescents in group treatment settings may be physically or socially punished by more aggressive peers for exhibiting behavior that is desirable from the clinicians' point of view, and that powerful peers can reinforce antisocial behaviors targeted by therapists for elimination, and he suggested ways of dealing with these perverse applications of operant principles.

Some persons do not respond to the contingencies in token reinforcement programs, and Kazdin (1977, 1982) suggested means of increasing responsiveness to this kind of treatment. These include altering the contingencies, using group contingencies, and working with the "economic" factors in token reinforcement programs (for example, saving of tokens by patients, exchange rates, token spending rates).

Generalization of Change

As noted frequently, the change in target behaviors occurring in institutional, residential, and other less-than-natural settings is frequently not maintained following termination of the operant treatment program and/or return of the antisocial adult or delinquent youth to the community. One group of methods for maintenance and transfer of behavior change involves expansion of stimulus control via establishment of a large number of environmental or internal stimuli that reliably elicit a desirable target behavior, so that it is performed in many situations and around many people. This can be accomplished by having many staff or family members or peers administer or withhold reinforcement, reinforcing or punishing target behaviors in several different areas of the treatment setting, introducing into the treatment setting elements of the setting to which the target behaviors need to be generalized, extending contingencies into the natural setting, analyzing and solving the problem of inappropriately narrow stimulus control, and training in self-instruction. These methods and problems associated with them were discussed by Kazdin (1977, 1982), Rimm and Masters (1979), Stumphauzer (1976b), and Varley (1984).

A second group of transfer and maintenance techniques involves manipulation of the relationship between the target behavior and its contingent consequences. Kazdin (1977, 1982) and Rimm and Masters (1979) suggested the following: gradually delaying the occurrence of the reinforcer, selecting target behaviors that are likely to continue to be elicited and reinforced in the natural setting, using naturally occurring reinforcers, moving from continuous to partial reinforcement, fading contingent relationships between target behaviors and reinforcers, providing noncontingent reinforcement in the natural setting, and stabilizing target behaviors prior to termination of treatment. Kazdin (1977, 1982) described the many practical problems associated with these deceptively easy-sounding prescriptions.

Agee (1979) and House and Stambaugh (1979) provided detailed descriptions of the use of several of the above methods in treatment of antisocial adolescents in a training school and a psychiatric hospital, respectively. These techniques were used to fade out external control within the institution and to transfer the gains in target behaviors from the institution to the home. Stumphauzer (1976b) and Stumphauzer, Veloz, and Aiken (1981) emphasized the need to change reinforcement contingencies in the community, which often seem to control juveniles' delinquent behavior. Much of Emery and Marholin's (1977) critique of the behavioral treatment of delinquency illustrates useful system-level change, including changing the environment to be more tolerant of delinquency and teaching delinquent adolescents to modify their teachers' "behavior" and, thus, attitudes toward the adolescents.

Conclusions

Token reinforcement programs (sometimes including other operant techniques) consistently produce change in target behaviors of delinquent adolescents or antisocial adults in prisons, other institutions, group homes, and employment settings. They are considered to be the best treatment for institutionalized adolescents (Blakely and Davidson, 1984; Varley, 1984). They have weaknesses, though. There is not enough meaningful outcome data, especially follow-up data, and there is little evidence that they result in long-term maintenance of behavior change once the program is removed and/or the institutionalized person is discharged to the community, although the rate of recidivism shortly after deinstitutionalization is sometimes reported to be better than with other kinds of treatment (Burchard and Lane, 1982; Davidson and Seidman, 1974; Gross and Brigham, 1980; Kazdin, 1977; Stumphauzer, 1976b, 1981).

The main advantage of token programs is the short-term behavior change they produce. Noninstitutional, community-based applications of token reinforcement seem to have more of an effect on delinquent adolescents' recidivism than do institutional programs (Burchard and Lane, 1982; Davidson and Seidman, 1974; Davidson and Wolfred, 1977; Gross and Brigham, 1980; Kazdin, 1977). Token reinforcement (and other behavioral) interventions in employment programs for adolescents are considered promising (Burchard and Lane, 1982; Davidson and Seidman, 1974). The evidence for positive outcomes in correctional hospitals or special units of psychiatric hospitals is more limited, but in-hospital and some long-term change seems to occur (Kazdin, 1977).

OTHER MEDIATED BEHAVIORAL INTERVENTIONS

Probation

Jesness (1975), Burkhart, Behles, and Stumphauzer (1976), and Wood, Green, and Bry (1982) trained juvenile probation officers in behavioral techniques, including operant conditioning. Jesness (1975), after 40 hours of classroom training and an average of 22 hours of consultation per probation officer, found that more problem target behaviors included in contingency contracts rather than not were eliminated in the short-term, but there was no difference in recidivism at six-month follow-up. Only a minority of the probation officers actually wrote contingency contracts that met the standards of the program after they completed training. Burkhardt et al. (1976) and Wood et al. (1982) described didactic and experiential behavioral training of juvenile probation officers, found it effective in increasing knowledge and competence, and, in the case of Wood et al., found that training reduced the number of problem behaviors observed by both the officers and the parents of the delinquent adolescents.

Polakow and Doctor (1974) and Polakow and Peabody (1975) described the operant "behavioral probation" of adult offenders. A woman on probation for child abuse benefited from contingency contracting so that, after 30 weeks, she was using positive reinforcement effectively with her son, and his acting-out had been reduced. In a group study, operant procedures including contingency contracting were used to encourage development of desirable target behaviors (for example, employment) in a group of drug offenders. In both studies, time off from probation was one of the elements of the contingency contract.

Mediation by Parents, Buddies, and Others

Henderson (1981) reported 10 cases of "individualized combined treatment" for 8-to-15-year-old outpatient boys with serious stealing problems. Relaxation training, biofeedback, self-instruction, and positive reinforcement of desirable behaviors were used. Parents monitored reinforcement at home. External control was faded out. There were four to five office sessions in the first week, two in week two, then fortnightly visits for another four to six weeks. After follow-up of at least two years, two boys had stolen once or twice, and the rest had not. Kent and O'Leary (1976) also used parents as mediators in behavioral treatment of their aggressive, impulsive boys. Teachers and parents of 16 elementary school boys were trained in operant procedures over a three-to-four-month period. They used positive reinforcement at home and school, with some response-cost, and parents tutored their boys at home. At the end of treatment, treated boys' social behavior was better than untreated boys', but the groups were not different at nine-month follow-up. Treated boys' academic behavior was superior at follow-up, but not at the end of treatment.

Fo and O'Donnell (1974, 1975) and O'Donnell, Lydgate, and Fo (1979) taught operant conditioning techniques to volunteer "buddies" between the ages of 17 and 65 and assigned them to develop behavioral treatment programs for predelinquent or delinquent adolescents. The buddies inexpensively reduced predelinquent problem behavior, especially truancy, and increased performance of homework and household chores. These interventions averaged six weeks. Compared to a no-treatment condition, the buddy system reduced major offenses among more serious delinquents who had recently committed major offenses, but increased major offenses in those without such a record, possibly because of the modeling of delinquent behavior afforded by the program.

Tharpe and Wetzel (1969) had college-educated "behavior analysts" train and supervisor peers, parents and relatives, and other adults involved with predelinquents and delinquents. At six-month follow-up undesirable target behaviors and contacts with police were reduced; however, there was no control group in this study. Davidson and Robinson (1975) provided treatment to severely delinquent adolescents via an undergraduate student and a teacher's aide. An average of nine weeks of daily, varied behavioral intervention produced short-term change and reduced arrest and institutionalization rates, the latter compared to nongraduates of the program. Commenting on mediated behavioral techniques. Training lasted at least one month and resulted Burchard and Lane (1982) suggested that it benefits prior offenders most, should not be used preventively, and should include positive regard by the service providers for the problem youth.

The Oregon Social Learning Project

Patterson (1974) described a treatment program involving didactic and experiential training of parents of predelinquent adolescents in behavioral techniques. Training lasted at least one month, and resulted in short-term improvement in aggressive and other disruptive behavior and some maintenance of improvement at 12-month follow-up, although Kent (1976) questioned the claim of 12-month maintenance of change. Patterson (1979) reviewed the work of the Oregon Social Learning Project. Ferber, Keeley, and Shemberg (1974) used a family treatment program similar to Patterson's but obtained less improvement and had difficulty both getting parents to carry out the behavioral treatment of their children and getting an accurate view of the target behavior in the home. Arnold, Levine, and Patterson (1975) found that the young siblings of children treated in the Patterson (1974) study also improved during treatment and maintained that improvement at six-month follow-up. Moore, Chamberlain, and Mukai (1979) followed up some children treated at the Oregon Social Learning Project for two to nine years and found that the treatment had been more successful for aggression than for stealing.

Short-term Behavioral Systems Therapy

Parsons and Alexander (1973) and Alexander and Parsons (1973) described a behavioral intervention to modify interaction patterns of families of delinquent adolescents. This focused on changing the families' communication and negotiation patterns while teaching them how to make contingency contracts. The adolescents were mostly guilty of non-criminal status offenses. Treatment of each family lasted an average of eight hours. These studies and one by Alexander, Barton, Schiavo, and Parsons (1976) found predicted changes in family interaction patterns by the end of treatment and significant reduction in recidivism at follow-up between six and 18 months after treatment, compared to families who dropped out or got nonbehavioral or no treatment. Klein, Alexander, and Parsons (1977) found that siblings of delinquent adolescents whose families had been treated in the Alexander and Parsons (1973) study had less recidivism than a nonbehavioral or no-treatment group. Weathers and Liberman (1975) obtained largely negative results with this kind of treatment, but Burchard and Lane (1982) suggested that more dropouts, more severe delinquency, and demographic differences between the two studies may have influenced the results. Alexander et al. (1976) suggested that the relationship skills of the therapist may be a crucial determinant of therapy outcome in this treatment.

Contingency Contracting

The use of this method in behavioral probation was mentioned earlier. It involves in-advance agreement by two or more parties on clearly spelled-out target behaviors and contingent consequences. Stuart (1971a,b) and Weathers and Liberman (1975) stated principles and procedures for developing contingency contracts with delinquent youth. They and others (Fitzgerald, 1974; Mills and Walter, 1979; Stumphauzer, 1976a; Stuart, Jayaratne, and Tripodi, 1976) described contingency contracts between delinquent adolescents and their parents in the home, their teachers in school settings, and their behavior therapists in an employment program and a probation work program.

Critical reviewers of contingency contracting have not been very enthusiastic about its use with problem adolescents (Burchard and Lane, 1982; Kirschenbaum and Flanery, 1983; Moss and Rick, 1981a; Stuart and Lott, 1973). Results are mixed in terms of short-term and later recidivism. Weathers and Liberman (1975) and Stuart et al. (1976) suggested that this method is more effective when combined with other behavioral treatments. Varley (1984) indicated that it is most helpful with nonaggressive adolescents when the payback to the adolescent is the elimination of some noxious behavior of the other party and when adolescents' attempts to coerce regarding the contract can be controlled.

Conclusions

Burchard and Lane (1982) suggested that the use of nonprofessional mediators of behavioral treatment and of relatively short-term mediated behavioral treatment seems warranted for delinquent adolescents. Similarly, Stumphauzer (1981) credited the behavioral probation of adult drug offenders reported by Polakow and Doctor (1974) with reducing recidivism and increasing very relevant desirable target behaviors compared to regular probation, resulting in shorter probation and reduced costs.

Burchard and Lane (1982) concluded that behavioral treatment changes family interaction in the short-term and, in some cases, for up to one year after treatment. They determined that it reduces problem behaviors of adolescents in the families, reduces recidivism in milder delinquency, and may reduce recidivism among hard-core delinquents. These treatments seem more effective if families are intact, delinquent adolescents are relatively young, characteristics of the family system are taken into account, and the target behavior is simple aggression rather than more complicated delinquent problems (Burchard and Lane, 1982; McAuley, 1982; Ulrici, 1983). Burchard and Lane (1982) suggested that the treatment of choice for the older adolescent from a less intact family would be contingency contracting with employment-related target behaviors.

DIRECT BEHAVIORAL TREATMENT

Behavioral Psychodrama

Stumphauzer (1976b) described this technique with delinquent adolescents. In a group setting, the delinquent youth demonstrates a typically poor response to a problem situation and receives criticism, modeling, role-playing, and social and tangible reinforcement for a new, more appropriate response to the problem and for maintenance of the behavior between sessions.

Operant Self-control and Modification of the Environment

Several authors have suggested that operant self-control techniques be taught to adolescents so that they can control relevant stimuli and consequate their own behavior (Gross and Brigham, 1980; Varley, 1984). In effect, an adolescent might be taught to modify his or her own behavior when adult assistance is not consistently available or when being weaned from token reinforcement. Fedoravicius (1973) taught predelinquent and delinquent youths to modify not only their own behavior but also that of their parents and others, in the process decreasing their own problem behaviors. However, Sohn and Lamal's (1982) review cast doubt on the efficacy of truly "self"-reinforcement.

Assertive and Social Skills Training

Assertive training has been used with both adolescent delinquents and antisocial adults, whose aggression is sometimes described as the result of a deficit in appropriately assertive behaviors or of unwillingness to use these (Rimm and Masters, 1979). Rimm and Masters also noted that assertive training is more effective when aggression is the result of anger rather than a means of achieving ends, and when it is overcontrolled rather than undercontrolled. The first is often true of adolescent aggression (Feindler and Fremouw, 1983), but the focus of assertive training with these treatment populations has been their undercontrolled anger. Shoemaker (1974) used group assertive training to teach delinquents to be more appropriately assertive rather than aggressive. Ollendick and Hersen (1979) used social skills training with adolescent groups to reduce aggression and increase more appropriate behavior.

Rimm, Keyson, and Hunziker (1971) described group assertive training in six one-hour sessions with male adults hospitalized primarily for antisocial aggression. The treatment seemed to result in less aggressive behavior by these patients, compared to a group that had only discussed the expression of anger. Rimm, Hill, Brown, and Stuart (1974) gave eight hours of group assertive training to nonhospitalized, antisocially angry males and obtained significantly greater self-rated improvement compared to placebo controls. Group assertive training for undercontrolled aggression is further illustrated by Rimm and Masters (1979). Assertive and social skills training seems to have some use with antisocial aggression and anger, but follow-up data are often lacking (Bornstein, Hamilton, and McFall, 1981).

Herrell (1971) described the use of systematic desensitization with a young soldier with chronically undercontrolled anger that had gotten him into trouble repeatedly, including expulsion from school, firing from a job, arrest, and current inability to accept orders without becoming extremely angry and even physically aggressive. Treatment involved 18 sessions in approximately 12 weeks. Physical aggression decreased during treatment, and there was no physical aggression and only one verbal outburst within eight weeks of termination. Bornstein et al. (1981) concluded that this technique has been little used with truly antisocial aggression.

COMMUNITY-LEVEL OPERANT PROGRAMS FOR ADOLESCENTS

A few behavioral programs have gone beyond the individual or even relatively small-group level to analysis of and intervention with delinquency problems at the community level, referred to as "behavioral ecology" by Moss and Rick (1981a). Stumphauzer et al. (1981) discussed their interest in etiology, measurement, and environmental maintenance of these problems on the community level, and they adapted a conceptual framework, suggested by Kanfer and Saslow (1969) for behavioral interventions with individuals, for use with communities. Moss and Rick (1981a) described three community-level programs that analyzed community problems from a behavioral point of view and provided large-scale behavioral intervention for adolescents in a high-crime area via token reinforcement programs.

COMBINING BEHAVIORAL AND PSYCHODYNAMIC INPATIENT TREATMENT FOR DELINQUENT ADOLESCENTS

Elements of operant conditioning and other behavioral procedures are implicit to some degree in most inpatient psychiatric treatment of juvenile delinquents. In some, they are more explicit. Crabtree (1982) described a basically psychodynamically oriented treatment unit in a general psychiatric hospital for a small group of adolescents, a significant number of whom had marked behavior problems with family, school, and the law. His focus was on "persistent delinquents" or "outlaw leaders." Rossman and Knesper (1976) described in some detail an operantly based component designed to meet initial therapeutic goals of controlling disruptive behavior so that adolescents could be engaged in psychodynamically oriented inpatient treatment at a university hospital. Jones (1984) reviewed principles of psychodynamic and behavioral treatment of angry and violent adolescents.

These writers conceptualized anger and aggression in psychodynamic terms and used behavioral methods to control acting-out so that the adolescent could become engaged in treatment. With the behavioral program putting a lid on reinforcing emotional discharge, internalized conflict would develop and the treatment program would not be severely disrupted, including by angry countertransference on the part of the treatment staff.

GENERAL CONCLUSIONS

Cognitive and cognitive-behavioral interventions offer some promise for problems of juvenile delinquency and antisocial personality disorder, but their research base with these persons is limited. Behavioral interventions clearly produce short-term change, but there is much less evidence that they produce long-term alteration of behavior. As Burchard and Lane (1982) have noted, few rehabilitation programs of any kind work very well for juvenile delinquents or criminal adults. Failure of institutional behavioral treatment approaches to maintain gains in the community has led to community-based applications of these technologies (Gross and Brigham, 1980). Community-based approaches may work better than institutional ones, but they too have their problems. What may be the crucial missing element is an aftercare component of either institutional or community-residential treatment; the programming should be extended into the community along with the former institutional or group-home resident (Burchard and Lane, 1982; Davidson and Seidman, 1974; Stumphauzer, 1981). Others have called for self-management training to encourage self-control when mediated treatment is not available in the community (Gross and Brigham, 1980; Stumphauzer, 1981). Outpatient behavioral treatment is not as well supported as is institutional or residential treatment (Burchard and Lane, 1982; Moss and Rick, 1981a; Varley, 1984).

Frosch (1983) stated firmly that, regardless of the treatment approach, resistance and countertransference are major problems in the treatment of adult antisocial personalities. Personal qualities of therapists and the quality of their relationship with delinquent adolescents and their families also seem important (Alexander et al., 1976; Burchard and Lane, 1982; Varley, 1984).

REFERENCES

Agee, V. L. (1979). *Treatment of the violent, incorrigible adolescent*. Lexington, MA: D. C. Heath.

Alexander, J. F., & Parsons, B. V. (1973). Short-term behavioral intervention with delinquent families: Impact on family process and recidivism. *Journal of Abnormal Psychology, 81*, 219–225.

Alexander, J. F., Barton, C., Schiavo, R. S., & Parsons, B. V. (1976). Systems-behavioral intervention with families of delinquents: Therapist characteristics, family behavior, and outcome. *Journal of Consulting and Clinical Psychology, 44*, 656–664.

Arnold, J. E., Levine, A. G., & Patterson, G. R. (1975). Changes in sibling behavior following family intervention. *Journal of Consulting and Clinical Psychology, 43*, 683–688.

Ayllon, T., Roberts, M., & Milan, M. (1977). *Behavior modification and prison rehabilitation: Toward an effective humanism*. New York: Wiley.

Bassett, J. E., & Blanchard, E. B. (1977). The effect of the absence of close supervision on the use of response cost in a prison token economy. *Journal of Applied Behavior Analysis, 10*, 275–279.

Bassett, J. E., Blanchard, E. B., & Koshland, E. (1975). Applied behavior analysis on a penal setting: Targeting "free world" behaviors. *Behavior Therapy, 6*, 639–648.

Blakely, C. H., & Davidson, W. S. (1984). Behavioral approaches to delinquency: A review. *Advances in Child Behavioral Analysis and Therapy, 3*, 241–272.

Bornstein, P. H., Hamilton, S. B., & McFall, M. E. (1981). Modification of adult aggression: A critical review of theory, research, and practice. *Progress in Behavior Modification, 12*, 300–350.

Bornstein, P. H., & Quevillon, R. P. (1976). The effects of a self-instructional package with overactive pre-school boys. *Journal of Applied Behavior Analysis, 9*, 179–188.

Budd, K. S., & Baer, D. M. (1976). Behavior modification and the law: Implications of recent judicial decisions. *The Journal of Psychiatry and Law*, Summer, 171–244.

Burchard, J. D., & Lane, T. W. (1982). Crime and delinquency. In A. S. Bellack, M. Hersen, and A. E. Kazdin (Eds.), *International handbook of behavior modification and therapy* (pp. 613–652). New York: Plenum.

Burkhart, B. R., Behles, M. W., & Stumphauzer, J. S. (1976). Training juvenile officers in behavior modification: Knowledge, attitude change, or behavioral competence? *Behavior Therapy, 7*, 47–53.

Camp, B., Blom, G., Herbert, F., & Van Doorninck, W. (1977). "Think Aloud": A program for developing self-control in young aggressive boys. *Journal of Abnormal Child Psychology, 8*, 157–169.

Cleckley, H. (1976). *The mask of sanity* (5th ed.). St. Louis: C. V. Mosby.

Cox, S. G. (1979). Rational behavior training as a rehabilitative program for alcoholic offenders. *Offender Rehabilitation, 3,* 245–256.

Crabtree, L. H. (1982). Hospitalized adolescents who act out: A treatment approach. *Psychiatry, 45,* 147–158.

Craighead, W. E., Kazdin, A. E., & Mahoney, M. J. (1981). *Behavior modification: Principles, issues and applications* (2nd ed.). Boston: Houghton Mifflin.

Davidson, W. S., & Robinson, M. J. (1975). Community psychology and behavior modification: A community-based program for the prevention of delinquency. *Journal of Corrective Psychiatry and Behavior Therapy, 21,* 1–12.

Davidson, W. S., & Seidman, E. (1974). Studies of behavior modification and juvenile delinquency: A review, methodological critique, and social perspective. *Psychological Bulletin, 81,* 98–1011.

Davidson, W. S., & Wolfred, T. R. (1977). Evaluation of a community-based behavior modification program for prevention of delinquency: The failure of success. *Community Mental Health Journal, 13,* 296–306.

Ellis, A. (1962). *Reason and emotion in psychotherapy.* Secacus, NJ: Lyle Stuart.

Ellis, A. (1977). The basic clinical theory of rational-emotive therapy. In A. Ellis & R. Grieger (Eds.), *Handbook of rational-emotive therapy.* New York: Springer.

Ellis, A. (1980). Rational-emotive therapy and cognitive behavior therapy: Similarities and differences. *Cognitive Therapy and Research, 4,* 325–340.

Ellis, A., & Grieger, R. (1977). The present and the future of RET. In A. Ellis & R. Grieger (Eds.), *Handbook of rational-emotive therapy.* New York: Springer.

Emery, R. E., & Marholin, D. (1977). An applied behavior analysis of delinquency: The irrelevancy of relevant behavior. *American Psychologist, 32,* 860–873.

Fagan, T. J., & Lira, F. T. (1980). The primary and secondary sociopathic personality: Differences in frequency and severity of antisocial behaviors. *Journal of Abnormal Psychology, 89,* 493–496.

Fedoravicius, A. S. (1973). The patient as shaper of required parental behavior: A case study. *Journal of Behaviour Therapy and Experimental Psychiatry, 4,* 395–396.

Feindler, E. L. (1979). Cognitive and behavioral approaches to anger control training in explosive adolescents. Unpublished doctoral dissertation. West Virginia University.

Feindler, E. L., & Fremouw, W. J. (1983). Stress inoculation training for adolescent anger problems. In D. Meichenbaum & M. E. Jaremko (Eds.), *Stress reduction and prevention.* New York: Plenum.

Feindler, E. L., Marriott, S. A., & Iwata, M. (1984). Group anger control training for junior high school delinquents. *Cognitive Therapy and Research, 8,* 299–311.

Ferber, H., Keeley, S. M., & Shemberg, K. M. (1974). Training parents in behavior modification: Outcome of and problems encountered in a program after Patterson's work. *Behavior Therapy, 5,* 415–419.

Fitzgerald, T. J. (1974). Contingency contracting with juvenile offenders. *Criminology, 12,* 241–248.

Fleischman, M. J. (1979). Using parenting salaries to control attrition and cooperation in therapy. *Behavior Therapy, 10,* 111–116.

Foa, E. B., & Foa, U. G. (1983). Strengthening the umbilical cord. *Advances in Behaviour Research and Therapy, 4,* 201–203.

Fo, W. S. O., & O'Donnell, C. R. (1974). The Buddy System: Relationship and contingency conditions in a community intervention program for youth with nonprofessionals as behavior change agents. *Journal of Consulting and Clinical Psychology, 42*, 163–169.

Fo, W. S. O., & O'Donnell, C. R. (1975). The Buddy System: Effect of community intervention on delinquent offenses. *Behavior Therapy, 6*, 522–524.

Franks, C. M. (1977). Clockwork Orange revisited: Travesty and truth about aversive conditioning. In O. L. McCabe (Ed.), *Changing human behavior: Current therapies and future directions* (pp. 83–92). New York: Grune & Stratton.

Franks, C. M. (1982). Behavior therapy: An overview. *Annual Review of Behavior Therapy, Theory and Practice, 8*, 1–38.

Frosch, J. P. (1983). The treatment of antisocial and borderline personality disorders. *Hospital and Community Psychiatry, 34*, 243–248.

Glasser, W. (1965). *Reality therapy: A new approach to psychiatry*. New York: Harper & Row.

Goldfried, M. R., & Davison, G. C. (1976). *Clinical behavior therapy*. New York: Holt, Rinehart, & Winston.

Goodman, D. (1983). Juvenile justice: Thinking right about doing wrong. *Corrections Magazine, 9*, 30–36.

Gross, A. M., & Brigham, T. A. (1980). Behavior modification and the treatment of juvenile delinquency: A review and proposal for future research. *Corrective and Social Psychiatry and Journal of Behavior Technology, Methods and Therapy, 26*, 98–106.

Hedberg, A. G. (1981). Professional and ethical issues in providing clinical services. In C. E. Walker (Ed.), *Clinical practice of psychology* (pp. 369–396). New York: Pergamon.

Henderson, J. Q. (1981). A behavioral approach to stealing: A proposal for treatment based on 10 cases. *Journal of Behaviour Therapy and Experimental Psychiatry, 12*, 231–236.

Herrell, J. M. (1971). Use of systematic desensitization to eliminate inappropriate anger. *Proceedings of the 79th Annual Convention of the American Psychological Association, 6*, 431–432.

House, A. E., & Stambaugh, E. E. (1979). Transfer of therapeutic effects from institution to home: Faith, hope, and behavior modification. *Family Process, 18*, 87–93.

Jesness, C. F. (1975). *The cooperative behavior demonstration project: Submitted as the final report to the Office of Criminal Justice Planning*. Sacramento: California Youth Authority.

Jones, F. D., Stayer, S. J., Wichlacz, C. R., Thomes, L., & Livingstone, B. L. (1977). Contingency management of hospital diagnosed character and behavior disorder soldiers. *Journal of Behaviour Therapy and Experimental Psychiatry, 8*, 333.

Jones, J. D. (1984). Principles of hospital treatment of the aggressive adolescent. In C. R. Keith (Ed.), *The aggressive adolescent: Clinical perspectives* (pp. 359–400). New York: Free Press.

Kanfer, F. H., & Saslow, G. (1969). Behavioral diagnosis. In C. M. Franks (Ed.), *Behavior therapy: Appraisal and status* (pp. 417–444). New York: McGraw Hill.

Kaufmann, L. M., & Wagner, B. R. (1972). Barb: A systematic treatment technology for temper control disorders. *Behavior Therapy, 3*, 84–90.

Kazdin, A. E. (1977). *The token Economy: A review and evaluation*. New York: Plenum.

Kazdin, A. E. (1982). The token economy: A decade later. *Journal of Applied Behavior Analysis, 15*, 431–445.

Kelly, G. A. (1955). *The psychology of personal constructs.* New York: Norton.

Kendall, P. C., & Finch, A. J., Jr. (1976). A cognitive behavioral treatment for impulse control: A case study. *Journal of Consulting and Clinical Psychology, 44*, 852–857.

Kent, R. (1976). A methodological critique of "Interventions for boys with conduct problems". *Journal of Consulting and Clinical Psychology, 44*, 297–302.

Kent, R. N., & O'Leary, K. D. (1976). A controlled evaluation of behavior modification with conduct problem children. *Journal of Consulting and Clinical Psychology, 44*, 586–596.

Kirigin, K. A., Braukmann, C. J., Atwater, J. D., & Wolf, M. M. (1982). An evaluation of teaching-family (Achievement Place) group homes for juvenile offenders. *Journal of Applied Behavior Analysis, 15*, 1–16.

Kirschenbaum, D. S., & Flanery, R. C. (1983). Behavioral contracting: Outcomes and elements. *Progress in Behavior Modification, 15*, 217–275.

Klein, N. C., Alexander, J. F., & Parsons, B. V. (1977). Impact of family systems intervention on recidivism and sibling delinquency: A model of primary prevention and program evaluation. *Journal of Consulting and Clinical Psychology, 45*, 469–474.

Lawson, R. B., Greene, R. T., Richardson, J. S., McClure, G., & Padina, R. J. (1971). Token economy program in a maximum security correctional hospital. *Journal of Nervous and Mental Diseases, 152*, 199–205.

Ledwidge, B. (1978). Cognitive behavior modification: A step in the wrong direction? *Psychological Bulletin, 85*, 353–375.

Ledwidge, B. (1979). Cognitive behavior modification or new ways to change minds: Reply to Mahoney and Kazdin. *Psychological Bulletin, 86*, 1050–1053.

Linkenhoker, D. D. (1974). Increasing the effectiveness of timeout from reinforcement. *Psychotherapy: Theory, Research and Practice, 11*, 326–328.

McAuley, R. (1982). Training parents to modify conduct problems in their children. *Journal of Child Psychology and Psychiatry and Allied Disciplines, 23*, 335–342.

McCullough, J. P., Huntsinger, G. M., & Nay, W. R. (1977). Self-treatment of aggression in a 16 year old male. *Journal of Consulting and Clinical Psychology, 45*, 322–331.

McKee, J. M., & Clements, C. B. (1971). A behavioral approach to learning: The Draper model. In H. C. Rickard (Ed.), *Behavioral intervention in human problems.* New York: Pergamon.

Mahoney, M. J., & Kazdin, A. E. (1979). Cognitive behavior modification: Misconceptions and premature evacuation. *Psychological Bulletin, 86*, 1044–1049.

Marzillier, J. S. (1980). Cognitive therapy and behavioural practice. *Behaviour Research and Therapy, 18*, 249–258.

Meichenbaum, D. H., & Cameron, R. (1974). The clinical potential of modifying what clients say to themselves. *Psychotherapy: Theory, Research and Practice, 11*, 103–117.

Meichenbaum, D., & Cameron, R. (1983). Stress inoculation training: Toward a general paradigm for training coping skills. In D. Meichenbaum and M. E. Jeremko (Eds.), *Stress reduction and prevention* (pp. 115–154). New York: Plenum.

Meichenbaum, D. H. & Goodman, J. (1971). Training impulsive children to talk to themselves: A means of developing self-control. *Journal of Abnormal Psychology, 77*, 115–126.

Milan, M. A., & McKee, J. M. (1976). The cell-block token economy: Token reinforcement procedures in a maximum security correctional institution for adult male felons. *Journal of Applied Behavior Analysis, 9,* 253–275.

Mills, C. M., & Walter, T. L. (1979). Reducing juvenile delinquency: A behavioral-employment intervention. In J. S. Stumphauzer (Ed.), *Progress in behavior therapy with delinquents.* Springfield, IL: Charles C. Thomas.

Moore, D. R., Chamberlain, P., & Mukai, L. H. (1979). Children at risk for delinquency: A follow-up comparison of aggressive children and children who steal. *Journal of Abnormal Child Psychology, 7,* 345–355.

Moss, G. R., & Rick, G. R. (1981a). Overview: Applications of operant technology to behavioral disorders of adolescents. *American Journal of Psychiatry, 138,* 1161–1169.

Moss, G. R., & Rick, G. R. (1981b). Application of a token economy for adolescents in a private psychiatric hospital. *Behavior Therapy, 12,* 585–590.

Novaco, R. W. (1976). The functions and regulation of the arousal of anger. *American Journal of Psychiatry, 133,* 1124–1128.

Novaco, R. W. (1977). Stress inoculation: A cognitive therapy for anger and its application to a case of depression. *Journal of Consulting and Clinical Psychology, 45,* 600–608.

O'Dell, S. L. (1985). Progress in parent training. *Progress in Behavior Modification, 19,* 57–108.

O'Donnell, C. R., Lydgate, T., & Fo, W. S. O. (1979). The buddy system: Review and follow-up. *Child Behavior Therapy, 1,* 161–169.

Ollendick, T. H., & Hersen, M. (1979). Social skills training for juvenile delinquents. *Behaviour Research and Therapy, 17,* 547–555.

Parsons, B. V., & Alexander, J. F. (1973). Short-term family intervention: A therapy outcome study. *Journal of Consulting and Clinical Psychology, 41,* 195–201.

Patterson, G. R. (1974). Interventions for boys with conduct problems: Multiple settings, treatments, and criteria. *Journal of Consulting and Clinical Psychology, 42,* 471–481.

Patterson, G. R. (1979). Treatment for children with conduct problems: A review of outcome studies. In S. Feshback and A. Fraczak (Eds.), *Aggression and behavior change: Biological and social processes.* New York: Praeger.

Polakow, R. L., & Doctor, R. M. (1974). A behavior modification program for adult drug offenders. *Journal of Research in Crime and Delinquency, 3,* 41–45.

Polakow, R. L., & Peabody, D. L. (1975). Behavioral treatment of child abuse. *International Journal of Offenders Therapy and Comparative Criminology, 19,* 100–103.

Reppucci, N. D., & Saunders, J. T. (1974). Social psychology of behavior modification: Problems of implementation in natural settings. *American Psychologist, 29,* 649–660.

Reid, W. H. (1981). The antisocial personality and related syndromes. In J. R. Lion, *Personality disorders: Diagnosis and management* (2nd ed.) (pp. 133–162). Baltimore: Williams & Wilkins.

Rimm, D. C., Hill, G. A., Brown, M. N., & Stuart, J. E. (1974). Group-assertive training in treatment of expression of inappropriate anger. *Psychological Reports, 34,* 791–798.

Rimm, D. C., Keyson, M., & Hunziker, J. (1971). Group assertive training in the treatment of antisocial aggression. Unpublished manuscript. Arizona State University.

Rimm, D. C., & Masters, J. C. (1979). *Behavior therapy: Techniques and empirical findings* (2nd ed.). New York: Academic Press.

Rossman, P. G., & Knesper, D. J. (1976). The early phase of hospital treatment for disruptive adolescents: The integration of behavioral and dynamic techniques. *Journal of the American Academy of Child Psychiatry, 15*, 693–708.

Schwitzgebel, R. L., & Schwitzgebel, R. K. (1980). *Law and psychological practice.* New York: Wiley.

Shore, M. F., & Massimo, J. L. (1979). Fifteen years after treatment: A follow-up study to comprehensive vocationally-oriented psychotherapy. *American Journal of Orthopsychiatry, 49*, 240–245.

Shoemaker, M. E. (1974). Group assertiveness training for institutionalized delinquents. Unpublished dissertation. Fuller Graduate School of Psychology.

Snyder, J. J., & White, M. J. (1979). The use of cognitive self-instruction in the treatment of behaviorally disturbed adolescents. *Behavior Therapy, 10*, 227–235.

Sohn, D., & Lamal, P. A. (1982). Self-reinforcement: Its reinforcing capability and its clinical utility. *Psychological Record, 32*, 179–203.

Stuart, R. B. (1971a). Behavioral contracting with the families of delinquents. *Journal of Behaviour Therapy and Experimental Psychiatry, 2*, 1–11.

Stuart, R. B. (1971b). A three-dimensional program for the treatment of obesity. *Behaviour Research and Therapy, 9*, 177–186.

Stuart, R. B., Jayaratne, S., & Tripodi, T. (1976). Changing adolescent deviant behavior through reprogramming the behavior of parents and teachers: An experimental evaluation. *Canadian Journal of Behavioural Science, 8*, 132–144.

Stuart, R. B., & Lott, L. B. (1973). Behavioral contracting with delinquents: A cautionary note. *Journal of Behaviour Therapy and Experimental Psychiatry, 3*, 161–169.

Stumphauzer, J. S. (1976a). Elimination of stealing by self-reinforcement of alternative behavior and family contracting. *Journal of Behaviour Therapy and Experimental Psychiatry, 7*, 265–268.

Stumphauzer, J. S. (1976b). Modifying delinquent behavior: Beginnings and current practices. *Adolescence, 11*, 13–28.

Stumphauzer, J. S. (1981). Behavior modification with delinquents and criminals. In W. E. Craighead, A. E. Kazdin, & M. J. Mathoney (Eds.), *Behavior modification: Principles, issues, and applications* (2nd ed.) (pp. 458–478). Boston: Houghton Mifflin.

Stumphauzer, J. S., Veloz, E. V., & Aiken, T. W. (1981). Behavioral analysis of communities: A challenge. *Psychological Reports, 49*, 343–346.

Templeman, T. L., & Wollersheim, J. P. (1979). A cognitive-behavioral approach to the treatment of psychopathy. *Psychotherapy: Theory, Research and Practice, 16*, 132–139.

Tharpe, R. G., & Wetzel, R. J. (1969). *Behavior modification in the natural environment.* New York: Academic Press.

Ulrici, D. K. (1983). The effects of behavioral and family interventions on juvenile recidivism. *Family Therapy, 10*, 25–36.

Varley, W. H. (1984). Behavior modification approaches to the aggressive adolescent. In C. R. Keith (Ed.), *The aggressive adolescent: Clinical perspectives* (pp. 268–298). New York: Free Press.

Watkins, J. T. (1977). The rational-emotive dynamics of impulsive disorders. In A. Ellis & R. Grieger (Eds.), *Handbook of rational-emotive therapy* (pp. 135–152). New York: Springer.

Weathers, L., & Liberman, R. P. (1975). Contingency contracting with families of delinquent adolescents. *Behavior Therapy, 6,* 356–366.

Wood, G., Green, L., & Bry, B. H. (1982). The impact of behavioral training on the knowledge and effectiveness of juvenile probation officers and volunteers. *Journal of Community Psychology, 10,* 133–141.

Yochelson, S., & Samenow, S. E. (1976). *The criminal personality, Volume I: A profile for change.* New York: Jason Aronson.

Yochelson, S., & Samenow, S. E. (1977). *The criminal personality, Volume II: The change process.* New York: Jason Aronson.

Zelie, K., Stone, C. I., & Lehr, E. (1980). Cognitive-behavioral intervention in school discipline: A preliminary study. *Personnel and Guidance Journal, 59,* 80–83.

8

The Treatment of Antisocial Syndromes: The Therapist's Feelings

Larry H. Strasburger

The psychopath is the least loved of patients. Patients with antisocial syndromes traditionally have been considered untreatable (Cleckley, 1964). Even a quick review of the literature suggests that a chapter on effective treatment should be the shortest in any book concerned with psychopathy (Suedfeld and Landon, 1975).

There are some valid reasons for therapeutic pessimism. These people are impulsive, unable to tolerate frustration and delay, and have problems with trusting. They take a paranoid position or externalize their emotional experience. They have little ability to form a working alliance and a poor capacity for self-observation. Their anger is frightening. Frequently they take flight. Their relations with others are highly problematic. When close to another person they fear engulfment or fusion and loss of self. At the same time, paradoxically, they desire closeness; frustration of their entitled wishes to be nourished, cared for, and assisted often leads to rage. They are capable of a child's primitive fury enacted with an adult's physical capabilities, and action is always in the offing.

Much therapeutic pessimism arises from the feelings sociopaths engender in their caretakers and treaters. It is difficult to be sympathetic toward delinquent, substance-abusing, and sometimes violent individuals. Therapists are likely to regard the coping behavior of psychopaths as sin more than sickness. They are bad, not mad. "The defense mechanisms that underlie sociopathy seem . . . as unbearably gross to the observer as a strong cigar in a crowded elevator" (Vaillant, 1975). Indeed, psychiatrists are involved in the same unconscious rejection of psychopaths that society openly admits through its punitive attitudes (Bromberg, 1953).

Sociopaths are people with primitive personalities who for some reason have avoided facing inner dysphoria through antisocial forms of enacting or sharing displeasure. They are not simply bad, hopeless, incorrigible people. They can be worked with in therapy like other primitive personalities if one understands and can utilize the effects the patient has on an average therapist.

There is, however, a depreciatory attitude toward individuals burdened with a character diagnosis. In many training institutions personality disorders are not regarded as "good treatment cases." They may sarcastically be referred to as "PD's," with knee-jerk suspiciousness about their motivation and treatability. They are, in effect, often extruded from a clinic's teaching population (Lion and Leaff, 1973). Clinical staff do not like their repeated demands for help, coupled with their insistence that their troubles always originate outside themselves. Their infantile manner, omnipotent demands, and lack of introspection cause them to be rejected. Their hedonism and requirements for instant gratification often clash head-on with the personal values of clinical staff.

The antisocial veneer does have a curious attraction. Clinicians often focus on it, treating these individuals superficially, as though they had no inner dynamics. The inner desolation or chaos may be intolerable to doctor as well as patient. Since the behavior is repugnant, however, the patient is dismissed as a "psychopath" and the opportunity to understand his underlying psychopathology is lost (Protter and Travin, 1983). This anti-psychological attitude—ignoring an individual's inner world—is dehumanizing, but mirrors the way the therapist is treated by the patient. It is an essential element in the traditionally pessimistic attitude toward treatment of the antisocial syndromes.

Although the individuals exhibiting antisocial syndromes may be depersonalized in this way by those who deal with them, their psychology can reveal familiar, often manageable, human processes. When avenues of escape through action are cut off, these people show the dynamics of other, more treatable primitive personality disorders. "This pejorative term, psychopath, is accurate only insofar as it describes the back of a patient fleeing therapy. If a psychiatrist sees the same patient in a prison hospital, he may doubt that such a disorder exists" (Vaillant, 1975) Underlying the antisocial epithets are familiar clinical syndromes. Depression, for example, often lies behind the behavior of the aggressive personality disorders (Lion, 1972). This depression, produced by ordinary frustrations, accompanied by a sense of personal weakness and helplessness, leads to the violence these people manifest. In the presence of a facilitating environment and a therapist who is a match for the task, the depression is treatable.

SUCCESSFUL THERAPISTS

Before looking more closely at the pathological collusions the psychopath tends to enact with his surroundings, trying to articulate the relevant processes in the therapist, and, where possible, suggesting techniques for managing them, let us examine certain characteristics of therapists who successfully deal with antisocial patients. The ideal therapist is a readily perceptible, accessible person, differentiated by sharply defined characteristics, so that the patient can form a clear picture of him as a model for identification (Adler and Shapiro, 1973). The therapist can usefully adopt an informal, self-revealing style (Lion, 1981). He must be warm and understanding, but not uncritical, because he needs to confront maladaptive behavior. "I'm OK, you're not OK" may have some therapeutic value, according to Lion, who advises, in appropriate context, a direct confrontation of the patient's lack of success using his pathological style. At the same time, the therapist must help his patient define "problem areas" rather than accept the patient's picture of himself as totally bad. It is very helpful to particularize problems, as these people usually have had very little realistic, nonpunitive feedback in their lives. Often they have experienced a pathological acceptance of their actual badness, along with unrealistic attributions. The therapist, therefore, must not collude in their black-white, polarized, global thinking. "Frank descriptions of one's own reaction to violent [individuals], given spontaneously, have the remarkable therapeutic effect of helping them separate themselves from . . . an illusionary omnipotence and to see themselves in a realistic mirror" (King, 1976).

The treatment of the antisocial syndromes requires active involvement rather than an expectant or nondirective approach. Therapist passivity has been correlated with a negative outcome for incarcerated delinquents. Those who respond positively to therapy judge their therapist to be firm, as well as warm and understanding (Persons and Pepinsky, 1966). "The effective therapist will make it clear that he sees through the manipulative attempts of the patient, and will continue to be realistically rather than gullibly supportive" (Suedfeld and Landon, 1975). The therapist must have the capacity to set clearly defined limits, well explained to the patient. The rules must be enforced firmly and promptly, otherwise the treatment structure is disrupted and essential respect for the therapist is lost.

Latent antiauthoritarian attitudes of the therapist quickly become manifest and are exploited (Macdonald, 1965). Patients may vicariously gratify unconscious wishes or fantasies of the therapist, which may be one reason therapists choose to work with such persons in the first place. Inmates do things to others about which therapists cannot allow themselves even to have conscious fantasies. When the therapist is intrigued with such stories of crime, inmates correctly perceive that they are admired or envied for their badness. Obviously, this jeopardizes treatment.

It is particularly important that the therapist be able to modulate and constructively discharge his own anxiety. Sociopaths, "brought up to believe that anxiety is too dreadful to be borne and too awful to confess [are] reassured that someone can be anxious and yet in control" (Vaillant, 1975). One must show the capacity to bear intrapsychically what the patient cannot—this is the model for identification.

Therapeutic modesty is a prerequisite. How little we really know about the treatment of personality disorders, despite the wealth of material which has been written on the subject! Therapeutic omnipotence, even enthusiasm, may lead to severe disappointment for both patient and therapist. Some individuals do benefit from treatment; many do not.

In sum, that elusive and difficult-to-define characteristic, maturity, is a critical element in the personality of those who would attempt the frustrating task of treating antisocial patients. One wonders how this is to be found in therapists who have led a relatively sheltered academic life in the long process of earning a doctoral degree. Sociopaths have lived more in the world, and have learned from it. Is it any wonder that the street-wise psychopath is such a difficult challenge to a therapist during training or the early professional stages of his career?

THE THERAPIST'S FEELINGS

Despite the emergence of theoretical knowledge and treatment modalities for the antisocial syndromes, one of the primary roadblocks to successful treatment is the therapist's own feelings. The treatment of neurotic patients does not arouse such strong feelings. This emotional constellation, this countertransference, poses a unique set of problems which must be resolved if treatment is to be useful.

Freud introduced the term "countertransference" in 1910 to refer to the neurotic conflicts of the therapist which were reactivated within the therapeutic setting by the transferences of the patient. "We have become aware of the 'counter-transference,' which arises in [the physician] as a result of the patient's influence on his unconscious feelings, and we are almost inclined to insist that he shall recognize this countertransference in himself and overcome it. We have noticed that no psychoanalyst goes further than his own complexes and internal resistances permit" (Freud, 1910). Subsequent writers have developed a view of countertransference less as a flaw in the therapist and more as a rich source of information about nonverbal communication. The less rigorous popular usage of the term, which will be employed here, defines countertransference broadly as any emotional reaction the clinician has toward his patient. It includes reactions to the patient's reality, his transference, and the setting in which he is treated—the totality of the therapist's reactions to his patient.

While countertransference reactions may represent the reemergence of neurotic character traits of the therapist, and thus be quite individualized, there is a set of reactions which are more universal. These reactions occur as a result of the patient's primitive defenses, such as splitting, denial, projection, and acting-out—defenses against poorly tolerated feelings. The reactions are based in the character pathology of the patients and are to be expected in the treatment of the antisocial syndromes.

The phenomenon of countertransference was originally viewed pejoratively; it was an aberration in the therapist, something basically wrong that had to be overcome. Current therapeutic technique, however, involves the active use of countertransference reactions as a part of the treatment rather than just things to be "overcome." It is not the countertransference or the feeling that interferes, but the therapist's use of it—whether it is unrecognized and collusively enacted or recognized and looked upon as a source of data.

Because countertransference is a reenactment of unrecognized elements of a patient's earliest relationships as he perceived them, it has the potential of providing valuable information about the nature of the patient's early formative relationships. These have not been internalized in such useful forms as memories and awareness. In situations in which words are not available or memories fail to describe the nature of early life, countertransference serves as a vivid, if primitive, mode of communication to the therapist about the emotional flavor of that early life. Countertransference, if the information can be decoded, becomes an invaluable tool for understanding the patient. "It is often the other people in contact with the patient who find themselves experiencing the affect he is avoiding" (Frosch, 1983). Problems, however, arise from repression of countertransference and, at the opposite pole, from becoming overwhelmed by it (Racker, 1957). When unconscious, countertransference may generate well-rationalized but destructive acting-out by the therapist.

Countertransference can prevent the therapist from being his best therapeutic self, interfering with his perceptions and thinking, as well as making him exquisitely uncomfortable. Immature characterologic defenses are contagious. "In the presence of a drug addict liberals become prejudiced; the masochist elicits our own latent sadism, and the malingerer our passive-aggression. When baited by their adolescent children, even the most reasonable and staid parents become hopelessly involved and utterly unreasonable" (Vaillant, 1975).

In addition to complicating the treatment of individuals, countertransference contributes to the attrition of personnel at institutions dealing with antisocial syndromes. The work is hard, more so because of the personal myths the inexperienced have about therapeutic work. Countertransference often undermines the staff's feelings of competence and self-respect, adding to the phenomenon known as "burnout."

Often rationalized as a realistic assessment of treatment results, the traditional therapeutic pessimism about psychopaths may be regarded as a countertransference response in itself. The bias against treating psychopaths is rationalized as well as reinforced by the myth of untreatability; in turn, the myth of untreatability is both a cause and an effect of countertransference.

SPECIFIC COUNTERTRANSFERENCE REACTIONS

Fear of Assault or Harm

Fear may be rational or irrational. Some anxiety is therapeutic wisdom, leading the therapist to monitor the relationship. When fear is rational, the first priority is safety rather than further analysis. Such fears must be carefully assessed, clarifying differences between fantasy and reality, between feeling and acting. Real dangers must not be minimized or denied. "Rarely, the patient may be so determined to provoke a rejection that in fact he gives the psychiatrist the choice of withdrawing or being destroyed. To persist in the treatment of a patient where there are substantial risks of this order is to fall into the ultimate snare of one's own narcissism, namely the unrealistic belief that one is physically invulnerable" (Maltsberger and Buie, 1974).

Fears of physical assault may be less rational. The therapist's frustration can produce anger, which is projected as a fear of ambush. A revival of memories of past events of violence in a therapist's life may lead to overestimation of the patient's potential for violence. Fear can lead to the abandonment of talking in favor of seclusion, restraint, or medication.

Fears of assault on the therapist usually diminish with experience. Although fantasies of the paranoid patient who kills his psychiatrist are common, in fact life-threatening assaults on therapists are very rare (Strasburger and Eddy, 1985). Learning to read the advance warnings of imminent danger and to determine what to do about them is part of developing clinical judgment. Although patients with aggressive impulses fear losing control of them and may become more agitated when they sense fear in others (Lion and Pasternak, 1973), the therapist who does not provoke or disclose his own difficulty with aggression will promote the patient's confidence in the stability required for treatment. Familiarity with the environment of the treating institution may also reassure one that security is adequate.

An unusual handling of countertransference fear is reported by Whitaker (1975):

One day in an initial interview with an adult veteran, I became terrified lest he kill me then and there. I excused myself, went across the
hall and got Dr. John Warkentin and brought him back into the interview. I told him and the patient of my fear. He said to the patient with
a perfectly straight face and in a serious tone, "I don't blame you a bit;
I've often wanted to kill Whitaker myself!" This confused me but it made
the patient's anger much more controllable, and we went on with a comfortable interview.

Wishnie (1977) describes a mismanagement of patients at a drug
treatment center, where staff members were terrified and sought to ap-
pease patients rather than confront and deal with their fears in more
productive ways. Unacknowledged fear reactions should be suspected
when there are unusual staff behavior patterns, such as calling in sick,
forgetting appointments, using excessive seclusion and restraint or higher
medication doses than needed, or early discharge of patients. In order
to enhance staff capacity to cope with fear-producing situations, staff
members, as a group, must be allowed to openly express fear.

Fears can also include fears of litigation (Haldipur, Dewan, and
Beal, 1982), increasingly so in the post-Tarasoff era, as courts sometimes hold therapists responsible for the behavior of their patients.
Paradoxically, when this fear is not acknowledged, it can produce its
own cause, as through the premature discharge of potentially violent
patients.

Helplessness and Guilt

Psychotherapy with antisocial patients is a difficult, slow-moving
task. The therapist cannot assume the existence of a collaborative
alliance. It is more probable that he will feel his efforts to help rejected
while he himself is devalued. The therapist often feels impotent in his
quest for change in the patient. Here the problem has to do in part
with the therapist's wish to do something to the patient rather than
to help him make more enlightened choices. Helplessness and guilt
about the patient's lack of improvement may lead to rage at the patient. This can become manifest either as emotional withdrawal or (by
reaction formation) as overresponsibility for what happens to the patient, with rescue attempts or "smothering."

Therapists in training or at the beginning of their professional careers
are particularly vulnerable to feelings of helplessness (Adler, 1972).

Patients project their own helplessness. The beginning therapist who feels inadequate due to his lack of experience believes his feelings are representative of the true state of affairs, rather than reflective of the countertransference.

Anticipatory guilt over harm to others as a result of inadequate or insufficient treatment is a common phenomenon. Beyond the rational concerns about patients who threaten others is the fantasy that the patient will commit a murder and the therapist will be held responsible. The anxiety is, of course, aggravated by recent legal decisions holding therapists responsible for injuries to third parties. This situation may actually represent the therapist's difficulty differentiating himself from the patient and his inappropriately holding himself responsible for the patient's behavior. It is a pervasive problem, for the therapist and the institutional setting have actually taken over some responsibility for the patient, when their task is, instead, to show the individual his responsibility for himself, his choice points, and their consequences.

Feelings of Invalidity and Loss of Identity

The therapist's idealized self-image as strong, loving, kind, etc., is threatened as the patient defends against assault on his fragile identity by producing a similar dilemma for the therapist. In a general sense, as the patient disowns his problems and ascribes them to the therapist, the therapist may come to feel that *he* owns them. Unwilling to experience this dysphoria, the therapist may engage in an unconscious counterprojective game of "you touched it last" as he attempts to wriggle free of the patient's attributions.

All therapists, whatever their level of professional experience, require validation (Adler, 1970). Devaluation is devastating, producing feelings of worthlessness, depression, fear, rage, guilt, shame, and envy. It represents an acceptance of the patient's projected badness. The devaluation experienced in the treatment of personality disorders removes our sense of "wholeness" about our own personality. The neophyte therapist is particularly vulnerable. He has little confidence in his abilities as he stands at the threshold of professional identity information, a process which will lead to self-awareness as a person with skills and knowledge of the worth and limits of his work. The patient who tells the therapist that his personal and professional doubts are correct touches a particularly vulnerable spot.

A more subtle problem occurs as a result of the cognitive styles of many patients who manifest antisocial syndromes. The literal, concrete conversation of such patients is often confined to monosyllabic responses to questions. The thinking of these patients is nonpsychological, reflecting an inner world without imagination or subtle nuances of feeling. They do not free-associate and often seem incapable of forming fantasies. Although impulsive, they seem at the same time to operate entirely on the basis of secondary process thinking. This style clashes with the therapist's modus operandi and thereby with his professional identity.

The therapist often feels as though something is keeping him from working in his usual way, something which threatens his professional autonomy. Since it may be hard for the therapist to identify the source of the trouble, it produces a subtle upset of his equilibrium. These patients, suffering from identity problems, lack a well-defined self-image, and view themselves basically as worthless, unlovable persons. "Their fundamental identity is unformed, and is essentially an amorphous, hollow shell, consisting mainly of the feeling of nonexistence. It is this vacuum that they project onto the therapist" (Giovacchini, 1972). The resultant painful feeling produces an existential anxiety in the therapist, which is often as persistent as it is difficult to decipher. It may take the form of professional rationalization, in which the patient is condemned as untreatable because he is too rigid and resistant.

Denial

"Denial is the most ubiquitous defense against anxiety generated by a violent patient" (Lion and Leaff, 1973). It may lead to a failure to elicit information about weapons, lethal skills, past criminal or violent acts, or even driving habits. "To face the issue of dangerousness is very threatening to the physician, much as it is to face the seductiveness of a female patient; the therapist's human vulnerability emerges" (Lion and Leaff, 1973).

The therapist may counterphobically place himself in a dangerous position. One inexperienced resident known to the author responded to two adolescents bullying a female patient by calling them "chicken." His chivalrous indiscretion was rewarded by their attempt to throw him from a third-story window.

Rejection

The patient deals with all transactions as current, conscious, and deliberate. The coin of interchange is action, struggle. Language is assaultive, locked in the moment, and nonreflective. "They blunt the unconscious, obviate the sympathetic, race past the rational, and exhibit no evidence of conscience" (King, 1976). It is easy to moralize about manipulation, impulsivity, and flouting of social conventions, yet an attitude of acceptance without moralizing is important. The therapist who treats this type of patient must maintain a delicate balance between a talion rejection of the patient and a "masochistic submission to unreasonable demands" (Frosch, 1983).

Rejection may take subtle forms, such as a lack of emotional investment on the part of the therapist. Boredom can be one sign of emotional withdrawal, with the therapist projecting his feelings at the expense of contact and activity with the patient.

Hatred

Transference hatred provokes countertransference hatred, a combination of aversion and malice. The patient may provoke countertransference hatred to substantiate his own projections. His basic questions about the reliability, worth, and integrity of other people amount to a transference assault on the therapist. Such assaults on the therapist's self-esteem arouse hatred. The narcissistic aspirations of the therapist to heal all, to know all, and to love all make him especially vulnerable.

Although the danger of a patient's suicide may be heightened by ignoring countertransference hatred (Maltsberger and Buie, 1974), the generation of that hatred may be a positive accomplishment for the patient (Winnicott, 1947). "If the patient can experience an affect such as hatred, and if he can provoke others to hate him, he is creating a situation where love can also exist. To hate someone means that his existence is acknowledged" (Giovacchini, 1972).

Rage and the Wish to Destroy

Rage tends to be a final common pathway for the emotions of both therapist and patient. Whether it be through reactively mirroring the emotion of his patient or through the more complex route of identification with the aggressor, the therapist will find anger to be a constant companion in the treatment of antisocial syndromes. Some of this has to do with the primitive interpersonal world of such people, in which the experience of pleasure in mutuality is nonexistent: I live; you die.

Often the rage is only perceptible through an awareness of the defenses against it. The patient's defiant, remorseless, threatening attitude provokes its punitive reaction, with which the therapist may deal outside his awareness. When there is a loss of the therapist's own ego boundaries, he often attempts to control the patient as though he were a dangerous aspect of himself (the therapist). The largest single problem in the work can be "the appearance in the dyad of an oppositional stance due to countertransference rage in the therapist stirred up by the patient—a stance that can lead, in turn, to fruitless struggle, recapitulation of infantile modes of relating, and suspension of useful investigation" (Gutheil, 1985).

Those interested in the treatment of antisocial syndromes are often people who have difficulty with their own expression of aggression, people who tend to internalize anger (Lion, 1981). As patients become demanding and manipulative, and as they begin to act out their thoughts and feelings, therapists become aware of their own irritation and anger. This is a distinct therapeutic challenge. What is needed is "an effective therapist who is comfortable with his own anger so that he is aware of it, can stand it without projecting it, can test how much really belongs to the patient, and does not lose his ability when faced with a frightened and frightening patient who never had that capacity or has lost it" (Adler and Shapiro, 1973).

SPECIAL PROBLEMS OF SETTINGS

The setting in which treatment of antisocial syndromes occurs can have a significant role in evoking countertransference responses, separate and apart from the role of therapist-patient interaction. Treatment often occurs in prisons or settings where a punitive philosophy is at odds with professional training emphasizing empathic caring and respect for others. Correctional personnel inevitably test mental health personnel, frequently with jibes and "jokes," in order to check their resilience, to see if they will retaliate, or to find out "whose side they really are on." Identification with this "sadism" is all too easy for mental health staff, who bring their own set of problems and issues to work with them at such institutions. At the opposite pole, anger at being witness to the cruelty which inmates suffer may produce an overidentification with them; this overidentification makes it hard to clarify the role inmates play in incidents or to help them accept responsibly (Adler, 1984).

The therapist working in a prison setting cannot avoid being characterized by his patients as an agent of the authoritarian system. Inmates externalize their sense of their own badness, generalizing about the badness of the world and of people in authority. There is an implicit question: Will the therapist act dishonestly, like a criminal? "An encounter with workers who acknowledge that they represent the authority in power, and, as a part of it, are honest, empathic, and nonpunitive can provide a new kind of experience that discourages [such] primitive generalization" (Adler, 1984).

Outside prison settings, the institution can still have a role in countertransference formation (Gendel and Reiser, 1981). When a chronically ill individual has a stable, sustaining relation with an institution, institutional countertransference can block change and contribute to hopelessness about treatment. In these situations the patient is often treated by a succession of trainees who never really get to know him. The therapist usually feels the patient is well-known to the clinic, even though little information about him may be available in the record. Because the patient's primary relationship is with the facility, the therapist often believes that he cannot be important to the patient. He may see no richness to the patient's inner life, fail to work toward developing his particular potentials, and believe that management of the institutional transference is the only important function of therapy. A banal form of "cookbook therapy" follows.

SOLUTIONS TO COUNTERTRANSFERENCE PROBLEMS

Solutions to the problems posed by countertransference can be found outside the therapist as well as in the therapist's inner world. The use of secure facilities has already been recommended. Some assistance with the intensity of countertransference may be found through treatment dilution, without withdrawing from the patient or giving up on him. The use of treatment groups, as opposed to individual treatment, is often recommended (Lion and Bach-y-Rita, 1970). Reduction of patient-therapist contact through infrequent meetings or the use of walk-in clinics has also been recommended. Short-term treatment, centered on specific task-oriented issues, has been proposed as a way of reducing countertransference issues. This approach has been attempted in a unique way in wilderness experience programs (Matthews and Reid, 1981). Some advocate simple incarceration as a treatment mode. This, of course, removes the issue of countertransference. It also avoids the patient's inner reality and is indistinguishable from punishment.

When the countertransference problem is institutional, the periodic staff conference may provide an opportunity to integrate and modulate countertransference reactions, as well as to improve overall morale within the institution. It provides an opportunity for staff reality testing of the countertransference, as well as for peer supervision. Staff awareness and agreement about limited goals and restraint of therapeutic omnipotence helps prevent pessimism, hopelessness, and the "burnout" phenomenon.

The inner world of the therapist—the locus of the countertransference experience—is perhaps the most fruitful place to focus efforts at countertransference resolution. Winnicott (1947) emphasizes self-knowledge: "However much he [the psychiatrist] loves his patients he cannot avoid hating them and fearing them, and the better he knows this the less will hate and fear be the motive determining what he does to his patients."

The therapist must learn to use his own personality as an instrument in the treatment process. Because his reactions to the patient are a means of understanding how the patient treats important others and how he feels treated by them, the countertransference can lead to identification and verbalization of the patient's previously inaccessible feeling states. Reacting to such transference-countertransference situations with interest rather than anxiety or anger is most helpful. This requires a capacity for reflection and self-observation. The therapist may feel anxious or angry "but his attitude about his fear and anger is non-anxious and benevolent. He is reacting and at the same time is analytically interested in his reactions" (Giovacchini, 1979, p. 488).

In his article on taking care of the "hateful" medical patient, Groves (1978) offers some suggestions which may be usefully applied to the treatment of the antisocial syndromes. He has grouped these individuals and the reactions which they evoke into four categories: "Dependent clingers" evoke aversion in the physician, with which he must deal by limiting his expectations of the treatment. "Entitled demanders" evoke anger and a wish to counterattack, which should be dealt with by acknowledging the patient's entitlement to good care. "Manipulative help-rejectors" evoke depression, which should be confronted through an acknowledgment to the patient that his pessimism is empathically shared. "Self-destructive deniers" evoke the physician's malice. In this situation the clinician must reduce his expectations that he can give perfect care and be willing to accept the possibility of suicide by his patient as ultimately beyond his control.

Giovachini (1972) believes that honesty is especially useful in one's approach to these patients. Again, in terms of identification, if the therapist acknowledges his mistakes and takes responsibility for them, he provides a model for the patient to do the same.

> To admit that it is possible that the patient may be correct and to investigate further what might have occurred shows respect for the patient's integrity as a sensitive observer, who is concerned about his self-esteem. Furthermore, it also demonstrates that the therapist is not ashamed of the irrational within himself, making the patient more accepting of his own inner primitive forces. A calm acceptance of the possibility of a countertransference reaction and a willingness to investigate further represent an active demonstration of the therapeutic process and a convincing example of the faith one has [in one's treatment method.] . . . Honesty is a pragmatic approach that makes sense in the therapeutic process (Giovacchini, 1972).

This is especially true with dishonest individuals.

Kernberg believes that the therapist's capacity to experience concern is important in overcoming the effects of aggression and self-aggression. Concern manifests itself in an awareness of the serious nature of destructive and self-destructive impulses in the patient. It is present in the authentic wish and need to help the patient in spite of his transitory "badness."

> In concrete terms, concern implies ongoing self-criticism by the analyst, unwillingness to accept impossible situations in a passive way, and a continuous search for new ways of handling a prolonged crisis. It implies active involvement of the therapist as opposed to narcissistic withdrawal, and realization of the ongoing need of consultation with and help from one's colleagues. The last point is important: willingness to

review a certain case with a consultant or colleague, as contrasted with
secrecy about one's work, is a good indication of concern (1965).

Kernberg's conception of concern would appear to have ethical as well
as pragmatic value, as ethics depend for their base on an affirmation of
life and caring feelings for others (Ciccone and Clements, 1984).

The treatment process which has been described is clearly a difficult
one. Why would a therapist want to undertake it? Is it simply an exercise in masochism or martyrdom?

I think not. Many antisocial patients are fascinating individuals.
They have things to teach about life in general, as well as about psychotherapy in particular. The benefits both to them and to society from
their rehabilitation can be most gratifying to those who treat them.
Is it absolutely necessary for the therapist to have such adverse feelings? They are an integral part of an intimate relationship with people who commit antisocial acts. Not to be adversely affected by such
people would be a denial of one's humanity. However, "being human
includes having failings. Possibly without such failings there would be
no treatment of patients who have so often been used by persons who
have to deny their own failings" (Giovacchini, 1979).

REFERENCES

Adler, G. (1970). Valuing and devaluing in the psychotherapeutic process. *Archives
of General Psychiatry*, 22:454–461.
Adler, G. (1972). Helplessness in the helpers. *British Journal of Medical Psychology*,
45, 315–326.
Adler, G. (1984). Correctional (prison) psychiatry. In Kaplan and Sadock (Eds.). *Com-
prehensive Textbook of Psychiatry*, (4th ed.). Baltimore: Williams and Wilkins.
Adler, G., & Shapiro, L. N. (1973). Some difficulties in the treatment of the aggressive,
acting out patient. *American Journal of Psychotherapy, 27*, 548–556.
Bromberg, W. (1953). The treatability of the psychopath. *American Journal of
Psychiatry* 110.
Ciccone, J., & Clements, C. (1984). Forensic psychiatry and applied clinical ethics:
theory and practice. *American Journal of Psychiatry, 141*, 395–399.
Cleckley, H. (1964). *The mask of sanity*. St. Louis: Mosby.
Freud, S. (1976). The future prospects of psycho-analytic therapy. In J. Strachey (Ed.
and Trans.) *The standard edition*. New York: Norton. *11*, pp. 141. (first published
in 1910.)
Frosch, J. (1983). The treatment of anti-social and borderline personality disorders.
Hospital and Community Psychiatry, 34, 243–248.
Gendel, M., & Reiser, D. (1981). Institutional countertransference. *American Journal
of Psychiatry, 138*, 508–511.

Giovacchini, P. (1972). Technical difficulties in treating some characterological disorders: countertransference problems. *International Journal of Psychoanalytic Psychotherapy, 1*, 112–27.

Giovacchini, P. (1979). *Treatment of primitive mental states.* New York: Jason Aronson.

Groves, J. (1978). Taking care of the hateful patient. *New Eng Journal of Medicine, 298*, 883–887.

Gutheil, T. (1985). Medicolegal pitfalls in the treatment of borderline patients. *American Journal Psychiatry, 142*, 9–14.

Haldipur, C., Dewan, M., and Beal, M. (1982). On fear in the countertransference. *American Journal of Psychotherapy, 36*, 240–7.

Kernberg, O. (1965). Notes on countertransference. *Journal of American Psychoanalytic Association, 13*, 38–56.

King, C. (1976). Countertransference and counter-experience in the treatment of violence prone youth. *American Journal of Orthopsychiatry, 46(1)*, 43–53.

Lion, J. (1972). The role of depression in the treatment of aggressive personality disorders. *American Journal of Psychiatry, 129*, 347–349.

Lion, J. (1981). Countertransference and other psychotherapy issues. In Reid W. H. (Ed.). *The treatment of antisocial syndromes.* New York: Van Nostrand Reinhold.

Lion, J., & Bach-y-Rita, G. (1970). Group psychotherapy with violent patients. *International Journal of Group Psychotherapy, 20*, 185–191.

Lion, J., & Leaff, L. (1973). On the hazards of assessing character pathology in an outpatient setting. *Psychiatric Quarterly, 47*, 104–109.

Lion, J., & Pasternak, S. (1973). Countertransference reactions to violent patients. *American Journal of Psychiatry, 130*, 207–210.

Macdonald, J. (1965). Acting out. *Archives of General Psychiatry, 13*, 439–43.

Maltsberger, J., & Buie, D. (1974). Countertransference hate in the treatment of suicidal patients. *Archives of General Psychiatry, 30*, 625–633.

Matthews, W., & Reid, W. (1981). A wilderness experience treatment program for offenders. In Reid, W. (Ed.). *The treatment of antisocial syndromes.* New York: Van Nostrand Reinhold.

Persons, R., & Pepinsky, H. (1966). Convergence in psychotherapy with delinquent boys. *Journal of Counseling Psychology, 13*, 329–334.

Protter, B., & Travin, S. (1983). The significance of countertransference and related issues in a multiservice court clinic. *Bulletin American Academy Psychiatry and Law 11*, 223–30.

Racker, H. (1957). The meanings and use of countertransference. *Psychoanalytic Quarterly, 26*, 303–357.

Strasburger, L., & Eddy, S. (1985). Violence to the therapist. Unpublished manuscript.

Suedfeld, P., & Landon, P. (1975). Approaches to treatment. In Hare, R., and Schalling, D. (Eds). *Psychopathic behavior: Approaches to research*, New York: Wiley.

Vaillant, G. (1975). Sociopathy as a human process. *Archives of General Psychiatry, 32*, 178.

Whitaker, C. (1975). Psychotherapy of the absurd with a special emphasis on the psychotherapy of aggression. *Family Process, 14*, 1.

Winnicott, D. (1958). Hate in the countertransference. In the *Collected papers.* New York: Basic Books. pp. 194–203. (first published in 1947.)

Wishnie, H. (1977). *The impulsive personality.* New York: Plenum.

9

Inpatient Treatment
of Antisocial Youth

William Shamblin

Adolescents with severely antisocial features are often unable to experience psychological growth or improvement in an outpatient treatment setting. Inpatient treatment may then be indicated. Work with this group of patients is interesting and rewarding, but also challenging and often lengthy. This chapter provides a brief review of the literature and a description of a theoretical point of view which can serve as a basis for inpatient work. Long-term treatment that provides structure, support, affection and education about health and psychopathology is helpful to these youngsters.

LITERATURE REVIEW

A short review of the literature will clarify some of the controversy regarding treatment of antisocial adolescents and also show some of the prevailing opinions about the elements of appropriate treatment. There are questions in the existing literature regarding the effectiveness of various treatments for antisocial persons. While Aichhorn (1935) claimed very positive results with long-term residential work, Levine and Bornstein (1972) find little evidence of positive change with treatment. Masterson (1967) has concluded that children with such serious character problems as antisocial behavior do not mature and improve without appropriate help.

Vaillant and Perry (1980) have suggested that severely antisocial individuals are reachable, understandable, and treatable in an institutional setting. They claim that the "uncaring and unreachable" characteristics described by Cleckley (1964) as applying to psychopaths in fact apply to antisocial persons who are in flight. Vaillant feels they are "all too human" when stopped from running away: "Once an antisocial personality feels that he is among peers, his lack of motivation for change disappears."

At Highland Hospital we asked parents of patients discharged from two to nine years ago 1) how much their child improved in hospital; 2) how much improvement occurred from hospital admission to the present; and 3) how much the hospital helped their child (Shamblin, 1985). Twenty-nine of the 47 patients in the study were judged to have significant antisocial features. Antisocial patients were thought by most parents to have improved in hospital and to have continued to improve after discharge. On average, parents thought the adolescent unit helped their antisocial child "a moderate amount." These antisocial patients were reported only slightly less improved than the non-antisocial patients studied. Improvements from admission to discharge and from admission to the time of follow-up were statistically significant ($p < .01$) for both the group of antisocial patients and the group of all patients studied.

Jenkins (1960) maintains that the antisocial person "suffers from inadequate inhibition over his behavior." He recommends teaching patients to establish internal controls by "maintaining a firm but accepting attitude toward the patient while imposing external limitations on his actions."

Kernberg (1975) has discussed in detail the intrapsychic functioning of certain character-disordered persons. He sees antisocial personality as being a "lower level" character disorder with basically borderline personality structure. He believes that treatability of antisocial personalities is related to the degree of superego development.

Rinsley (1980) has described the basic requirements for milieu treatment of a variety of ill youngsters and their families, including borderline youth described as "delinquent" and having "superego defects." He also comments on the intrapsychic, family, and social attributes of antisocial youngsters and recommends "more humane, individualized and in-depth treatment." Marohn, Dalle-Molle, McCarter, and Linn (1980) and McCord (1982) have described well-organized residential treatment programs and found them to produce lasting good effects.

Lewis and Balla (1976) found resistance in treatment personnel to looking beyond antisocial features to other diagnosable problems, saying that "it is clear that the frequency of neurological and psychopathological conditions that can either contribute to or mimic antisocial behavior is high" and that these problems "might be helped with appropriate treatment" if diagnosed.

Meeks (1980) discusses conduct-disordered children, who are likely to have a "bleak future" because of sociopathic tendencies. He says that active treatment is indicated for these youngsters and that an inpatient unit or residential treatment center is often necessary. "Most successful treatment programs seem to use a combination of behavior modification techniques, family therapy, relationship psychotherapy and peer pressure in treating the behaviorally disturbed child and adolescent." He encourages families and staff to be prepared for a long and difficult course of treatment.

A TYPICAL CASE

John is now 21 years old and doing reasonably well. He has a regular job. He has not been in trouble with the law for four years. He sees his psychiatrist weekly and, in addition, whenever he feels the need. He has a girlfriend and a positive but limited relationship with his disorganized family.

John began to seek help from mental health professionals when he was 13. He went to a mental health center after having problems with fighting at school and stealing. He was given a diagnosis of "adjustment reaction of adolescence." His divorced parents had two sessions in which consistent discipline was discussed. John talked about his feelings for two sessions. He seemed to be somewhat improved, so further sessions were not offered, even though the parents thought John had "deep-seated problems" that hadn't been discussed or worked through. John remembers that he was confused and angry about his parents' recent separation. He now says that he had been stealing and fighting frequently since age nine.

Soon thereafter, his mother moved to another town with her new boyfriend; John went with them. She was permissive and easy for John to manipulate, unlike his father, who was rigid, stern and sometimes brutal in his discipline. John missed a lot of school just because he didn't want to go. He was involved in drug abuse. He was picked up by police for selling drugs and for stealing, and was put on probation. He decided that he was getting in too much trouble living with his mom and made arrangements to move back in with his dad (who now had a new wife). His mother agreed.

John developed a "tough guy" reputation at school. In spite of being rather small, he would fight anybody. He later said that this was a good way to take out the anger he felt. He also remembers thinking that, sooner or later, he would be killed, and that that would be good.

John had great difficulty getting along with his father. He felt unaccepted and unliked by his new stepmother. He spent a lot of time away from home "hanging out" with his friends. At times his father and stepmother condoned and encouraged this but at other times they attempted to restrict him.

At school, John was thought to be bright and was well liked by some teachers, in spite of being unable or unwilling to study or attend consistently.

John was arrested for breaking and entering after he and a group of friends stole food and other things from a house. He was living away from home at the time, moving from place to place. His lawyer asked that he have a psychiatric evaluation because of the reckless abandon with which he approached his crime and his possible prison sentence. An inpatient evaluation was allowed by the court.

John was an inpatient for 19 months. After a six-week evaluation, the psychiatrist recommended inpatient treatment prior to trial. By the time of trial, John had been able to understand how he had been acting out his anger at his parents and himself by putting himself in dangerous situations that would sooner or later prove destructive to him. He had seen how his verbal skills were significantly below his nonverbal skills and had been able to relate this to his school difficulties. Even though he had many arguments with hospital staff and had been enraged to realize that the hospital could and would control him, John had been able to understand something about the harshness of his conscience (like his father), and its inconsistency (like his mother). He had been able to find some real interest in how this problem with his conscience was affecting his life. He had little trust in anyone, but was somehow able to tell the court that he wanted to stay in the hospital for treatment (even if he might be sentenced later for his crimes).

Hospitalization was very difficult for both John and the staff. Underlying borderline personality features were played out in interpersonal interaction with staff and peers. John set some staff up to be like his mother. He was very "nice" to them, expecting to be able to take from them without being disciplined by them in return. He treated other staff in provocative ways that tended to bring out harsh criticism, re-enacting the pattern he had with his father.

When staff and the patient group began to point out these behaviors, John was furious. Then he was thoughtful. For a while he took pride in being able to fool staff; then he began to see how much trouble and paranoia he was bringing into his life just to prove that he could not be completely controlled by others.

At first, work with his parents was very difficult, but eventually they were able to work together. Each had been using him to prove that the other had been at fault in their unsuccessful marriage. The mother attempted to prove that she had been right by making John like her and like living with her. The father tried to show that he could make John mind and obey rules when his ex-wife could not. When the parents were able to give up proving each other wrong through John, he was able to feel better about himself and his family.

Many of John's important lessons were ideas to which he could not listen unless he first heard them from the patient group. He was so used to arguing with and mistrusting adults that he automatically became defensive when staff tried to advise him. When his peers began to say similar things, however, he was able to pay more attention. He later said that the hospital staff provided necessary structure and limits while the peer group encouraged him to look at his problems.

John got a volunteer community service job to demonstrate unself-ishness to the court and staff. At first, he complained about "working for nothing" and said his heart wasn't in it. He was fairly dependable, however, and later liked the idea. As is often the case, real personality change was preceded by *pretending* to be different. John was also able to get a paying job while in the hospital. This seemed to be a real psychological turning point; the job allowed him to feel more secure and to have more self-esteem. He tended to set his supervisors up as parent figures, however, and in the beginning needed much help from hospital staff to avoid reenacting old family patterns at work.

While John continued to have the same kinds of problems during hospitalization and after as he had before admission, their frequency and severity were less. After more than a year in the hospital, he was better able to talk about his feelings and to make and keep agreements about misbehavior. Discharge plans were made. The court decided to keep him on probation for a lengthy period. John was able to realize that this would probably be helpful to him.

After discharge, he had some rough times. While he lived on his own, he was able to talk problems out with hospital staff he had come to trust and with his probation officer, instead of engaging in serious antisocial behavior as he had before hospitalization.

John's life is still troubled. He works in weekly psychotherapy to keep improving his approach to himself and others. Psychiatric hospitalization was very important in helping him toward a reasonably happy, productive life.

DISCUSSION

Often youngsters like John are not considered for inpatient treatment, even though they may have the financial resources that would make psychiatric hospitalization possible. Parents and some people in the helping professions don't want to think of the antisocial adolescent as mentally ill. Many third-party payers reinforce this idea, because inpatient treatment is relatively expensive in the short run. Here are some facts about psychiatric hospitalization which will allow people in the helping professions to make good decisions about referring patients for inpatient work:

1) There are logical criteria which indicate the appropriateness of inpatient treatment for a child or adolescent.
2) Antisocial youngsters who are appropriate for inpatient treatment also regularly demonstrate other "lower-level" character pathology (antisocial, schizoid, paranoid, narcissistic, infantile, or borderline). These problems, as well as affective, developmental, attention deficit, and other problems, deserve attention and treatment along with the antisocial disorder.
3) Youngsters with lower-level character pathology (antisocial and other) often improve in specially designed inpatient settings.
4) Effective treatment units must offer high levels of control, positive staff attitude, interpretation of pathology, and teaching of healthy alternatives to pathological behavior and psychodynamics.

5) Successful treatment of these patients occurs in predictable stages (resistance and testing, productive work, termination and transition) over many months of treatment.

6) As these patients improve, their psychodynamics and behavior change from unstable, mistrustful, dishonest, and manipulative to more stable, more trusting and more honest. A communicating-negotiating style of thinking and behaving emerges, along with a healthier superego and ego.

1) Criteria for Inpatient Treatment

Rinsley (1980) has enumerated the criteria of various authors for admission to long-term inpatient treatment, and added criteria of his own. He suggests that inpatient treatment is warranted by (a) behavior which is dangerous, unmanageable, or intolerable in nonpsychiatric settings; (b) psychological developmental failure of a serious nature which has been unresponsive to outpatient treatment; or (c) various sorts and degrees of psychopathology which have been shown to require inpatient treatment for substantial improvement. Youngsters with severe antisocial features often satisfy all three criteria.

Young patients should be given a chance to demonstrate that they can and will improve in the context of family life and outpatient treatment, unless it is very clear from the seriousness of their pathology that outpatient work will be futile. Those who can't or won't improve with good outpatient work should be placed in inpatient units.

Antisocial youngsters are often able to evade thorough evaluation and treatment in even the best-designed outpatient settings. Work in the outpatient setting should incorporate a clear schedule for steady improvement, which, if not met, would mandate inpatient treatment.

2) The Appropriateness of Mixed Lower-level Character Diagnosis

The stereotypic purely antisocial (without moral or superego development) adolescent who cannot be reached by treatment does not really exist. In the author's experience, (a) none of these youth are completely without moral development; (b) all have significant other lower-level character pathology in addition to and other than antisocial pathology; (c) many have affective, developmental, attention deficit, and neurological disorders as well; and (d) not all families of these patients are seriously pathological. Heredity, biology, and characteristics of temperament sometimes encourage the development of the problem in a way that cannot be effectively dealt with by the resources of a family, but can be managed by an inpatient unit. The antisocial features may have been so compelling that family and even mental health professionals overlooked the almost inevitable presence of other pathology.

The current practice of encouraging "conduct disorder" diagnoses for many of these children can contribute to poor and superficial diagnosis. Some describe them as having "behavior problems," as if the pathological behavior were not based on pathological thinking and feeling. This superficial behavioral diagnosis leads to superficial treatment that seeks only to modify behavior. This is not as helpful as the multi-dimensional treatment that can come from deeper understanding of the child.

3) Lower-level Character Pathology Is Often Improved by Long-term Inpatient Treatment

I know of no well-controlled, prospective studies that could prove the effectiveness (or lack thereof) of long-term inpatient work in this area.

McCord (1982, p. 262) concluded that a "progressive psychiatrically oriented" milieu dramatically helped antisocial youngsters to "develop consciences, absorb new codes of ethics, and identify with helpful adults." He compared those youngsters with similar youth in a traditional reformatory that taught strict discipline and vocational skills. The children in the reformatory neither improved nor learned very much compared to those in the psychiatric milieu. Marohn et al. (1980) conclude that useful, lasting improvement of juvenile delinquents is frequent after inpatient work in their specialized setting.

While there are numerous examples of improvement in antisocial youngsters after inpatient treatment, the prognosis for all patients with lower-level character problems must be guarded. Even so, an adequate inpatient trial is indicated for these children, since their prognosis without treatment is so grim (Masterson, 1967). In my opinion, at least two years of appropriate treatment without any appreciable improvement is required before we can think about labeling a child "untreatable."

4) Characteristics of Effective Programs

Rinsley (1980) has described characteristics of good treatment and good treatment settings for these children, while Marohn et al. (1980) have written about inpatient work with antisocial youth in particular. Some of their suggestions are discussed below.

Prepubertal children should not be treated on the same units with adolescents. Adolescent pathology has an overwhelmingly negative, destructive influence on younger patients.

The inpatient unit must have facilities for complete patient-family evaluation. It must be capable of high levels of control of patient behavior. The staff must be capable of high levels of communication and cooperation, while tolerating much interpersonal and intrapsychic conflict. Staff must point out, and teach patients about, both pathological and healthy thinking and behavior. This often takes place in an atmosphere of social and emotional turmoil; discrimination and awareness of countertransference are crucial. Both the unit and the institution must be able to patiently carry out treatment for many difficult months, offering a full program of therapeutic school, individually designed activities, vocational training, and individual, group, family, and milieu therapy.

Evaluation. Full psychiatric-psychological-medical-neurological-educational evaluation must be avalable for each patient. Some programs prefer that evaluation be done prior to admission. Others admit patients who seem to need long-term treatment and complete the full evaluation after admission. Neuropsychological testing is often indicated, as are special tests for learning disabilities. Each child should have a complete medical history and physical exam. Neurological problems should be ruled out with examination, EEG, and CAT scan as appropriate. Family dynamics must be expertly evaluated.

Control. To be successful, an inpatient setting must be able and willing to stop behavior which is judged to be unhealthy. If behavior control is not carried out promptly and thoroughly, patients will avoid treatment and improvement by acting-out.

This process requires (a) a set of rules and a general understanding by ward staff about what is and isn't approved and healthy behavior; (b) regular and effective monitoring and evaluation of patients' behavior; and (c) staff in sufficient numbers to enforce rules and decisions even if the patient actively resists. Patients must know that the staff is in charge. Antisocial patients must learn to go by and then respect even seemingly illogical or unimportant rules, because these rules are the way that groups and individuals in society communicate and live with each other.

Communication. Staff must be good at communicating and cooperating, so that they will really function as a treatment team. The team must have a clear leader who acts with authority when necessary. Decisions are best made by team consensus, however, with the leader functioning as the leader of an orchestra of professionals who know well how to do their individual jobs.

The treatment team must present a solid wall of therapeutic management to the patient on an around-the-clock basis. The leader must keep each member of the team working toward appropriate therapeutic goals. Each shift of staff members must be able to work with other shifts.

Tolerance. Staff members in such treatment settings must like their work and genuinely like their patients. It is often very difficult to maintain constant disapproval for even minor misbehavior, constant concern for patients' improvement, and constant vigilance for the well-being of others, while liking the patient all the while. These patients have often been resented and rejected by parents who really did not want them. They know how to ward off and protect themselves from people who don't like them.

Staff members should keep in mind that they must treat the patient in the way that they want the patient's *conscience* eventually to treat the patient. If genuine positive regard is not expressed by a staff member, the introject of that staff person (which could become part of a more healthy superego constellation) will not be positive and encouraging and will not be useful to the patient. It is important in this regard for staff to schedule good times and playful situations that encourage real enjoyment; however, one should avoid the unrealistic overinvolvement that most lower-level patients and occasional staff seek. Therapeutic interchanges must be firm, but always done with kind concern. Continuous harsh negative confrontation is destructive.

The treatment team, and the hospital itself, must be comfortable working for one to three years or more with patients who don't get better quickly and who have to demonstrate and discuss the same problems over and over again. Staff must have a basic understanding of the slow process of real character change and of the stages of inpatient treatment.

Staff teaching. The program must have staff with sufficient therapeutic knowledge and skill to recognize and interpret pathology and to demonstrate healthy alternatives to the patient. Patients must learn about the psychological roots of pathological and healthy behavior if they are to mindfully continue healthy patterns after discharge. They must be confronted over and over again about their faulty, irresponsible, and pathological thinking. Keeping antisocial (or any other) patients so busy and controlled that they don't have time or opportunity to misbehave is of little use to lasting incorporation and generalization of healthy behavior.

Staff should be as well trained as possible in psychodynamics, including object relations theory related to lower-level character disorders. An understanding of primitive defenses and ego-boundary pathology is important. Such knowledgeable staff should be available to work with the patient in individual, group, and family therapy and in the ward milieu work.

Program breadth. The treatment program should have a therapeutic school, an activities program, a vocational program, and supervised social opportunities. Antisocial youngsters regularly have problems in each of these areas; these become useful grist for the therapeutic mill in individual, group, family and milieu therapy. Classes and activities should be designed to put patients face to face with various aspects of their pathology, as well as to teach new skills.

5) Treatment Stages

Treatment tends to proceed in three predictable stages (Rinsley, 1980). Several months to a year will be spent in some form of resistance. Then there will be some months (perhaps 12 to 24) of productive work, with some regression and backsliding. At some point the patient will be ready to continue to grow and improve as an outpatient. Discharge should then follow one to four months of inpatient termination work.

The initial resistance is usually negative and argumentative, but may be passively compliant or pseudo-cooperative. The essence of the patient's resistance is a wish to continue basic pathology and to test the integrity and worth of the treatment program.

Understanding the patient's wish and need to resist and test the integrity of the system before working in treatment is very important. The mistrustful, manipulative, and dishonest patient cannot at first believe that an honest situation, which is very clear and which values the patient, could exist. In the first few months, especially, patient behavior may be consciously or unconsciously designed to ask:

- Can I make them dislike or reject me?
- Can I turn staff against each other and thereby discredit them all?
- Can I catch them being dishonest or breaking rules?
- Can I overwhelm them with my pathology?

Only after much testing of staff's strength, honesty, knowledge, and kindness will the patient try to work in therapy.

There will be inevitable disappointments, frustrations, and attempts to escape treatment. Staff should be very dependable (but not try to be perfect) regarding their kindness, honesty, knowledge and strength, and point out the testing to the patient.

6) Improvement

As these patients improve, they become better able to make and keep good agreements. In the beginning they are very unstable in their views of themselves and others (as one would be predict from primitive defenses and shifting ego states). They trust no one except fleetingly and magically, and believe that everyone is much like them. They manipulate in a dishonest way instead of communicating and negotiating. Their goal is "to seem" rather than "to be." They have scarcely experienced the quiet satisfaction of honest competence or accomplishment. They fear getting better will be boring; they cannot imagine how healthy people can be happy with modest achievements and experiences. Their intrapsychic themes are of attacking and escaping in one form or another.

Little by little, all this gives way to a more trusting and stable communicating and negotiating that produces better and more useful agreements. Alongside this process a useful conscience is developing, in addition to more realistic internal objects and internal object relations. The patient then can live without his "mask."

REFERENCES

Aichhorn, A. (1935). *Wayward youth*. New York: Viking Press.

Cleckley, H. (1964). *The mask of sanity* (4th ed). St. Louis: Mosby.

Jenkins, R. (1960). The psychopathic or antisocial personality. *Journal of Nervous & Mental Disorders*, 131:318.

Kernberg, O. (1975). *Borderline conditions and pathological narcissism*. New York: Jason Aronson.

Levine, W., & Bornstein, P. (1972). Is the sociopath treatable? *Washington University Law Quarterly* 693.

Lewis, D., & Balla, D. (1976). *Delinquency and psychopathology*. New York: Grune & Stratton.

Marohn, R., Dalle-Molle, D., McCarter, E., & Linn, D. (1980). Juvenile delinquents: Psychodynamic assessment and hospital treatment. New York: Brunner/Mazel.

Masterson, J. (1967). The symptomatic adolescent five years later: He didn't grow out of it. *American Journal of Psychiatry, 123,* 1338–1345.

McCord, W. (1982). The psychopath and milieu therapy: A longitudinal study. New York: Academic Press. pp. 262.

Meeks, J. (1980). Conduct disorders. In Freedman, A., Kaplan, H., & Sadock, B. (Eds). *Comprehensive Textbook of Psychiatry III, Vol. III*. Baltimore: Williams and Wilkins. pp. 2816–26.

Rinsley, D. (1980). *Principles of therapeutic milieu with children: Treatment of emotional disorder in children and adolescents*. New York: Spectrum.

Shamblin, W. et al. (1985). Unpublished research on outcome of adolescent inpatient treatment.

Vaillant, G., & Perry, J. (1980). Personality disorders. In Freedman, A., Kaplan, H., & Sadock, B. (Eds), *Comprehensive Textbook of Psychiatry III, Vol. II*. Baltimore: Williams and Wilkins. pp. 1562–1588.

10

A Therapeutic Milieu for Treating the Antisocial, Substance-abusing Adolescent

Richard D. Selman

In this chapter I will attempt to outline a program designed to treat the major emotional imbalance and subsequent behavioral manifestations of substance-abusing, antisocial adolescents.

Many severely disturbed adolescents with behavioral and antisocial disorders can be described using Cleckley's (1976) list of characteristic symptoms: superficial charm and good intelligence; absence of delusions and other signs of irrational thinking; absence of "nervousness" or psychoneurotic manifestations; unreliability, untruthfulness, and insincerity; lack of remorse or shame; inadequately motivated antisocial behavior; poor judgment and failure to learn by experience; pathologic egocentricity and incapacity for love; general poverty in major affective reactions; specific loss of insight; unresponsiveness in general interpersonal relations; fantastic and uninviting behavior with drink and sometimes without; suicide rarely carried out; sex life impersonal, trivial, and poorly integrated; and failure to follow any life plan.

Treatment approaches to these antisocial adolescents are unlikely to be successful without an understanding of the typical motivations, defensive maneuvers, and styles of relating of these adolescents. These adolescents are often hyperalert, extremely observant, and capable of developing elaborate and well-conceived plans for engaging in disapproved behavior without detection and punishment. They are experts in manipulative behaviors. These are highly narcissistic adolescents for whom manipulative behavior becomes an end in itself. They use denial, projection, rationalization, and displacement to justify their behavior and have perfected the interpersonal skills necessary to maintain this outlook. These youngsters are skilled at provoking anger and mistreatment by others so that they can justify their misbehavior and avoid guilt (Meeks, 1979). Often impulsive acting-out and substance abuse are major problems. These adolescents are treatable, but often only in highly structured inpatient settings.

THE HOPEWELL PROGRAM

"Hopewell" is an adolescent substance abuse program at Highland Hospital designed to treat adolescents who suffer from two concurrent problems—a substance abuse problem along with another treatable psychiatric illness. Often the behavioral manifestations of this illness are clearly antisocial. Hopewell was patterned after a program developed by John E. Meeks, M.D., for the treatment of drug-involved antisocial adolescents. It is not intended for all psychiatrically disturbed adolescents—most of these adolescents have, even in the absence of drug use, symptoms and behaviors which can be described as antisocial.

The Patients

Often the adolescents entering Hopewell have a history of maladaptive behaviors dating back to early childhood. Behaviors include defiance and disobedience, manipulative and provocative behaviors, lying, stealing, running away, persistent truancy, vandalism, breaking and entering, firesetting, and outbursts of rage and violence. There are repetitive and persistent patterns of aggressive and/or nonaggressive conduct in which either the basic rights of others or major age-appropriate societal norms and rules are violated. Referral diagnosis, in addition to a substance abuse problem, is often conduct disorder or a personality disorder with antisocial features. Frequently, our patients have not responded to other, perhaps less-intensive, forms of treatment. In some cases, the drug abuse has not been addressed in treatment.

Deke was a 16-year-old high school student referred to Hopewell after not responding to outpatient psychotherapy and several brief hospital stays. Initially he had been referred for outpatient treatment by his school counselor for repeated truancy, running away, poor school performance, and family problems. During the next six months of outpatient psychotherapy, his drug abuse was apparent; however, it was felt to be a symptom which would resolve itself after the underlying problems of depression and low self-esteem were resolved. He was then hospitalized twice during the next month, first for a suicide attempt and again after physically attacking his mother when she questioned him about what time he would be home. At this point, he was referred to Hopewell. It became apparent that he had been high for each of his psychotherapy sessions and could remember little of what was discussed.

Another adolescent with a similar history was initially treated only for his problems with alcohol and marijuana. Since the underlying emotional difficulties were not addressed, when he left that chemical dependency program without having developed the internal controls necessary to remain abstinent, he resumed his previous patterns.

Components of the Program

At Hopewell, we utilize a locked 12-bed adolescent unit. All patients are involved with individual psychotherapy, group psychotherapy, family therapy, activity therapy, and Narcotics Anonymous meetings; most attend school on the hospital grounds at Homewood School. I would like to focus on several other components of our program which are utilized in the treatment of the severely disturbed substance-abusing adolescent.

Of particular importance are the therapeutic milieu programs. Gunderson's (1978) review of the literature reveals three qualities of a milieu that positively influence therapeutic outcome. They are: 1) distribution of responsibility and decision-making power; 2) clarity in treatment programs, roles, and leadership; and 3) high level of staff/patient interaction. He also described five milieu techniques which augment the psychotherapeutic process in the psychiatric hospital milieu. These techniques are containment, support, structure, involvement, and validation.

According to Gunderson (1978), "the function of containment is to sustain the physical well-being of patients and to remove the unaccepted burdens of self-control or feelings of omnipotence." Through the use of our locked, highly structured unit, serious acting-out is controlled and limits are set on behavior. Such limit-setting achieves one of the first treatment goals, which is to help the patient gain control over his or her destructive actions, so that meaningful psychotherapeutic work can begin.

"Support refers to conscious efforts by the social network to make patients feel better and to enhance their self-esteem" (Gunderson, 1978). While support is essential, too much emphasis on support can give the adolescent the message that he/she is not responsible for his problems or their solutions.

Gunderson continues, "Structure is all aspects of a milieu which provide a predictable organization of time, place, and person. A function of structure is to promote changes in the patient's symptoms and action patterns that are considered socially maladaptive." Through our highly structured program, we help the adolescent to consider consequences and to delay acting upon dysphoric feelings or impulses. Patients respond best if rules, regulations, expectations, rewards, and penalties are clear and consistent. Our ward rules and consequences for antisocial behaviors are written and presented to patients on admission, as well as available on the unit for patients and staff.

"Involvement refers to those processes which cause patients to attend actively to their social environment and interact with it. The purpose is to utilize and strengthen the adolescent's ego and to modify aversive interpersonal patterns" (Gunderson, 1978). Means of facilitating involvement, which will be described later, include open rounds, patient-led groups, the identification of shared goals, mandatory participation in milieu groups, community activities, verbalization of problems, and opportunities for self-assertion. We attempt to foster a prosocial value system among our patients. We also control acting-out through frequent and consistent staff/patient interactions. Positive emotional bonds enable staff members to provide a constructive social model, as well as to directly assist the adolescent in controlling his behavior.

Validation refers to the ward processes that affirm a patient's individuality. These techniques eventually help the adolescent successfully terminate from the program and the hospital.

Behavioral Principles

We utilize positive reinforcement as part of our overall behavioral program. The reinforcers are both material (points) and social (praise, attention, affection, recognition, approval). While we have clearly stated penalties and consequences for misbehavior, a primary focus is the reinforcement of appropriate and desired prosocial behaviors; the adolescents earn points that can be exchanged for specified privileges and improved status. All patients are aware of certain target behaviors which are used to determine points on a daily basis. Some examples of these target behaviors are as follows:

1) Improve interactions with parents and other authority figures
2) Self-esteem
3) Appropriate interactions with peer group and being able to say "no" to peer pressure
4) Insight into treatment needs
5) Exploring one's own feelings and being able to express feelings verbally
6) Control of anger
7) Activity and group attendance and participation
8) Taking responsibility
9) Supportive of peers and helping the community as a whole
10) Dealing with the reality of substance abuse.

Points are assigned on a range from 1 to 5, with 5 being the most healthy. Specific behaviors are clearly set out for each level. The written criteria are available on the unit for patients and staff. For example:

1) Improve interactions with parents and other authority figures:
    (a) Arguing or verbal abuse directed at parents or authority figures (1 point)
    (b) Avoiding interactions with staff or discussions of problems; poor attitude towards family (2 points)
    (c) Minimal interaction or discussion with staff about problems with staff initiation (3 points)
    (d) Minimal interaction or discussion of problems with staff at patient initiation (4 points)

(e) Demonstrates a willingness and ability to have meaningful interactions or discussions with staff (5 points)

Points are determined three times a day at the end of each nursing shift, i.e., at 3 p.m., 11 p.m., and 7 a.m., with the 11 p.m. to 7 a.m. shift using a somewhat different rating system. To earn privileges and advance in status, patients need a certain (usually large) number of points, written approval from all three nursing shifts, and a majority vote of the patients.

Other aspects of the behavioral program include the withdrawal of positive reinforcement, e.g., time-out and response-cost. Time-out involves the immediate removal of the individual from a given situation. It is especially useful with provocative behavior which could escalate without some intervention. Response-cost is the application of fines and penalties for inappropriate behaviors.

A Prosocial Atmosphere

We encourage a pro-therapy and prosocial atmosphere in the community through a patient government with considerable patient input into the decision-making process. The expectation of positive and prosocial group functioning is further conveyed by holding the entire patient group responsible for serious infractions or misbehaviors. Thus, the entire unit could be restricted for the serious acting-out of an individual. This might appear unequitable; however, in our experience, major acting-out episodes (e.g., running away, procurement of drugs) usually involve substantial group collusion. Often group members were involved with the planning or had prior knowledge of the event which was not shared with staff. This process encourages peer confrontation, thinking before acting, and taking responsibility for one's action. Much of this process occurs during regularly scheduled daily groups, as well as in crisis groups which are held with patients and staff immediately after major acting-out has occurred and been resolved.

Special Groups

Another important part of our overall program is psycho-social-educational groups to address the needs of substance-abusing adolescents. These groups assist adolescents in becoming more informed about the drugs of abuse, more familiar with their own physiological and psychological selves, and more aware of environmental influences as they relate to their daily lives. These groups run on a six-week cycle, several at a time. Three areas are addressed:

1) Familiarization with the categories of social-recreational drugs. Basic to understanding some of the fundamental dangers involved in abusing drugs recreationally is knowledge about the substance being used or abused. We assist patients in gaining a more realistic perspective of the dangers they have exposed themselves to, as well as a base of information to assist them in making healthier and more knowledgeable decisions in the future. Often adolescents' decisions concerning drug use are based on common street knowledge and "folklore." This knowledge can be dangerously inaccurate, and the results can be lethal. These groups help to dispel the folklore and replace it with accurate information.

Topics discussed in this area include the following drug categories: depressants, stimulants, narcotics, hallucinogens, cannabis, and trash inhalants. In considering depressants, for example, we discuss the therapeutic use and misuse of these drugs, reasons for abuse, dangers of abuse, tolerance and physical dependence, alteration of sleep patterns, and the specific dangers of mixing drugs in this category. Specific emphasis is given to the concept of alcohol as a drug and to the use of drugs while driving. The other drug categories are discussed in a similar manner.

2) Familiarization with self physiologically and psychologically. The goal here is to address these questions: How do our bodies work? How are our personalities formed? How do our physiological and psychological selves interact? How do drugs affect these areas? We attempt to demystify the effects of drugs and to make apparent the real dangers of recreational substance abuse. A component of this educational group, which often fits in nicely with the concurrent individual, group, and family therapy, is our attempt to help these adolescents identify within themselves reasons for their drug abuse. Another goal is the development of skills that will significantly reduce their perceived need to use drugs. The topics discussed include the following: anatomy and physiology, central nervous system functioning, pharmacology, the tasks of adolescent development, self-esteem, addiction and personality, assertiveness, leisure education, problem definition, and problem-solving.

3) *Familiarization with the environment.* We attempt to help the adolescent increase his awareness of pervasive environmental influences: media, advertising, family dynamics, societal norms and expectations, etc. Our goal is to instill insight as to how our environment is perceived and a sense of responsibility as to how we interact in the context of this environment. The topics which we discuss in this section include the chemical world in which we live, peer pressure, families, first aid, and drug emergencies.

As an illustration, let's look at what we do in the group concerning "our chemical world." In this group we discuss the nature of our environment regarding drugs and make an effort to put drugs and drug abuse in context. We discuss the four categories into which all drugs can be placed: environmental, food, medical, social-recreational. We examine each of these in relation to our definition of a drug (any substance that brings about a biochemical change in a person) and look at its impact on our lives. We identify positive and negative qualities of drugs and attempt to show that drugs are not inherently bad; rather, it is how they are used that determines whether they are good or bad. It is emphasized that we live in a world full of drugs and that, if we are to survive and lead productive lives, we must learn to make healthy, realistic decisions about drugs. We also explore social pressures that influence our use of drugs (role-modeling, peer pressure, the media) and lead the discussion toward healthy conclusions that are used in formulating our "drug values."

Another group, in the evenings, the self-improvement workshop series, also runs on a six-week cycle. The staff utilizes didactic presentations, group discussions, group exercises, role-playing, assertiveness training, and other group techniques. Each week the group addresses a different topic, moving from self-awareness to self-esteem, relationships, communication, conflict, and finally social skills. The topics become increasingly application-oriented and move outward from the self, starting with the most basic experiences and sensitivities and progressing to experiences which increasingly involve others' presence and feelings. With the last week on social skills the discussion comes full circle—from self-awareness through other-awareness and back to self-awareness again.

The activity therapy program emphasizes the use of leisure time and positive socialization, as well as exploration of alternatives to substance abuse and antisocial behaviors. The patients also take part in an Inward Bound experience, utilizing an outdoor environmental program consisting of a rope and obstacle course on the hospital grounds. During the Inward Bound experience a social microcosm is developed in which each participant contributes. Patients are confronted about inappropriate interactions and behaviors, and given opportunities to learn and experiment with new ways of relating productively in a group situation. We have found that this experience is especially effective in dealing with issues of trust and group cohesion, as well as in improving self-esteem, frustration tolerance, and creativity.

Other aspects of the Hopewell program include random drug screens, an autobiography and daily journal. On admission, each patient writes an autobiography, which is shared with patients and staff. Then he or she is asked to keep a daily journal; this is used in discussions with staff and is helpful as the adolescent learns to verbalize feelings rather than act them out. In this way the adolescent learns to think about actions and feelings and to see the resulting consequences.

Staff Considerations

The active, informed, and consistent participation of all members of a multidisciplinary team is necessary in the treatment of these adolescents. An enormous potential for negative countertransference feelings exists and requires open and honest discussion in treatment team meetings. While the members of nursing staff are not police, as some patients claim, they are involved with the daily confrontation, clarification, and limit-setting of patients' behaviors. At times, the staff's need to avoid being "outsmarted" can seriously interfere with empathy and emotional sensitivity. New and inexperienced staff should be supervised closely. Some, while seeming to be able to set reasonable limits, may be unable to function on the unit without becoming angry and punitive or being caught up in the patient's rationalization, thus being inconsistent and too lenient.

After the adolescent completes our substance abuse program, specific recommendations are made to him and his family. If longer-term psychiatric hospitalization is needed, referral may be made to Highland's adolescent program, where continuity of care is possible.

Working with these severely disturbed adolescents is difficult for all members of the treatment team. However, they can experience success and see improvements in these adolescents in a highly structured inpatient setting using a combination of treatment modalities.

REFERENCES

Cleckley, H. (1976). *The mask of sanity*. 4th edition. St. Louis: Mosby.

Gunderson, J. (1978). Defining the therapeutic processes in psychiatry milieus. *Psychiatry. 41*, 327–355.

Meeks, John E. (1979). Behavioral and antisocial disorders. *Basic handbook of child psychiatry*. New York: Basic Books.

11

Comprehensive Inpatient Treatment of a Severely Antisocial Adolescent

Leo J. Potts, William D. Barley, Kathleen A. Jones, & Peggy K. Woodhall

The patient discussed here is representative of antisocial persons who present to a private hospital for treatment. A brief introduction will be presented, followed by a discussion of work with the patient and his family, an individual behavioral modification program, and an extensive activities therapy program. It is important to note that the overall treatment provided in this case reflected a consolidated team and nursing effort, with a significant amount of time spent each week coordinating therapeutic efforts and interventions, working on treatment goals, and maintaining a consistent approach and attitude toward the patient.

THE PATIENT

The patient (here called "Peter") was admitted to the hospital in the fall. He was an unmarried, late adolescent, white, high-school dropout. He was an only child from his mother's first marriage. There were no step- or half-siblings.

Reason for Admission

The patient was admitted after a court hearing which found him in violation of a probation order. Probation was continued, with the provision that he be hospitalized, as recommended by his treating psychologist, in order to provide extended, intensive inpatient treatment and rehabilitation of his antisocial behavior. The patient had been in treatment with a psychologist for over one year but had attended irregularly and had not been responding to outpatient therapy.

Peter's problems began to appear at age 12, when he changed schools because of a rezoning of school boundaries. No major behavioral or developmental problems were reported up to that time. He was unsuccessful in team sports at the new school. He started abusing drugs, including marijuana, hashish, Quaaludes, and alcohol. His parents noticed a gradual deterioration in his behavior in addition to his abuse of drugs and alcohol. He became belligerent at home, started breaking rules, and at times was physically threatening to his parents. He made a habit of carrying a knife and was reported by his parents to have a sawed-off shotgun at home. Six months before admission to hospital, he was convicted of making harassing phone calls and was placed on probation, including a curfew. Three months before admission, he was charged with property damage, malicious injury, and violation of probation. He admitted to stealing from his parents and others. His parents reported repeated lying, repeated violations of rules at home, and increasing frequency of being late or absent from home at night.

Peter had been truant; his grades had deteriorated. He had been terminated from special education programs and classes because of lack of response. His local education authority refused to sponsor any further schooling unless he demonstrated a significant change in his attitude toward school. He minimized or denied the problems reported, but did admit that he had been abusing many different drugs.

Family History

Peter's natural father died when he was five years old. His natural father was described as "wild, a heavy drinker," and as exhibiting many antisocial characteristics. He married the patient's mother when the patient was two years old. The father later deserted the family for a time, was injured in a motorcycle wreck, and eventually died from an unrelated illness. The patient's mother remarried three years later, when the patient was about eight. Peter is said to have encouraged her second marriage and was, at that time, fond of his stepfather.

Peter's great-aunt, with whom he spent much of his time, was easily manipulated. She allowed him to smoke marijuana and to sleep with girls at her home. His maternal uncle was a substance abuser who occasionally provided the patient with alcohol, marijuana and possibly other drugs.

Medical History

Medical history was negative except for a gastrointestinal condition which responded to brief medication.

Physical examination was normal. Laboratory tests (including serology, CBC, urinalysis, and chemistry profiles), chest and skull X-rays, and EEG were all reported normal. The patient was discovered to be carrying a dangerous-looking knife at the time of admission. He had several tattoos.

Mental Status

Peter looked his age, was attractive, well-dressed, and neatly groomed. He was of athletic build and had long hair. Throughout the interview, he was guarded and defensive. He was anxious, and minimized the extent and degree of his substance abuse and antisocial behavior. He showed no evidence of any thought disorder or delusional thinking, and he denied paranoia or hallucinations of any kind. There was no evidence of any affective disturbance or organic central nervous system disturbance. His intelligence was judged normal.

Psychological testing included a WAIS, a neuropsychological screen, an Intake Booklet, TAT and MMPI. The patient was in the "bright normal" range of intelligence. There was no evidence of an organic brain syndrome on neuropsychological testing, nor evidence of any thought disorder or perceptual disturbance. Emotionality was poorly controlled. The patient did not seem to be significantly depressed or characterologically anxious. He was noted to be subject to situational anxiety, primarily in punishment situations. Self-esteem was based on his perception of himself as physically important and dangerous. It was thought that he might fantasize excessively about this. Acting-out was seen as the primary defense. The diagnostic impression was Conduct Disorder, Undersocialized, Aggressive type. A comprehensive treatment program was recommended, including individual therapy, confrontive group therapy, and firm external controls on acting-out, with the aim of making his incipient characterological features ego-dystonic.

PROGRESS IN HOSPITAL

Peter was hospitalized for approximately 14 months. During the first
three months, he continued to push and test limits. He was hostile and
abusive to staff. His attitude was negative. He was involved in episodes
of drug abuse, such as smoking marijuana and attempting to sniff paint,
and was noted to repeatedly lie about these episodes. He developed
a reputation among peers and staff as being manipulative, self-centered,
impulsive, and minimally concerned about the rights and needs of other
patients. He was not concerned about the impact of behavior on other
patients or on his family. These behaviors were responded to by reduction in responsibility levels, ward restrictions, etc., but this had little
impact on his behavior. He denied responsibility for his behavior,
usually suggesting that it was somebody else's fault. A frequent response
was "I can't," which seemed to reflect "I won't." There was an apparent
lack of any concept of concern for the feelings of others, both peers
and family, and an apparent inability or unwillingness to put himself
in another's place. His ward behavior was characterized by lack of effort, unwillingness to cooperate, complaints of boredom, and repeated
excuses. He was not trusted by staff or other patients. He seemed to
study other patients and staff and to use this knowledge to control patients and situations.

At the end of three months, the diagnosis and treatment program
were revised by the treatment team. We decided to revise the diagnosis
to that of antisocial personality disorder and to focus specifically on
the antisocial aspects of the patient's thinking in individual and group
sessions, daily patient/treatment team meetings, activity therapy group
meetings, and all other contacts with the patient and his family.

Peter began a specific behavioral program which is discussed in detail
later in this chapter. He also was to keep a diary with at least twice-
daily entries related to what he had done and what he was thinking
(not what he was "feeling"). The premise in this approach is that antisocial thinking precedes antisocial activity, that what the patient is
thinking determines what is most likely to be carried out.

For several weeks, Peter struggled against his new program. On
many occasions he lost day-to-day privileges, missed activities and outings, or missed visits with his family. Six months after admission he
was given a four-day therapeutic leave home to assess progress. His
parents reported no improvement since admission.

Following his return, Peter continued on a locked unit. On one occasion he absconded for several hours. Several weeks later, two other patients absconded for a short period of time. They had planned to leave with Peter, but it turned out that he had had no intention of leaving; he had simply set up "his friends" in order to settle an old score with them. Peter's peers soon voiced their strong disapproval, and very direct confrontation ensued in ward meetings, daily patient/treatment team meetings, other group meetings and individual sessions. Over the next several weeks, the disapproval generated ongoing confrontation by peers and staff about other aspects of his antisocial activity.

This period became a turning point in Peter's treatment. He began to make some significant changes in his behavior and interactions with others. His behavior modification program was adjusted as needed. During this time he was involved in regular, group, and individual psychotherapy and weekly joint telephone conferences with his family and social worker. There was an overall impression of continuing improvement in his behavior, a softening of his attitude, some sense of concern for consequences, some sense of guilt and shame, and a new sense of concern for others, particularly his mother.

Soon thereafter, Peter became emotionally involved with an attractive female patient. His involvement increased over the next month, in spite of initial advice against any intense relationship and finally in spite of prohibitions. His response was to distance himself from treatment and to return to limited acting-out. He began to disengage himself from treatment in spite of the efforts of staff and other patients, and in spite of efforts on the part of other staff working with the female patient. Within a week of her discharge a few weeks later, the patient signed out of the hospital against medical advice. His plans were to live with his female friend in his great-aunt's residence. His parents refused to have him live with them as long as he was leaving hospital without a regular medical discharge and to live with an ex-patient. No medication was prescribed on discharge; the only medication during hospitalization was lithium carbonate 300 mg. q.i.d., which was discontinued after four months because of no apparent benefit.

PSYCHOTHERAPY ISSUES

Psychotherapy proved to be a critical element in treatment. Peter's group therapy experiences resulted in frequent and forceful confrontation and intervention by his peers in a generally supportive setting. This was especially so when confrontation was by other antisocial patients well advanced in treatment who quickly identified in Peter defenses, interpersonal strategies, and differences in thinking that they were working on or needing to change themselves. The adage that "it takes one to know one" took on a new enhanced meaning for all concerned.

In group and individual sessions material was regularly generated from his daily journal of how and what he was thinking in regard to events as they occurred each day. It revealed typical antisocial defenses and strategies. They included minimizing or denying responsibility for behavior and the degree of his antisocial activity. Strategies used to achieve this included evasion, attempting to confuse, generalizing to a point of absurdity, lying, diverting attention and accusing or blaming others, angry silences, angry outbursts, and verbal intimidation. The primary and consistent intervention was the idea that society holds us accountable for our behavior, that one has choices about what one does, and that there is a need to find adaptive, reasonable ways of behavior and "survival."

Other specific areas of confrontation and working through included issues typically seen in antisocial persons: the "victim" stance of displacing responsibility and blaming others, saying "I can't" and meaning "I won't," lacking a sense of injury or empathy for others, distorted attitudes about ownership and possession, distorted values and defective sense of conscience, problems with trust and the need to achieve power over and control of others, and the failure to think things through or look at possible consequences of behavior.

As in the treatment of any patient, psychodynamic issues will become apparent as treatment progresses. They will require attention, clarification and resolution to the degree possible. The issues listed above simply reflect those areas we most frequently encounter in working with antisocial aspects of personality. We do find when dealing with other dynamic issues in antisocial patients that it is important to prevent patients from using other dynamic issues as a means of "excusing" or rationalizing and justifying antisocial behavior and avoiding responsibility for their actions.

FAMILY INTERVENTION

The families of severely antisocial adolescents or of young adults with antisocial personality disorder have special problems and needs that differ considerably from the needs of families of other patients in the general psychiatric population. Families of most psychiatric patients have functioned under the strain of everyday crises for many years, experiencing problems that they never anticipated. However, the families of psychopaths tend to view major crises as if they were a "normal" experience. These families often accept horrible and sometimes frightening experiences without question. They make remarkable, albeit misdirected, sacrifices for the offspring or spouse.

This pattern of misdirected aid develops slowly over many years. The parents' or spouse's behavior has been subtly and unconsciously trained by the psychopath from early childhood. Families soon realize that he or she is the center of their lives. They may have buried the family pet killed by their child, settled with irate storekeepers after petty thefts, dealt with neighbors after vandalism, spent many sleepless nights worrying about car accidents, brought their child home from jail after charges have been filed against him, etc. From this basic understanding, one begins work with the family.

When the patient arrives for admission, time is set aside to meet with the family. A social history elicits material about the patient, and the bud of a relationship begins to form between the family and the social worker. The first task after this history-taking session is to ally oneself with the family. It is important to give the family permission to relax and to try to regain some energy to cope with crises yet to come. Family members should be warned that the patient, while in hospital treatment, will continue to display the same problems presented in the past. We ask the family members for their help in setting limits and in abiding by the limits set by the hospital.

The family members may be encouraged, for the first time, to have some control over their lives and the life of the patient. Families are instructed about the games the patient will play in the hospital. They are told that the patient will state that he is "in danger from all the crazy patients," that the staff is mean, that the doctor is mean, and that he wants to come home. When the pressures of hospitalization are on, the patient is very unhappy. He will prey on his family's previously helpless stance and try to manipulate them once again. It is important to try to help the family members see themselves as part of the consolidated front to "contain" the patient.

Simultaneously, an educational process must begin. Families need an explanation of the process in which they—the family—have been functioning. One should avoid explaining how the psychopath has developed. Most parents and family members blame themselves enough without addressing the errors they may have made trying to raise these children. What is addressed is the hope that they can begin to learn different ways to deal with existing problems.

The second step is to help them understand that they have been used and abused. They have been trained to accept being cajoled, charmed, conned, and exhausted by the adolescent or psychopath. Through the years, these behaviors and the family's responses to them have slowly taken form. The family bears the brunt of any punishment that is intended for the psychopath.

Our program makes an effort to interfere with the family's rescuing behaviors. We interrupt all contact except letters, so that any attempt at manipulation takes days instead of minutes to complete. From the beginning, the family is given a rest from the day-to-day ups and downs of living with the patient. Most families do not rescue willingly; they rescue under the threat of embarrassment, humiliation, and notoriety in the community. (Who wants it known that his child beat up a teacher or robbed a neighbor?) With the patient in the hospital, there are some controls; they have the freedom to let the patient take the consequences for his behavior. The family members' lives and livelihoods no longer hang in the balance. They can begin to piece together what is left in his wake without consideration of his needs and wants.

If the family repeats old patterns when crises arise during the hospitalization, intervention can be initiated. When families are confronted with the patient's first request to take him out of treatment because other patients are "bothering him," they can be reminded of their child's problem. They can face the situation head-on and realize who is really the offending party.

The family members need to distance themselves from the antisocial offspring as much as possible. Once they are free of the day-to-day problems, they are never quite the same. They experience outrage at their previous way of life. They begin to see how horrible their lives have been and to recognize the cause: the child they have been trying to "save."

As the family sees that the brunt of the problems in the hospital is shared by all staff, they begin to see that they have taken on far more than necessary. In the community, these families usually function in isolation. They have so many secrets and feel so much like failures that they never share their life experiences with others. They have few ways of getting support because of their reluctance to admit that they cannot control the child or spouse—or even their own lives. Once families experience the relief of separation from the patient during hospitalization, they see that they never could have been successful in dealing with the psychopath alone.

The effective family conference is another helpful tool. These conferences are not like traditional family therapy sessions. These are carefully orchestrated events. The patient is told that a conference will be held and that the family wants to convey to him the impact of his behavior on the family unit. The conferences are preceded by a brief session without the patient, in which the family is instructed about what needs to be accomplished in the joint session: The patient must be confronted with all of his trangressions against the family. He is faced with the tragedy he has caused by the people he thought he could count on for support. It is very dramatic when a family shows the patient for the first time that they know what is going on and they are not happy!

The patient usually shows two different reactions to this kind of intervention: 1) He becomes angry and refuses to listen; and 2) after a period of bravado, the patient begins to see that he abuses his own family. Another helpful aspect of this conference is that the patient becomes aware that the staff knows what is going on; he can no longer deny or minimize it. The patient also realizes that the last safe arena for acting-out has been taken away. The accustomed abuse of the family must stop.

These conferences are lengthy and grueling for all involved, but worth the investment of time and energy. Families prove once again how powerful they are. It takes much work and preparation to get a family ready for such drastic a break with tradition. Daily intervention for weeks or months may be necessary. The rewards are great, however. Even if the changes in the patient are not readily apparent, this kind of intervention has a very positive impact on the family.

In Peter's family this process went relatively smoothly. His mother and stepfather were ready for help and were extremely cooperative and trusting of the hospital staff. His mother and one of the authors worked especially closely during his hospitalization. She was bright, articulate and "sick and tired of being sick and tired." She was an ideal parent to work with in this respect. She had little energy left to try to continue to rescue Peter all by herself. She entered enthusiastically into

Peter's program. She agreed to send staff members rewards for Peter to earn in the program that was designed for him. She followed all guidelines set when Peter returned home for brief visits and refused to lie for him when he requested it. She was able to confront him with his behavior in a factual, nondemeaning way. His stepfather was a caring man who participated in Peter's treatment as much as his work allowed. Even when the stepfather was not present at family conferences, Peter learned that his parents were now functioning as a unified couple. Peter reestablished a productive relationship with his stepfather, following some extremely hostile periods prior to his hospitalization.

There was one family member, Peter's great-aunt, who was estranged from the rest of the family and caused some difficulties in his treatment. She continued to support Peter's rebelliousness. She was very careful to work with the family counselor, but undermined the treatment at every turn. It was she, in fact, who provided a home for Peter when he left the hospital against medical advice.

As mentioned earlier, Peter left the hospital against medical advice and his parents' wishes. After a period of continued acting-out and problems with the police, he was able to reorder his life to some extent. His parents continued to refuse to support his psychopathic way of life. When he was able to make reasonable goals for himself and to begin to accomplish these goals, they agreed to allow him to return to their home. At this writing, he has held the same job for over a year and recently entered technical college.

It is important to remember that the family of a psychopath or antisocial adolescent can make strides *independent of the patient*. If this can be accomplished with families, then they can return to the kind of life they planned for themselves, rather than being manipulated and punished once again.

COGNITIVE AND BEHAVIORAL TREATMENT

About four months after Peter's admission, the treatment team decided to implement an individual cognitive and behavioral treatment program for him. Peter had not responded to the general treatment program, milieu therapy, and individual and group psychodynamic psychotherapy. The team began to focus more specifically on the antisocial aspects of his thinking and behavior. The "behavioral" part of the new emphasis was a contingency management program, specifically a token point system. The "cognitive" aspects of the revised approach followed suggestions of Yochelson and Samenow (1976, 1977).

Peter was required to monitor his thinking over the course of each day and to make a written record of his thoughts available to the treatment team. He had to keep a diary with entries at least twice daily, related to what he had been doing and what he was thinking at the time. His compliance with this requirement and the material that he produced were reviewed and critiqued frequently by the psychiatrist, social worker, and activity therapist. Elements of "criminal thinking" were identified, confronted, and modified by this means.

There were several reasons for using a token point system. We wanted to provide the treatment team and ward nursing staff with frequent opportunities to confront Peter's thinking and behavior; if expectations for his thinking and behavior were made more explicit, then confrontation might occur more consistently. The treatment team wanted to extinguish certain of Peter's antisocial actions. Positively reinforcing behaviors incompatible with antisocial actions and withdrawing positive reinforcement after antisocial actions offered some promise of achieving this goal. Finally, a general psychodynamic rationale for containment of antisocial behavior in a hospital setting is to encourage engagement by controlling the disruptive behavior that can make the milieu unpredictable and even hostile for the patient. One may also force the development of internal dysphoria and self-dissatisfaction by blocking the emotional discharge that accompanies antisocial behavior (Crabtree, 1982; Jones, 1984; Rossman and Knesper, 1976). A token point system might not only extinguish some of Peter's misbehavior, but also influence Peter to respond to his impulses in a more internally focused and less action-oriented fashion. Thus, the behavioral part of Peter's treatment was intended to achieve immediate behavioral goals, as well as to influence his thinking and other internal processes.

Several basic questions were addressed before the behavioral treatment program was developed. These questions had to do with Peter's suitability for this program and with the ability of the treatment team and ward nursing staff to carry it out. We had to face the fact that it might someday be necessary to control Peter physically. He was judged to be manageable, and staff members decided that they could control him if it became necessary.

It was very important that some extraordinary external constraints and incentives be available, since Peter had no internal motivation for change. Because of a suspended sentence and probation which overlapped with most of his hospitalization, Peter faced the threat of jail if he did not cooperate with his treatment. His probation officer was quite interested in our work. The nursing staff were willing to expend additional time and effort on the behavioral program. Finally, we decided it was reasonable to expect Peter to change. His age and our previous experience with others like him led us to believe that a behavioral program would be helpful.

The program was developed by active cooperation of the treatment team, consisting of psychiatrist, clinical psychologist, social worker, activities therapist, and representatives of the nursing staff on Peter's ward. We also involved all members of the daytime nursing shifts on Peter's ward. Many details had to be worked out after the general direction of the behavioral program had been decided. Peter's new token point system had to be overlaid on extant ward- and hospital-wide policy; it had to be practical and "do-able" in our environment. The primary policy in this regard was the hospital's "ad lib" system of increasing privileges contingent upon improvement in a patient's behavior. Second, nursing staff expressed a strong preference for behavioral programming based on positive reinforcement principles rather than punishment. Third, the hospital does not have a ward devoted entirely to behavioral treatment; the nursing staff's role in the new behavioral program would be an additional responsibility for them.

Target behaviors, reinforcers (both attractive to Peter and under treatment team control), and the contingent relating of target behaviors and reinforcers were then established. As many nursing staff and treatment team members as possible were to be involved in evaluating and acting on Peter's behavior. The degree to which we could deprive Peter of privileges enjoyed noncontingently by other patients on the same ward was a difficult issue. It was necessary to develop a schedule of positive reinforcers and their withdrawal that was theoretically effective as well as practicable wherever the patient's treatment might occur. Weekly meetings were held with ward nursing staff to rehearse contingency-management and token-system principles and their application to Peter's treatment.

It was hoped that the behavioral changes would generalize to nonhospital settings. Following Kazdin's suggestions (1977), we discussed ways to build in behavioral maintenance and transfer to posthospital

living. These included: 1) choosing target behaviors that would naturally have consequences outside the hospital; 2) removing the contingent
reinforcers gradually; 3) involving as many reinforcing agents as possible to obtain broad stimulus control; 4) using both short- and long-
term reinforcers to build in delayed reinforcement; and 5) using the
cognitive aspects of Peter's treatment to encourage self-reinforcement
of his prosocial behavior and to modify the self-speech that we thought
had contributed to impulsive antisocial behavior in the past.

The token-point system, which we initiated after about one month
of preparation, was the product of repeated consultation with Peter,
his treatment team, and ward nursing staff. It was modeled generally
after principles and examples discussed by Kazdin (1977) and Rimm
and Masters (1979). A detailed, written description of the program
was prepared, distributed to the treatment team, nursing staff, and the
patient, and discussed at length. Peter was expected to exhibit specific
behaviors in order to receive points which qualified him for short- and
long-term rewards. The behaviors included attendance at each scheduled activity, appropriate participation (as judged by the activity leader), good manners and consideration for others (as judged by the activity leader), personal hygiene acceptable to the ward nursing staff,
a clean and orderly room (as judged by the nursing staff), washing of
his clothing as necessary, adherence to all written rules of the hospital and ward, appropriate behavior toward female patients (as judged
by any staff member), and generally nonmanipulative and honest behavior toward others (as judged by staff). Once each hour, nursing staff
or other staff members having had contact with Peter assessed whether
the sum of his behavior during that hour met the standards for reinforcement. If it did, he earned a point for that hour, which was recorded
on a Daily Record Form kept on the ward.

Points awarded for these target behaviors qualified Peter for rewards
over the course of each day, including the privilege of eating lunch and
dinner in the cafeteria rather than in isolation, going to a pleasant activity each afternoon or at night, swimming and playing basketball,
and going to the hospital snack bar. Accumulated points would also
allow Peter to use his stereo in his room on the following day.

Once-weekly rewards were contingent upon the achievement of a
certain percentage of the total possible points over the course of the
previous week. Peter was contingently allowed to participate in much-
sought-after activities on Saturdays and Sundays, to obtain favorite

items of personal decoration such as motorcycle patches, to enjoy an increased level of hospital-wide freedom of movement, and to go escorted into town on weekends. We also provided for longer-term reinforcers, including major off-grounds outings and solo trips into town, contingent on a certain percentage of total possible points earned over a several-week period. Previously earned points could be lost when his behavior did not meet these expectations.

The Daily Record Form was used not only to record accumulations of points, but also to alert ward nursing staff to the level of privileges that Peter had earned up to that time in the day, as well as to the reinforcers he might expect to earn by the weekend should he continue functioning as he had up to that time. Ward nurses were the primary agents of reinforcement and its withdrawal, as they had the most consistent contact with Peter and the most control over his movement.

The written program description distributed within the hospital gave instructions for initial verbal cuing of Peter to perform the target behaviors and for fading of these cues over time. Staff members were also encouraged to pair social reinforcers such as praise, handshakes, and pats on the back with hourly points awarded and with the privileges the points allowed. The importance of modeling desirable behaviors was stressed, although he already had most of the desired behaviors in his repertoire. A second handout discussed with the treatment team and nursing staff described the cognitive "errors" peculiar to antisocial patients (Yochelson and Samenow, 1976, 1977), and specified the kinds of staff responses that would be therapeutic and consistent with the treatment team's approach.

The program was maintained for approximately nine months. Weekly team and nursing staff meetings often suggested changes in the program based on changes in Peter's behavior or practical problems. For example, we quickly learned that when he did not earn a point for an hour he stopped trying and gave up. Consequently, criteria for earning the daily positive reinforcers were briefly lowered. Later, the longer-term reward of an unescorted trip to town after four weeks of very good behavior was suggested. "Appropriate behavior toward members of the opposite sex" did not become a target until about one month into the program, when ward nursing staff noted that Peter's behavior toward a young female patient was becoming very sexually provocative. As time passed, more emphasis was placed by nursing staff on offering weekly reinforcers, so that Peter would have continued incentive to earn points even if earlier points were lost. Meetings with treatment team and ward nursing staff members were also occasions for rehearsal of their roles in various aspects of the program, primarily "consequation" (implementing consequences) of the target behaviors, recordkeeping, and identification and confrontation of antisocial thinking.

Peter's response to the idea of a token-point program was positive. He made a list of what he thought were his problem behaviors, possible solutions for them, and ultimate behavioral goals. Some of his ideas were incorporated into the first version of the system. Once the program began in earnest, though, Peter requested a transfer to another treatment team. The request was refused because it was clear that it was the direct result of his dissatisfaction with the increased focus and systematic consequation of his behavior.

Some of the target behaviors ceased to be problems after the point system went into effect. For example, there were no violations of expectations for personal hygiene and washing of clothes. Some presented only minor difficulty: Peter's room was almost always orderly, and his participation in scheduled activities, not bad early in the program, improved slightly. Other target behaviors improved markedly during the program: attendance and promptness at scheduled activities, manners and overt consideration for others, and nonmanipulative attempts to solve problems. Behavior in some areas became worse. Peter's frequency of inappropriate actions toward female patients increased, and he more frequently violated written ward and hospital rules as the months passed.

The percentage of waking hours per week in which his behavior was acceptable in all respects ranged from 88% to 100% during the program's existence. There was no overall trend in a "better" or "worse" direction during that time. As noted by Crabtree (1982) and Yochelson and Samenow (1976, 1977), the overt behavior of the antisocial patient in confinement is not always a problem. This is why the treatment team placed such great emphasis on psychodynamic and cognitive change and generalization, in addition to behavioral changes.

ACTIVITY THERAPY

The activity therapy staff (art, horticulture, music, occupational, recreational, and vocational therapists) facilitates each patient's therapy through an individualized treatment plan. Our expectations for Peter were:

1) to be responsible for his behavior;
2) to be open and listen, without interruption, to feedback from others;
3) to honestly look at and alter his thinking errors;
4) to exhibit "prosocial" behavior.

The staff was to confront Peter's antisocial behavior in a neutral, matter-of-fact manner. We encouraged him to examine how his thinking led to antisocial actions. Appropriate consequences were established for negative behavior and prosocial behavior.

Much of our work with the antisocial patient is done in groups. These groups contain a variety of types of patients, varying in their treatment progress. We encourage and expect patients to confront each other's behavior. Frequently, this is an educational process for non-antisocial patients, since they initially succumb to the antisocial patient's charm. As patients in the group learn about antisocial behavior and thinking errors, they are asked how they feel about such things as put-downs, thinking errors, or the "victim" stance. The other patients help to reflect the views of society. Antisocial patients frequently hear criticisms of their behavior more clearly from other patients than from staff.

Peter participated in a daily activity therapy group with the other patients served by the team. This group of patients was together in treatment team, rounds, group therapy and often lived on the same unit. They became well acquainted with each other. They usually knew who was conning and who was working. The purpose of the activity therapy group was to help patients grow and learn about themselves through action-oriented processes and to motivate them to interact in healthy ways. Through the relationship that developed among therapist, patient, and group, an atmosphere of trust and risk-taking grew. We used a variety of activities to develop this trust, to explore ideas and values, to gain insights, and to try out new behavior patterns in the here-and-now. Seven elements of Peter's work in this group can be described: communication skills, value clarification, self-awareness activities, assertiveness training, problem-solving activities, leisure skills and pursuits, and creative expressive activities.

Communication skills. Peter was encouraged to develop listening skills. He was often asked simply to repeat feedback others had given him. Corrective guidance was important in this process since misinterpretations, often to his own advantage, were frequent. When he talked with others, he was expected to give clear, open messages, with no vague or hidden meanings.

Values clarification. This took place in activities, discussion groups, and games in which Peter compared his values with those of others in the group. His values clearly reflected errors in his thinking process. Peter would perceive himself as the "victim" of society, his family, patients, and staff of the hospital. It was necessary to point out repeatedly that (and how) he was the persecutor, while society, his family, his fellow patients, and the hospital were his victims. One example of this type of behavior follows:

> During a group discussion, Peter learned that another group member worked at the public library. He appeared very interested in her library job, asking numerous questions. It soon became apparent that Peter had ulterior motives. He told the group that he had several overdue books from the library and, after repeated notices, the library had the "audacity" to send him a bill. He stated that the fines were more than the original books cost, and he complained about unfairness. If he returned the books and paid the fine, the library would have made money on him! He accepted no responsibility for the fact that he kept the books long after they were due.
>
> Because of his persuasiveness, his "victim" stance soon had others in the group siding with him against the "authoritarian" library. Someone then asked why he had not returned the books on time. He stated that, while he had read a few of the books, he had not finished all of them. He had not bothered to renew them by calling the library, because that was too inconvenient. He was not truly interested in the librarian/patient and her job, but saw this as a way of using her to his own advantage, i.e., getting the books back without paying the fine. We encouraged Peter to look at other choices he had, such as taking out fewer books, calling for a renewal, accepting responsibility for his behavior, and accepting the consequences of his irresponsible behavior by returning the books and paying the fine. We also pointed out his attempt to use the librarian and how this may have injured her reputation.

Self-awareness activities. Peter was expected to challenge his own thinking. Inappropriate behavior or comments were examined, enabling him to see faulty thinking patterns. During these exercises, Peter frequently became defensive and anxious. Using a matter-of-fact, non-attacking approach, the therapist encouraged him to reflect upon his thinking and its product, antisocial behavior. We required that he be responsible for his behavior and his thinking style. Choices were advocated. As time went on, his defensiveness decreased; however, his anxiety increased. Reduction of anxiety was not attempted since it was felt he would not attempt change unless he was uncomfortable with himself.

The concept of emotionally hurting others was foreign to Peter. He only understood how he could hurt others physically. He appeared surprised to realize the psychological pain, as well as the financial burden, he had caused his parents and family. This only became clear to him after social work family conferences, in which his mother talked about the anguish he had caused in the family. This information was used during the activity therapy group to remind Peter of his responsibility.

These activities were used to bring behavior into conscious awareness, reduce his denial system, and force acceptance of consequences for his antisocial thinking and behavior. They also created an opportunity to point out appropriate thinking and behavior. We stressed change in how he thought about life, people, and situations as the foundation for change in his antisocial behavior.

> A discussion centered around how each person felt about the food in the cafeteria. Some talked about how good the desserts were; others talked about how hard it was to diet; another hoped that lunch would not be "the same old thing again." Peter wondered how much money would be in the cash register, how many staff would be between him and the nearest exit, and how far he could get from the hospital to find a little "chick" and have a good time. When confronted, he stated he was "just kidding." He wasn't really planning anything; besides, he would probably get caught. The group persisted in pointing out that his thinking differed from that of the other group members, that his thinking was antisocial, and that it was necessary for him to change his thinking patterns if he were to improve.

Goal-setting talks were included in self-awareness activities. Peter was to write down problem areas, then to write solutions to the problems. An example from his record late in the program:

Problem	*Solution*
1) Too much pleasure-seeking.	1) Try to be more content with certain situations instead of looking for a good time; think of others' feelings when tempted to make fun of them for my good time.
2) Sometimes have trouble with authority telling me what to do.	2) Realize when authority is trying to help or looking after my interests.
3) Using drugs and alcohol for a "good time."	3) Try to find other sources of recreation that are legal and unharmful.
4) Need to think of consequences instead of taking action.	4) Just stop and think before I act; talk out any problems.
5) Not using time wisely or to my advantage.	5) Instead of using time for pleasure, use time for helping myself —like reading, writing, or listening to other people's ideas.
6) Testing limits of authority and peers.	6) Stop pushing people just to see how much they can take. Accept people as they are.
7) Lying	7) To be truthful.

Goal: To become a productive citizen in my community, with a successful career. To be more enjoyable to associate with.

This list of problems, solutions and goals reflects definite changes in Peter's thinking. There was more awareness of others and how his behavior affected others. He also left loopholes in words such as "try." The amount of energy he put into "trying" remained less than our expectations; however, it was a good beginning.

Assertiveness training. The patients were videotaped playing various roles which were then played back for group discussion. Peter was encouraged to look at himself, and his interactions with others, with a critical eye. His aggressive self-centeredness was obvious. He liked his physical appearance but attempted to deny his behavior and outward impression. He was encouraged to become more assertive in interactions with others, but not to expect to get his way. Being assertive meant learning to listen to and compromise with others. Expectations were that he would continue to practice assertive behavior throughout his hospitalization and eventually develop a generalizable skill.

Problem-solving activities. Learning to work with a group—to look at choices, compromise, and come to one group decision—was a challenge for Peter. It was necessary for him to take others into consideration instead of impulsively tackling a task. Talking out choices from beginning to end—and looking at consequences of their enactment—was part of the exercise.

An example of this is our Inward Bound program, in which group interaction and working well together are essential for the success of a group task. The recreational therapist in charge of this program challenges the group with a physical task (e.g., getting the whole group over a 20-foot wall, getting a car tire and a truck tire over the top of a telephone pole, having the group traverse a gully by using five tire swings). The more agile, capable persons have to plan so that those less skilled are involved as useful members of the group. The challenge was good for Peter. He developed positive leadership skills. He was pleased that his planning skills were used in a positive manner.

Leisure skills and pursuits. Since many antisocial persons use their leisure time negatively (drugs, alcohol, illegal activities), awareness of and participation in leisure skills were felt to be important. Peter was frequently bored when his time was not structured. He was encouraged to be involved in evening and weekend activities and to gain skills in a variety of leisure activities.

The activity therapy group included a physically active game each week (e.g., volleyball, softball). Peter was extremely competitive in these games. He had a greater need to win than the other group members. He ridiculed other players for not being as quick and agile as he. His expectations for them were far above their playing ability. He frequently played the whole court rather than staying in his position, or he and another antisocial patient would monopolize the ball. When reminded to play his position, he would become angry and threaten to quit. He also wanted to quit when his side was losing. When this happened, we pointed out that perhaps his behavior was part of the reason his side was losing. If his side happened to be ahead, Peter took all the credit.

When talking in group sessions, Peter apparently had little feelings for his fellow players. Instead of giving them a chance to improve their skills, he saw them as impediments to his winning. Peter was regularly confronted by other group members regarding how they felt when he took over their plays. They told him how his behavior and attitude affected the team spirit. We also discussed how his anger affected both people individually and the mood of the game. Limits were placed on Peter for not conforming to expectations, as per his cognitive-behavioral program.

Creative-expressive activities. Collages were frequently used. For example, each group member's body was outlined on a large sheet of white paper. Inside the outline each person was to make a collage of what was inside of himself, using pictures or words from various magazines. Peter's collage was very sparse. He included the words "sincere," "style," and "unique," and pictures of a bottle of liquor, a pack of cigarettes, and an attractive girl in a bikini. When he presented this to the group, he stated he "had sincerity" and "style" and he had to be number one. He also felt that he was a very rare person—the best. The liquor, cigarettes, and woman represented his likes and possessions. The collage was very similar to those of other antisocial patients in this group. The need to be "number one," to feel that they had a "sincere heart," and that they were different from and better than others (and truly liked this difference), was striking.

Other group members made collages of their impressions of Peter. One patient's perception of him was riding a motorcycle with hair streaming in the wind. The title was "Get Down and Party" and "Rock 'til You Drop." We highlighted Peter's sparse collage, focusing on the comparison between his values and those of others. We discussed how his values got him into difficulty with the law and how his behavior affected his family and those who loved him. He was shown how he constantly put his needs first, with little thought or concern for others.

Other activity groups included art, music, and occupational therapy. *Art therapy* is an expressive activity, emphasizing nonverbal expression of thoughts and feelings. Peter initially began by drawing pot leaves, drug paraphernalia and motorcycle symbols. He enjoyed the attention and laughter he got, especially from a few young girls in the group. While drawing he told the art therapist that he was working hard in therapy and felt he was really changing. The therapist told him his drawings reflected what he was thinking, and his thinking continued to revolve around drugs and the fast life. Again, he was led to see his thinking patterns.

He slowly gave up these types of drawings and began to appear more uncomfortable in this group. He began structuring his drawings by using masking tape and rulers to block off sections of his canvas to paint. By using these external controls, Peter gave his drawing a less impulsive quality. He had to plan before he acted. With the greater controls, he seemed to feel more inner anxiety, i.e., cracking his knuckles, rubbing his hands repeatedly on his pants. "Sweet talk" and "charm" were confronted in a matter-of-fact manner by the art therapist. As time went on, projects that could be finished in a day gave way to work that required one or two weeks.

Verbal expression is expected in the *music therapy group*. Early in treatment Peter was asked to select a song that would reflect his thinking. He chose Billy Joel's *My Life*, which includes several lines about independence and freedom from authority. Peter said that was how he was thinking. He said he was tired of people probing and prodding and making him look at himself, his behavior, and his thinking.

Where other, non-antisocial patients were prompted to explore and verbalize underlying feelings, Peter was asked to state what he was thinking and then shown how this thinking was indicative of his "world view." While others were given appropriate support for their own views on issues and encouraged to be assertive, Peter was confronted about how his views had victimized others in order to gratify his own needs. This obvious difference in approach created some discrepancy within the music therapy group, making it necessary to keep divergent treatment approaches at hand and learn how to quickly change from one to the other. When this became easier, the process of giving Peter responsibility for his own attitude and behavior, rather than minimizing or rationalizing, became more fluid.

Peter's demanding, self-centered and attention-getting behavior was apparent in the task-oriented *occupational therapy group*. He would monopolize the therapist for 10–15 minutes at the beginning of each hour by "needing" answers or requiring assistance, materials, or special tools. The therapist pointed out that she was there for the whole group, not just to take care of his needs. History showed that he had the capacity to solve problems; he could plot elaborate schemes. Peter was encouraged to put these problem-solving skills to more appropriate, constructive use. Each day he was to take the first few minutes of the group to plan for all his needs for the day's task. Peter soon became less impulsive and demanding and more organized. He tolerated the delay of immediate gratification.

In occupational therapy, Peter was a "sprinter" rather than a "long distance runner." He would be very enthusiastic about starting a project, but his enthusiasm would quickly fade. One such project was a latch-hook rug. This activity is very tedious, because it is repetitious and, once one learns how to manipulate the tool, has few challenges. It was pointed out that this was a long-term project, that it would be very tedious, and that once he started it he was expected to complete it before starting anything else. He remained eager and initially seemed to like the challenge. He was not willing to consider the time element. He quickly became bored.

In his boredom, he used his energy to instigate friction between two other patients, then stepped back to enjoy the conflict. He tried to avoid his rug project by making somatic complaints, skipping occupational therapy, hiding his rug, attempting to give it to others, and offering another patient money and cassette tapes to finish it for him. Each time one of these issues came up, we would discuss his thinking and behavior, and appropriate limits/restrictions would be given according to his behavior modification program. Peter finally realized he could not manipulate the therapist. He began to compete with himself, setting an initial goal of a certain number of rows and improving on that number in ensuing days. After completing this project, Peter received positive feedback from the therapist and others and, one hopes, learned more about delay of gratification and frustration tolerance.

This continuous, daily confrontation in all the activity therapy groups, as well as in group therapy, individual therapy, and group treatment team rounds, appeared to have a positive affect. Peter began seeing himself as he really was rather than as he wished to be. After the patients realized how he set them up before going AWOL, they became even more confrontive. Soon after the joint family conference was convened, the activity therapy department had more material for confrontation—the hurt and pain his thinking and behavior had brought to his family. Slowly we began to see change. There was less acting-out in the activity therapy groups. He appeared more serious. His productions were less antisocial; there was less testing of limits. He took more responsibility for himself and did not assume the victim role as often.

His language improved. He was more able to accept confrontation and would ask opinions about his thinking, using a slightly more critical eye. He violated rules less frequently and began to receive rewards. Through the various activities used in the activity therapy group, as well as the specialized groups of art, music and occupational therapy, Peter was confronted in all spheres of his being, his verbal and non-verbal: attitude, verbalizations, thought content (including symbolic representations), work habits, and general behavior around peers and staff. His disruptive and antisocial behavior was contained in a consistent manner. The resulting anxiety made Peter more accessible to the treatment approach used.

CONCLUSION

Follow-up data covering almost two years since Peter's discharge indicate that, after a rocky start, he has lived quite adaptively and with only one minor scrape with the law. We have seen a wide range of outcomes in our inpatient work with antisocial adolescents and adults, and we think that the possibility that these persons will achieve an adaptive way of life makes the effort worthwhile. We believe that treatment is possible, in spite of opinion to the contrary. We have difficulty accepting the logic of an identified DSM-III diagnostic category being excluded from inpatient treatment intervention efforts based on diagnosis, unless there is clear evidence of failure to respond during inpatient therapy based on a case-by-case review. It is clear to us that there are degrees of psychopathy. Experience tells us that the younger patient with more recent symptom onset responds better to treatment than does the hardened, psychopathic, criminal adult, who is rarely seen in the hospital setting. Further, some kind of motivation and decision to change is a prerequisite for doing so, whether deriving from internal dissatisfaction or external pressure, e.g. family or legal pressure.

We think that a comprehensive treatment program involving cognitive, behavioral, family, and psychodynamic work is a necessity. The treatment environment must be made predictable to everyone involved. Acting-out must be contained. Pressure for change from the patient's peers must be harnessed. Motivational issues must be worked through. The patient's family must be taught and learn not to rescue—itself a positive therapeutic outcome for the family. Troublesome countertransference must be dealt with. All of this requires a highly coordinated effort by treatment staff. The result may not be a "cure," but improved, more adaptive functioning is clearly possible for a significant number of these patients.

REFERENCES

Crabtree, L. (1982). Hospitalized adolescents who act out: A treatment approach. *Psychiatry, 45*, 147–158.

Jones, J. (1984). Principles of hospital treatment of the aggressive adolescent. In C. Keith (Ed.), *The aggressive adolescent: Clinical perspectives.* New York: Free Press.

Kazdin, A. (1977). *The token economy.* New York: Plenum.

Rimm, D. & Masters, J. (1979). *Behavior therapy: Techniques and empirical findings* (2nd ed.). New York: Academic Press.

Rossman, P. & Knesper, D. (1976). The early phase of hospital treatment for disruptive adolescents: The integration of behavioral and dynamic techniques. *Journal of the American Academy of Child Psychiatry, 15*, 693–708.

Yochelson, S. & Samenow, S. (1976). *The criminal personality, Volume 1: A profile for change.* New York: Jason Aronson.

Yochelson, S. & Samenow, S. (1977). *The criminal personality, Volume 2: The change process.* New York: Jason Aronson.

12

Manipulativeness in Entrepreneurs and Psychopaths

Ethel Spector Person

Manipulation is a specific kind of interpersonal interaction. Initiated by one individual to influence the feelings and behavior of another, it may serve intrapsychic purposes or goal-oriented aims or both. The manipulator is determined to get what he wants, to have things his way. Acutely sensitive to interpersonal cues, he intuitively knows how to use the emotions, needs and weaknesses revealed to him for his own ends. He rarely responds with empathy or exhibits a sincere desire to help.

Manipulation, of course, takes many forms. In *David Copperfield* Dickens characterized humility as a disguise for manipulativeness in the character of Uriah Heep:

> His hypocritical assumption of humbleness, his damp bony hands, his fawning hatred of those he has deceived, his calculated dependence upon these loyalties and affections, his ingenuity in spinning his web, make him despicable and dangerous. . . . Uriah Heep can worm his way into the confidence of an experienced man of affairs, gradually get the upper hand of his weaknesses, and reduce him to subservience.

The American version of humbleness and self-deprecation more often takes the form of assuming a "country boy" pose:

An earlier version of this paper was presented to the Michigan Psychoanalytic Society on March 11, 1978.

Ike, one of the better political generals the army has produced, may have sometimes out country-boyed Lyndon Johnson when (Majority Leader) Johnson didn't know it. Ike, too, was a fine actor and not a bad manipulator of men (Bobby Baker quoted by Wills, 1978).

The kind of manipulation utilized by psychopaths, however, is generally based on charm. The manipulator appears to be helpful, charming, even ingratiating or seductive, but is covertly hostile, domineering, or, at best, neutral in interaction with another individual (object). This object is perceived as an aggressor, a competitor, or merely as an instrument to be used. The manipulative maneuver is related to the seduction of the aggressor as described by Lowenstein, a topic to be explored later in this chapter.

The purpose of manipulation varies with different personalities in different situations, but it usually falls into one of three categories: the pursuit of personal gain, the stabilization of self-esteem, or the symbolic destruction or domination of the object, all under a guileless façade. Manipulation in the interpersonal field can serve both as an adaptive technique and as a defensive maneuver, and is found across a wide spectrum of personality types and occupational groups. However, it is the hallmark or signature of psychopaths and of some other individuals who come for treatment, in particular some entrepreneurs.

There are important differences between psychopaths and other manipulators, such as entrepreneurs. Entrepreneurs often lead successful and productive lives, while a downward drift in the lives of psychopaths is inevitable. In the entrepreneur, manipulation may be bent purely to intrapsychic aims, but is more often linked to goal-oriented behavior. Even when it is used simply to establish dominance, manipulation is subject to and qualified by reality demands, and internal demands may be delayed. In the psychopath, the urgency of intrapsychic needs is such that manipulation inevitably becomes the end-all and is no longer qualified by the reality principle. In entrepreneurs, manipulation is elective; in psychopaths, it is obligatory. Manipulation, in and of itself, is a neutral technique which may issue in positive or even creative endeavors, or may be the vehicle of destructive and self-destructive aims.

Although the current trend in psychiatric discourse is to focus almost exclusively on diagnostic categories or specific disorders, it remains critically important to evaluate defense mechanisms and personality styles, since they are predictive of particular transference struggles. Only by understanding the centrality of manipulation as the modus operandi in the mental life of certain patients can a successful therapeutic relationship sometimes be negotiated. Therefore, reliance on interpersonal manipulation as a defense mechanism is the central focus of this chapter.

PSYCHOPATHS AND ENTREPRENEURS

Greenwald (1967) noted, perhaps ironically, that we usually reserve the term psychopath for the "unsuccessful" psychopath. He quotes the observation by the sociologists Sorokin and Lundeen that the moral behavior of the ruling group tends to be more criminal than that of the ruled population. They also contend that the lack of morals and apparent lack of guilt characteristic of psychopaths can be found to exist among many persons of power and influence. Some successful entrepreneurs might also be "successful" psychopaths.

Greenwald's remarks underscore the fact that the hallmark characteristic of the psychopath must extend beyond his antisocial behavior and his reliance on interpersonal manipulation as his modus vivendi. The psychopath is set apart by the downward drift in his life. By definition, the psychopath is not successful.

Traditionally, the psychology of psychopaths has not been a topic for psychoanalysts, since psychopaths are almost universally considered unanalyzable. More recently, there have been psychoanalytic characterizations of the antisocial personality as a variant of the borderline or narcissistic personality (Kernberg, 1975). Unfortunately, however, in these formulations the psychopath is not sufficiently distinguished from among a variety of antisocial personalities. In particular, psychopathic behavior should be separated from criminal behavior. It varies significantly from stealing, destruction of property, and truancy.

Kernberg reiterates, "There is nothing new in mentioning the absolutely hopeless prognosis for the analytic treatment of antisocial personalities . . . " (1975, p. 254). He goes on, however, to make the extremely important point that there is a continuum between the narcissistic personality and the antisocial personality, which he sees "as an extreme form of pathological narcissism with, among other features, a complete absence of integrated superego."

The author is in agreement with Kernberg's general observations and would suggest further that there is a continuum — which will be described herein—between the psychopath, as one subset of the antisocial personality, and the narcissistic personality. The type of narcissistic personality encompassed in this continuum is often encountered among entrepreneurs who seek psychiatric treatment.

The entrepreneur is a member of society whose social worth is well-recognized, while the psychopath is generally described in more perjorative terms. The thesis presented here is that some entrepreneurs—those with narcissistic features—and psychopaths, despite their obvious differences, share certain characteristic ways of mediating between internal demands and external reality. They share characteristic ways of defending against anxiety, depression, and conflict. In particular, both groups employ sophisticated manipulative techniques both defensively and adaptively.

What entrepreneurs share with psychopaths is a finely honed skill, the ability to turn interpersonal maneuvers to their own ends. Such a capacity in the psychopath, while structurally similar, is often antisocial, usually some variant of the "con." It need not be antisocial in the entrepreneur, although it sometimes is. Narcissistic entrepreneurs and psychopaths exist on a continuum in which similar defensive structure and adaptive modalities are embedded in personalities with widely disparate levels of ego integration, ranging from mature to neurotic to borderline.

ENTREPRENEURS[1]

There are virtually no psychoanalytic investigations of businessmen, whether managers or entrepreneurs. The common characteristics of businessmen are not deemed relevant to psychoanalytic scrutiny. Therefore, it might be argued that it is difficult to make psychoanalytic observations on a group of individuals distinguished only by career choice

---

[1]Although the author has seen a number of patients who were successful entrepreneurs, and is herself convinced that they share certain personality features, my sample cannot be considered representative of entrepreneurs as a general class. First, by virtue of having sought treatment, they represent one subgroup only. Second, as reported elsewhere (Person, 1983), certain men preferentially seek female therapists when they have intensely competitive problems with other men. The following account of some few entrepreneurs who sought treatment with a woman may be of general interest, however, for the light it sheds on manipulation as a defensive style in a sizable group. For purposes of narration, the broad term "entrepreneurs" will be used when in fact the reference is to one subgroup only—essentially entrepreneurs with narcissistic personalities.

rather than by unconscious material or symptomatology, character, and defensive structure. Yet there has been a long-standing psychoanalytic interest in artists and creative individuals, despite the absence of shared personality organization among them. Many entrepreneurs, as a particular subgroup of businessmen, share a predominant style or adaptive modality which warrants observation.

In general, entrepreneurs elude definition, since the word "entrepreneur" has been used in many different ways by economic theorists and sociologists.[2] Entrepreneurs are usually concerned with the creation or reorganization of a business, while "managers" are primarily involved in its operation. In contrast to a manager's desire for stability and ordered growth, the entrepreneur is interested in creating the dynamics of a new business organization. He is not primarily interested in management and may best be viewed as an impresario, a kind of producer or director. By this definition, however, we have excluded many of the classical concepts and categories of entrepreneur, including the owner-proprietor of a small business whose primary purpose is to insure a steady living.

Entrepreneurs who are innovative like to view themselves as at the cutting edge of social change. Whereas the social importance of certain characteristics of the entrepreneur has long been recognized, particularly in technological innovation, the entrepreneur's motivation has been narrowly interpreted and rationalized merely as the wish for profit. For example, the economist Joseph Schumpeter (1954) emphasized the importance of the entrepreneur for technical progress. He felt it was the possibility of making profits that prompted businessmen to seek more efficient methods and take the risk of introducing them.

From the psychological point of view, entrepreneurs may have as much invested in the ongoing excitement of risk-taking as in the possibility of profit. It is the opportunity to make one's mark on the external world, not simply profit, which motivates entrepreneurs. The difference in motivation is expressed in a quote attributed to Andrew Carnegie and cited by Maccoby (1976): "It is the pursuit of wealth that enlivens life; the dead game, the fish caught, becomes offensive in an

---

[2]Corporations are staffed predominantly by managers, though some entrepreneurs may flourish in them. Paradoxically, as Zaleznik, (1977) has stated, "the irony of the managerial ethic is that it fosters a bureaucratic culture in business, supposedly the last bastion protecting us from the encroachment and controls of bureaucracy in government and education."

hour." Most entrepreneurs, though they wish for success, live for the game, for the ongoing interactions and interpersonal maneuvers which give birth to business ventures. They prefer acquiring wealth through short-term speculative coups and deal-making rather than through long-term consolidation and slow, painstaking labor.

The way this type of individual asserts his creativity is quite characteristic. Entrepreneurs exert their influence by interpersonal manipulation, which may be mediated through charm and contagious enthusiasm. One patient calls this the "seduction trick." As such, the entrepreneur can be described as a salesman, although the product to be sold is his idea or his preeminence. He has both dramatic flair and the boyish enthusiasm of adolescence. Entrepreneurs have the ability to inspire those around them, to elicit enthusiasm for projects which they have proposed, and to lend their energies to those who, while quite competent and efficient, lack the fire and imagination to initiate change. Entrepreneurs often are able to tap the resources of those gifted people who must be brought to life by outside forces. Paradoxically, it is the fire entrepreneurs are able to ignite in others which illuminate their own image in a way that stabilizes self-esteem. They are often energized by these interpersonal encounters and use them to spark their imaginations and spawn more and more ideas. Some other personalities can learn to be manipulatively adept but tend to find such encounters depleting, not replenishing.

There are many others, like entrepreneurs, who attempt to mediate between the demands of instinctual life and external prohibitions by intervening in the external world, people who may therefore be said to rely heavily on alloplastic adaptations. Scientists, craftsmen, and builders usually eschew introspection and attempt to put their imprint on the external world; control and mastery are thus externalized. However, they focus on manipulation of the inanimate, or at least the nonhuman, part of the environment. In contrast, entrepreneurs are dependent on manipulation of people as their major mode of adaptation. It is positive feedback from others which affords gratification, not control of the inanimate world.

Entrepreneurs change the organization of economic and social life; but unlike the visionary or idealist, they do not wish to impose an internal vision onto the external world. The entrepreneur is essentially a loner; he is seldom a political zealot of any stripe, although he will favor whatever political program he perceives as benefiting him personally. It is his "flexibility" in preserving his self-interest that lends him a chameleon-like quality. Like the successful statesman, who does not oppose the prevailing trend but adapts to it, the entrepreneur senses the possibilities implicit in the economic and psychological world and operates within them in order to assert his mastery, achieve recognition, and gain profits. Even so, entrepreneurs are innovative rather than reactive, at least in response to the interpersonal part of the external world.

What is the underlying meaning of manipulation per se for the entrepreneur? Although manipulation may be rationalized as the most direct means of achieving conscious rational ends, it serves other functions as well. Manipulation is the primary method of eliciting admiration, "love," and even envy. It is also a favorite technique for expressing aggression without the threat of retaliation, because the aggression is masked. Self-contempt is discharged by projection onto the person who has been manipulated; the pleasure in making a fool of him repairs self-esteem. At the same time, admiration is sometimes the reward, as well as concrete proof that the aggression has gone unnoticed or, at least, unpunished.

Entrepreneurs operate on a spectrum ranging from charm to cutthroat competition; the types are seldom pure. At each end of the spectrum entrepreneurs share one or the other of the two predominant characteristics of psychopaths. Those who rely on brute force express the aggression which is veiled in psychopaths; those who rely on charm most closely resemble the psychopath in terms of surface behavior.

The entrepreneurial personality appears to be primarily competitive with other men. Success is determined by the man's ability to establish ascendancy over another male by his charm or importance. The need for domination is seldom contaminated with so much aggression that relatively stable hierarchical relationships become impossible. In other words, the narcissistic entrepreneur can deal with other men, and even be supportive, so long as his ascendancy is not fundamentally challenged. The more successful the entrepreneur, the less he wants "yes" men. He admires other men's gifts and welcomes their contributions, so long as they are not competitively entrepreneurial. He wants to surround himself with first-rate managers, so long as he remains the star. Men who represent real competitive threats are poorly tolerated.

A few entrepreneurs apparently resolve this potential problem with men by staffing their organizations with women. This solution simply reflects the fact that so few women are essentially entrepreneurial in style — an entrepreneurial threat from a woman would not be any better tolerated than one by a man. Thus, a man may gain a reputation for respect for women and be viewed as a feminist, while the truth is that he has not found the woman he takes seriously as a competitive threat.

In contrast to his relationship with men, the entrepreneur's relationship with women is motivated less by the need for dominance and more by the need for approval and admiration, although sexual dominance may be an important feature of his affective life. If a significant woman is not found to be appreciative of the entrepreneur's gifts, he becomes enraged and hostile. He often defines himself by the gleam in a woman's eye. The narcissistic entrepreneur is often blatantly unfaithful to his wife, but would be devastated by her unfaithfulness to him. The most paradoxical element in the makeup of the entrepreneur is his veiled dependence, particularly on women. He enjoys, for instance, being teased by a woman about his "wickedness."

Although the need for preeminence is striking, admiration must be expressed constantly by persons in the immediate environment. For him, feeling good is contingent on the admiring response of a significant other. The entrepreneur utilizes action to ward off feelings of passivity and depression, but he also requires admiration from others. He is frequently fighting off an identification with a failed father figure.

The ego and defensive organization of the narcissistic entrepreneur depend on certain mental attributes: paranoid sensitivity coupled with intelligence, imagination and a facility with both ideas and words. Good entrepreneurs know they will have to initiate many ideas or projects for every one that succeeds. Their stream of mental activity is usually accelerated. (Dr. Lionel Finkelstein has remarked that some persons with entrepreneurial personalities need to be distinguished from manic-depressives in the manic phase.[3]) Although their best ideas are usually triggered by the presence of someone else, the more creative and mature individuals can tolerate a certain amount of solitude. The necessity for constant action is significant; the entrepreneur frequently passes his leisure time in gambling or competitively strategic sports. If a gambler, his preference for particular forms of gambling gives some clue to his operative dynamics. Gambling which relies primarily on luck (e.g., casino gambling), rather than on skill (e.g., gin rummy), betrays

[3]Personal communication.

a more primitive insistence on the symbolic smile of a maternal figure ("lady luck," perhaps) and less reliance on self to outmaneuver the competitor.

Entrepreneurs are distinguished by their boldness, the impulse to gamble, and a lack of guilty restraint. Unlike obsessives, who may also be capable of great achievement, entrepreneurs are little concerned with detail and little inhibited by a need to obey the letter of the law. Because of their lack of guilt, entrepreneurs are not long-suffering people. In narcissistic entrepreneurs, problems often take the form of a "garlic neurosis"; the problems bother someone in the entrepreneur's environment more than they bother him. If he comes to treatment, it is most often following some blow to self-esteem that results in depression. This depression is often colored by lethargy, a failure of nerve, and fears of impoverishment, sometimes despite actual affluence. There is fear of being a washed-up has-been and resentment that the outside world will not permit him to rest on his past achievements, along with immense envy of those who are currently successful. Business reversals are frequently translated into potency disorders, which compound the depression. The reversal of the depression in treatment is not difficult, although real analytic engagement is seldom achieved. Entrepreneurs usually come to treatment to repair or improve their skills, not to change their characters.

It is clear that these subgroups of entrepreneurs exhibit certain features which form part of Kernberg's classic outline of the narcissistic personality (1975). They have a charming and engaging surface, but underneath may be cold and ruthless. Their conflicted concept of self, coupled with the need for external love, admiration, and tribute, reflects a disturbance in self-esteem and self-regard. These characteristics are related to a specific disturbance in internalized object relationships.

Kernberg (1975, p. 231) speculates that "there is a fusion of ideal self, ideal object, and actual self images as a defense against an intolerable reality in the interpersonal realm, with a concomitant devaluation and destruction of object images as well as of external objects." However, this structure leads the narcissistic personality to divide the world into overidealized "objects" and contemptible ones. Furthermore, the self-esteem system is precariously balanced. As already noted, the patient comes for treatment following blows to his vulnerable self-esteem, at which time he may present with feelings of worthlessness and thoughts of suicide. At the same time, he feels entitled to control, possess, and exploit others without guilt (Kernberg, 1975). There are areas of healthy superego consolidation; patients generally act within the letter — if not the spirit — of the law. The level of overall personality organization varies among patients, and prognosis differs accordingly.

Unlike the psychopath, the entrepreneur can foresee the consequences of his behavior. He perceives the future as a reality and can therefore restrain certain behavior. He can delay action when necessary without the threat of personality disorganization. The psychopath, in contrast, must struggle to stabilize his *identity* or *self*, and not just his self-esteem.

PSYCHOPATHS

The typical psychopath, as described in the psychiatric literature of several years ago (Cleckley, 1964; Henderson, 1939; Kahn, 1931; Karpman, 1948, 1954; Palmer, 1957), is attractive, impressive, and charming. His personality is permeated by an excessive reliance on the psychopathic maneuver as his predominant defensive and adaptive modality. The basic psychopathic maneuver is the interpersonal manipulation already described, except that it is almost invariably contaminated by antisocial or destructive aims.

The psychopath's insight is always directed toward his internal needs. These needs are not what they appear to be. He is not predominantly hedonistic, although some of his behavior, particularly sexual, might lead one to think so. Instead, he is motivated primarily by the need to dominate and humiliate either the person he is "taking" or, very often, someone connected to a person with whom he is involved. He may, for instance, seduce a friend's girlfriend.

While his behavior is riddled with aggression and even sadism, he both protects himself and humiliates his victim by the overlay of charm. Psychopaths generally agree that it is easier to "con a con" than anyone else, because the former is so susceptible out of his own needs. When a con is not so needy, he has a keen eye for seeing through other people's manipulations. The psychopath is a curious mixture of cynicism coupled with a magical belief that fortune will smile on him.

Many psychopaths make and lose money cyclically; however, a downward drift in their lives is the general rule. Despite a lack of cognitive impairment and periods of success and even brilliance, the psychopath will eventually fail in certain significant areas of his life. The cause of this downward drift has been generally understood as a variant of masochism, the need to fail out of some unconscious guilt. Bursten (1973) does not share this misconception and offers a much more cogent explanation for manipulation in his excellent book, *The Manipulator*. He recognizes the preemptory quality of the need to manipulate, not guilt, as the central problem in psychopathic patients.

Affect

Psychopathy can be viewed as an impulse disorder in which the short-term relief of anxiety is more important than any long-term consequence. Anxiety, precipitated by a sense of disorganizing rage, is relieved through the psychopathic maneuver.

This conclusion is reinforced by the way psychopaths describe their need to be "in action." When they are jailed or involuntarily hospitalized, one often sees the emergence of an empty depression, anxiety, and other affects usually viewed as absent in the psychopath. (Vaillant, 1975, also makes this point.) The psychopathic maneuver has the same urgency for the psychopath as the fix has for the heroin addict. In both, dreaded affect must be avoided at any cost.

Although the ultimate effects of psychopathic behavior may be devastating, the underlying purpose of the apparently self-destructive act is not to fail, but to allay anxiety and depression. The psychopath wards off negative affect much as the heroin addict given free access to drugs avoids painful affect by taking a fix. Personality disorganization is continuously threatened by the constant pressure of rage, except when the rage is discharged in the psychopathic maneuver. Simultaneously, the psychopath reassures himself with the admiration he elicits in his victim-audience.

From the psychopath's point of view, his behavior is not reprehensible. He usually sees himself as acting defensively in order to avoid being taken advantage of himself. Greenwald (1967) believes the psychopath's subjective experience simulates that of the Jew living under the Nazis; on some level he feels so persecuted that all of his behavior is justified. Glover (1960) has also pointed out that the psychopath's hostility is tied to a sense of grievance. It is the psychopath's fundamental belief in the justice of his resentment which may give his performance so much credibility. He lies coolly, calmly, unflaggingly, and with apparent frankness, even when discovery is inevitable. Despite the apparent intellectual insight he can muster in admitting past mistakes and making future plans, his repetitious actions show that he learns nothing from his past experiences; he will continue to display defective judgment.

He appears to prefer a perception of himself as bad rather than as neurotic or "sick." When it becomes impossible to deny the facts of his misconduct, he becomes exceedingly apologetic and remorseful and plans to make restitution in the future. His future actions make it clear, however, that anything he may feel at the moment is only transient. (This phenomenon is apparent in the active addict or alcoholic as well and suggests the similarities in the ego defects in the several groups.) More likely than not, he is only saying what he thinks is of personal advantage at that moment. This dichotomy is indicative of splits in the ego as depicted by Kernberg (1975) in his descriptions of borderline pathology.

One can understand the psychopath's psychodynamics by referring to several interrelated theoretical models. From the classical point of view, certain predominant dynamics are apparent. A psychopath spends his life directly and indirectly recreating the never-resolved oedipal constellation and symbolically reenacting, over and over, the oedipal struggle of the little boy who hopes to best his father and take on his possessions. The wish to best the father is usually extended into the wish to discredit and destroy him. This may be veiled by the psychopath's devaluation of this father as weak, passive, and ineffectual, and his mother as controlling and castrating; yet he is symbolically vying for her. However, it is the projection of oral rage and the internalized object relation related to the infantile experience of oral range that are defining for personality organization.

Mr. A, who had been in both individual and group psychotherapy, was referred to me by his former therapist after the patient had seduced the therapist's mistress. The patient revealed his conquest to the group, thus creating havoc not only in his therapist's personal life but in his professional life as well. The patient had made and lost several fortunes (in the millions) while still in his twenties. He often borrowed money from his father's friends, never paid it back, and occasionally cheated these same friends outright. He continually blamed his parents for his difficulties and yet coerced his father, a wealthy man, into rescuing him by implicating his father's friends.

During the course of his treatment with me, he achieved preeminence in a particular field absolutely new to him and was offered a partnership in a lucrative business. He promptly undermined his new success, again by seduction, this time of both the mistress and the wife of his new partner.

This patient's dynamics are quite typical. He constantly strove to stave off fears of castration and establish his masculinity by seducing women involved with father substitutes and by cheating his father's friends and peers. At the same time, regressive trends were revealed in the coercion he exerted on his parents and on me to save him. For example, he arranged to cheat a number of pimps. This necessitated his hospitalization in order to elude the pimps, who threatened to murder him. While in the hospital, he was briefly depressed but quickly organized a rebellious patient government.

For this particular patient, a favorite sideline was to have sex simultaneously with a woman and a psychopathic male playmate, make her "crazy with pleasure," and then abandon her. Certain latent homosexual trends ere obviously present, but these are by no means universal among psychopaths.

The problem remains as to why success, in this patient and others, does not temper low self-esteem and restrain those impulsive interactions which undermine both fortune and, sometimes, safety. The psychopathic disorder is more than an impulse disorder coupled with a defect in resolution of the oedipal complex and in superego formation. There is an underlying problem in both self-identity and the self-esteem system; both must be constantly restabilized by the use of the psychopathic interpersonal maneuver, which vents aggression and externalizes an intrapsychic fantasy. In other words, self-identity can only be stabilized (however temporarily) in fluctuating partnerships. Lack of empathy is ego-defensive only in those few psychopaths who are treatable; in others, it appears as a structural defect related to the absence of good internal objects. This defect in self-esteem and in the internalization of good objects is much more prevalent than the oft-cited "superego lacunae," and prevents the psychopath from learning from experience. Gratification does not lead to any shift in this psychic organization.

The major defensive organization in psychopathy is contingent on feedback from a real partner. The victim and the admiring audience are often two separate people. Identity and stabilization of the self-system depend on the ability to elicit a variety of responses from an object. Why this maneuver must take place in reality rather than in fantasy is a question which has never been adequately answered; in this regard psychopathy resembles the full-blown perversions, in which the perverse script must be enacted in order to be effective (Ovesey and Person, 1976).

COMPARING PSYCHOPATHS AND ENTREPRENEURS

In their personality styles, both psychopaths and entrepreneurs are action-oriented and innovative rather than reactive and inhibited. In particular, they utilize manipulation of the interpersonal field. This is predominantly stereotypic and defensive in the psychopath, whereas it also serves adaptive purposes in the entrepreneur. The fundamental difference between the two groups resides in the different nature of personality organization.

In the entrepreneur, domination and the will to power are incorporated into the ego ideal and therefore stand at a considerable psychic distance from primitive sadistic wishes. Furthermore, any weakness of the superego may not stem from disordered development at all. It may reflect incorporation of parental inhibitions which are lax relative to the cultural norm, or it may be indicative of immersion in a subculture which does not provide a holding environment for the maintenance of superego structures (Morgenthau and Person, 1978).[4] The entrepreneurial personality, while sometimes reflecting narcissistic and paranoid trends, is not necessarily pathological. Its defensive organization may well allow for a healthy adaptation.

The entrepreneurial personality organization is not just predicated on acting-out, externalization, and the avoidance of consciousness of inner life; these conditions may be found in a variety of personalities. The ability to perceive interpersonal nuance is equally important. Above all, the entrepreneur is committed to the initiation of activity and the avoidance of passivity. Whether activity represents a healthy identification or a reaction formation against passive strivings is the

---

[4]This is well illustrated in the intellectual conversion of a liberal businessman: Initially opposing corporate bribes abroad on moral and ideological grounds, he has become convinced that American free enterprise cannot be fettered by prohibitions that do not obtain among foreign corporations without dire consequences for the American economy.

measure of the degree of healthy integration in the individual entrepreneurial personality.

The "choice" of defensive organization is probably multidetermined, but one hypothesis can be suggested as to the predisposition to develop manipulation as a predominant personality mode. Lowenstein (1957) described "seduction of the aggressor" as the ability in a child to change an unloving attitude in the parent into a loving one, noting that success depended on the ability of the infant to perceive the mother's emotions. He suggested seduction of the aggressor as a possible precursor of masochism. This author would suggest that this is only one possible fate of "seduction of the aggressor." When it develops in the active rather than the passive form, manipulation and the will to power predominate over masochism. In the manipulative maneuver, revenge accompanies the aim of reversing the object's negative affect.

In many entrepreneurs, underlying passivity and reaction formation against dependency needs are revealed in early feelings of helplessness and shame which persist and must be overcome. These feelings emerge quite readily in the depressive crises to which these patients are prone. It is striking, despite their intense competition with men, that nearly all of the author's entrepreneurial patients came from families in which the father was relatively weak and ineffectual or died early.

At the same time the mother adored her precocious son but predicated that adoration on his performance. Seduction of the aggressor as the precursor of manipulation more likely than not derives from an early interaction with the mother rather than with the father. Hostility is transferred to the father in order to preserve the mother as a good and adoring object, and out of resentment at the father for having failed to provide a strong male role model.

In contrast to the personalities just described, psychopaths reveal weakness of both superego and ego ideal, so that the interpersonal dramas which are enacted are much closer to primitive id material than one sees in the more highly developed entrepreneurial personality. Most important, there are significant ego splits and the personality is riddled with rage and sadism. Sadism must be vented in order to preserve the sense of self; sadism saturates the interpersonal enactment of intrapsychic dramas and ultimately leads to the downward drift in the lives of psychopaths.

TREATMENT

Analytically-oriented treatment of the true psychopath is of dubious value. However, narcissistic entrepreneurs who rely on manipulation may well benefit from the analytic method. In general, one must follow the procedures recommended in the treatment of narcissistic patients.

The transference paradigm usually begins with overidealization, in which every interpretation is treated with reverence. Initially, these patients appear to make extremely good use of interpretations; however, the utilization appears to be intellectual even when it leads to apparent shifts in behavior. The patients are also apparently very candid in reporting their failings. This is only pseudo-candor; it is almost as though their "brutal" honestly neutralizes excesses in their behavior. This is particularly true in reports of outbursts of rage, some attached to physical violence. The patient is eased by his "confession." One forms the impression that these patients quickly become able to use the "specialness" projected onto the analyst as a means of overcoming depression and reintegrating at the prior level of functioning. It remains difficult for the patient to establish more far-ranging goals for change. He tends to use the analyst as a magic talisman to be resurrected in times of crisis.

Underneath superficial admiration of the analyst lurks the potential for reversal of the manifest transference from admiration to denigration. In those patients who are treatable, the manifest idealization and lurking condescension must be brought into treatment. The risk is not the disintegration of the patient's personality, but rather the disruption of the treatment when the patient mobilizes his condescending rage toward the analyst. In order to denigrate the goodness of the psychiatrist, the patient may voice a brief "trial" criticism without affect, trusting the therapist to overlook it and thereby enabling the patient to accuse him of insensitivity or cowardice.

The analyst faces two special problems. First, since many narcissistic entrepreneurs are extremely successful, and some famous, the analyst must overcome her/his awe of the patient and not identify with his grandiosity. The psychiatrist must not self-identify as a special doctor who can magically preserve the patient's productivity. Insofar as one is involved with pride in the patient's successes, one repeats the parental error (real or at least perceived as such by the patient) that the psychiatrist (parent) loves the patient for his accomplishments, not for himself. There is a grave danger for those psychiatrists who become "shrink to the stars."

The analyst's fear of the magnitude of the aggression he senses in the patient may be just as important. There may be a tacit agreement to set the anger aside. The psychiatrist must be committed to gradually uncovering the full extent of rage and to tolerating it within the transference.

One must be scrupulous about maintaining procedures. These patients are constantly searching for imperfections and superego lacunae in the analyst. One must give full time (not taking minutes away from the hour to make a phone call or go to the bathroom), neither lend nor borrow books, not make exceptions either for the patient or for oneself, not park illegally in a place where that patient sees the car, and so forth. While these are good practice with all patients, any lapses have more dire consequences with antisocial patients.

MANIPULATION AND THE CULTURAL MILIEU

Greenwald (1967) commented on the general rise of psychopathy over the 15 years preceding his article. The entrepreneurial personality appears to be on the increase as well, and even replacing the "organization" man of the 1950s (see Maccoby's comparison of "The Gamesman" and "The Organization Man"). Not only has the expression "going entrepreneurial" been heard much more frequently among business people during the past ten years, but the shift may be seen even in the *Encyclopaedia Britannica*. Entrepreneurism is given a separate listing beginning with the 1971 edition. These changes parallel the concurrent rise in narcissism noted by a number of authors (Modell, 1975; Morgenthau and Person, 1978; Sobo, 1977). They reflect the relationship of psychopathology and character to culture and, in part, stem from the erosion (or change) of culturally validated values.

The contemporary social climate mandates a concluding addendum: Why are psychopaths and entrepreneurs predominantly male? The reason is really quite simple. The entrepreneurial personality is predicated on the prevalence of self-generating behavior over reactive behavior. Whether cultural or developmental in origin, the common prevalence of reactive behavior in women tends to yield a paucity of female entrepreneurs. The female equivalent of the psychopath might be seen as the high-priced call girl, while the female equivalent of the entrepreneur may be a version of the *femme fatale*. But one should not be surprised by the emergence of the female entrepreneur, after the classic model, in the very near future.

REFERENCES

Bursten, B. (1973). *The manipulator: A psychoanalytic view*. New Haven, CT and London: Yale University Press.

Cleckley, H. (1964). *The mask of sanity*. St. Louis: Mosby.

Glover, E. (1960). *The roots of crime*. New York: International Universities Press.

Greenwald, H. (1967, Spring). Treatment of the psychopath. *Voices*.

Henderson, D. (1939). *Psychopathic states*. New York: Norton.

Johnson, E. (1952). *Charles Dickens: His tragedy and triumph*. Vol. 2. New York: Simon and Schuster.

Kahn, E. (1931). *Psychopathic personalities*. New Haven, CT: Yale University Press.

Karpman, B. (1948). The myths of the psychopathic personality. *American Journal of Psychiatry, 104*, 523–534.

Karpman, B. (1954). *The sexual offender and his offenses*. New York: Julian Press.

Kernberg, O. (1975). *Borderline conditions and pathological narcissism*. New York: Jason Aronson.

Lowenstein, R. (1957). A contribution to the psychoanalytic theory of masochism. *Journal of American Psychoanalytic Association, 5*, 197–234.

Maccoby, M. (1976). *The gamesman: The new corporate leaders*. New York: Simon and Schuster.

Modell, A. (1975). The ego and the id: Fifty years later. *International Journal of Psycho-Analysis, 56*, 57–68.

Morgenthau, H. & Person, E. (1978). The roots of narcissism. *Partisan Review*, 337–347.

Ovesey, L. & Person, E. (1976). Transvestism: A disorder of the sense of self. *International Journal of Psychoanalytic Psychotherapy V*: 219–235.

Palmer, H. (1957). *Psychopathic personalities*. New York: Philosophical Library.

Person, E. (1983). Women in therapy: Therapist gender as a variable. *International Review of Psycho-Analysis, 10*, 193–204.

Schumpeter, J. (1954). *Capitalism, socialism and democracy*. New York: Harper and Row.

Sobo, S. (1977). Narcissism as a function of culture. *The Psychoanalytic study of the child, 32*, 155–172.

Vaillant, G. (1975). Sociopathy as a human process: A viewpoint. *Archives of General Psychiatry, 32*, 178–183.

Wills, C. (1978, July 20). A guy like I. *New York Review of Books, XXV*, 12.

Zaleznik, A. (1977, May–June). Managers and leaders: Are they different? *Harvard Business Review*.

Name Index

Adler, G., 193, 198, 199, 202, 203
Agee, V. L., 175
Aghajanian, G., 147
Agren, H., 143
Aichhorn, A., 208
Aiken, T. W., 175
Alexander, J. F., 178, 179, 184
Allen, V., 40
Angel, C., 133, 135
Anolik, S., 31
Arato, M., 143
Arieti, S., 7
Arlow, J., 101
Arnold, J. E., 178
Arnold, L., 143, 146, 147
Asberg, M., 132, 143
Atwater, J. D., 173
Axelrod, J., 135
Ayllon, T., 171

Bach-y-Rita, G., 203
Bader, M., 90
Baer, D. M., 167, 168
Baer, M., 138
Baker, B., 257
Balla, D., 210
Ballenger, J., 145, 146, 148
Banki, C., 143
Barley, W. D., 159–84, 231–55
Barnes, L. W., 8
Barton, C., 179
Basseches, M., 45
Bassett, J. E., 171, 172
Beal, M., 198
Beaumont, J. G., 22
Behles, M. W., 176
Bell, B., 143, 146, 147
Bell, D., 82
Bellak, L., 100, 101, 102, 104, 105, 109,
    111, 113, 114, 117, 119, 121, 124, 125,
    126, 127, 128
Bender, L., 100
Bennet, B., 142
Bensman, J., 78n

Beres, D., 101
Berrettini, W., 143, 147
Bertilson, H. S., 15
Beskow, J., 135
Bioulac, B., 141, 142, 146
Blackburn, R., 28
Blackman, D., 136
Blakely, C. H., 175
Blakeney, C., 66, 67
Blakeney, R., 66, 67
Blanchard, E. B., 171, 172
Blatt, S., 100, 130
Blom, G., 165
Blumberg, A., 82
Bohman, M., 32, 35, 36, 37, 38, 40
Bornstein, P. H., 165, 182, 208
Branchey, L., 145
Braukmann, C. J., 173
Brenner, C., 101
Brigham, T. A., 161, 169, 173, 176, 181,
    183
Bromberg, W., 192
Broughton, J., 45
Brown, G. L., 132–48
Brown, M. N., 181
Bry, B. H., 176
Bryden, M. P., 22
Budd, K. S., 167, 168
Buie, D., 197, 201
Bunney, W., Jr., 136
Burchard, J. D., 165, 166, 167, 169, 172,
    173, 176, 178, 179, 180, 183, 184
Burkhart, B. R., 176
Bursten, B., 266
Bushing, J., 133
Buss, A., 138

Cadoret, R., 28–41
Cain, C., 32, 33, 37, 40
Calogeras, R., 121
Camen, P., 143, 146
Cameron, R., 164, 165
Camp, B., 165
Cantwell, D., 30

Carnegie, A., 260
Chamberlain, P., 178
Charalampous, K., 137
Cherek, D., 146
Christiansen, K. O., 12, 31
Christmas, A., 135
Ciaranello, R., 135
Ciccone, J., 206
Clark, L., 135
Cleckley, H., 3, 4, 7, 8, 15, 16*n*, 21, 22,
    24, 45, 46, 59, 68, 75, 89, 93, 98–100,
    119, 161, 191, 209, 221, 265
Clements, C. B., 171, 206
Cloninger, C., 32, 35, 36, 37, 40
Cobliner, W., 134
Coles, M. G. H., 10
Connolly, J. F., 13, 22
Cook, J. O., 8
Coscina, D., 133
Cox, D. N., 10
Cox, S. G., 163
Crabtree, L. H., 169, 182, 241, 245
Craft, M. J., 7
Craigen, D., 10
Craighead, W. E., 167
Crawley, J., 134
Crowe, R., 34, 38
Cunningham, L., 35

Dahl, A., 102
Dahlstrom, W. M., 6, 138
Dalle-Molle, D., 209
Davidson, W. S., 173, 175, 176, 178, 183
Davison, G. C., 164
Deluca, D., 133
Dengerink, H. A., 15
Dewan, M., 198
Dickens, C., 256
Doctor, R. M., 176, 180
Dominguez, M., 133
Domino, E., 147
Dorr, D., 98–130, 159*n*
Durkee, A., 138
Durkheim, E., 88, 94, 95

Eddy, S., 197
Edwards, J., 35
Eichelman, B., 133
Eisenhower, D. D., 257
Elkind, D., 47
Ellis, A., 162, 164
Ellul, J., 94
Emery, R. E., 167, 168, 175
Endicott, J., 137
Erikson, E., 69, 106

Everitt, B., 136

Fagan, T. J., 160
Farrington, D., 30, 31
Fedoravicius, A. S., 181
Feindler, E. L., 165, 166, 181
Ferber, H., 178
Fernstrom, J., 142
Finch, A. J., Jr., 165
Finkelstein, L., 263
Fischer, D., 31, 40
Fitzgerald, T. J., 179
Flanery, R. C., 179
Fleischman, M. J., 169
Fleiss, J. L., 19
Fleming, R., 143, 146, 147
Flor-Henry, P., 21
Fo, W. S. O., 177
Foa, E. B., 162
Foa, V. G., 162
Fodor, E., 59
Fowler, J., 46, 56
Fowles, D. C., 25
Frank, S., 57
Franks, C. M., 166, 167, 168, 169
Frazelle, J., 10
Freedman, D., 133
Fremouw, W. J., 165, 166, 181
Freud, Sigmund, 82, 84, 94, 106, 117,
    119, 123, 127, 132, 195
Freud, Sophie, 45*n*
Freundlich, D., 57
Friedrichs, D., 81, 82
Fromm, E., 94
Frosch, J. P., 183, 196, 201
Fuller, R., 147
Fyro, B., 147

Gabrielli, W., Jr., 28, 35
Gardner, D., 33
Gardner, H., 46
Gath, A., 37
Gediman, H., 100
Gendel, M., 203
Gerth, H., 86, 88
Geyer, M., 133
Gibbon, M., 137
Gilligan, C., 45
Giovacchini, P., 200, 201, 204, 205, 206
Glasser, W., 164
Glenn, M., 89, 94
Glover, E., 266
Glueck, E., 28
Glueck, S., 28
Goffman, E., 84, 87

Gold, S., 57
Goldfried, M. R., 164
Goldsmith, L., 100, 101
Goodman, D., 164
Goodman, J., 165
Goodwin, D., 29, 37
Goodwin, F. K., 132–48
Gough, H. G., 18
Grant, L., 133
Green, A., 136
Green, L., 176
Greene, R. T., 171
Greenwald, H., 258, 266, 272
Grieger, R., 162
Gross, A. M., 161, 169, 173, 176, 181, 183
Grossman, S., 133
Grove, W., 37
Groves, J., 204
Gunderson, J., 223, 224
Gutheil, T., 202
Guze, S., 29, 30, 34, 35

Haldipur, C., 198
Hamilton, S. B., 182
Hare, R. D., 3–24
Harrington, A., 89, 94
Hart, S., 4, 21
Hartmann, H., 100, 101, 115, 124, 127
Hayward, E., 37
Hedberg, A. G., 167
Hegstrand, L., 133
Hellige, J. B., 24
Helzer, J., 37
Henderson, A. F., 45n
Henderson, D., 265
Henderson, J. Q., 177
Herbert, F., 165
Hermansen, L., 37
Herrell, J. M., 182
Hersen, M., 181
Hesselbroch, M., 36
Heyert, M., 65
Hickey, J., 57
Hill, G. A., 181
Hoeldtke, R., 138
Hollister, L., 138
Horn, J., 34
Horney, K., 94
Horvat, B., 82
House, A. E., 170, 175
Hudgins, W., 57
Huntsinger, G. M., 165
Hunziker, J., 181
Hurvich, M., 100

Hutchings, B., 28, 35, 36
Huttunen, M., 142

Iverson, S., 136
Iwata, M., 165

Jackson, D. N., 17
Jacobson, E., 100
Jayaratne, S., 179
Jenkins, R., 209
Jennings, J. R., 10
Jennings, W., 57, 59
Jequier, E., 133
Jesness, C. F., 176
Johnson, L. B., 257
Jones, F. D., 171
Jones, J. D., 183
Jones, K. A., 231–55
Jonsson, G., 30
Jurkovic, G., 59
Jutai, J. W., 4, 11, 12, 13, 23

Kahn, E., 265
Kanfer, F. H., 182
Kantak, K., 133
Karpman, B., 7, 28, 265
Kaufmann, L. M., 165
Kazdin, A. E., 161, 162, 166, 167, 168, 169, 171, 172, 173, 174, 175, 176, 242, 243
Keeley, S. M., 178
Kegan, R., 45–76
Kelly, G. A., 164
Kendall, P. C., 165
Kent, R. N., 177, 178
Kernberg, O. F., 100, 115, 205, 209, 258, 264, 265, 267
Keyson, M., 181
Kilkenny, R., 57, 59
King, C., 193, 201
Kirigin, K. A., 173
Kirschenbaum, D. S., 179
Klein, N. C., 179
Knapp, S., 147
Knesper, D. J., 183, 241
Koshland, E., 171
Koe, B., 133
Kofoed, L., 41
Kohlberg, L., 46, 53, 57, 58, 59
Kraemer, G., 134
Krause, R., 147
Kreusi, M., 142
Kris, E., 115, 119
Kropp, R., 4, 21
Kulkarni, A., 133

Lacey, B. C., 10
Lacey, J. I., 10, 14
Lamal, P. A., 181
Lamprecht, F., 135
Landon, P., 191, 194
Lane, T. W., 165, 166, 167, 169, 172, 173, 176, 178, 179, 180, 183, 184
Lanyon, R., 138
Lasch, C., 90, 94, 121
Lawson, R. B., 171
Leaff, L., 192, 200
Leckman, J., 143
Ledwidge, B., 161
Lehr, E., 163
Leventhal, B., 133
Levine, A. G., 178
Levine, W., 208
Levy, J., 24
Lewis, C., 29, 30, 36, 37
Lewis, D., 210
Liberman, R. P., 179
Lidberg, L., 141, 142
Lifton, R. J., 88
Lindner, R., 88, 94
Linkenhoker, D. D., 168
Linn, D., 209
Linnoila, M., 141, 142
Lion, J., 192, 193, 197, 200, 202, 203
Lipsky, A., 135
Lira, F. T., 160
Livingstone, B. L., 171
Loehlin, J., 34
Loevinger, J., 46, 57, 58
Loftus, R., 35
Longo, V., 133
Lott, L. B., 179
Lovenberg, W., 133
Lowenstein, R., 257, 270
Luchins, D., 133
Lydgate, T., 177
Lykken, D., 5, 7, 9

McAuley, R., 180
McCarter, E., 209
McClarren, G., 78*n*
McClure, G., 171
Maccoby, M., 260, 272
McCord, J., 7, 94, 95
McCord, W., 7, 78*n*, 94, 95, 209, 215
McCullough, J. P., 165
Macdonald, J., 194
McFall, M. E., 182
McKee, J. M., 171
McKinney, J., 29, 30
McKinney, W., 134

MacMillan, J., 41
McPherson, L. M., 4, 21, 23
Magnusson, D., 40
Mahler, M., 100, 115
Mahoney, M. J., 161, 162, 167
Mailer, N., 89, 94
Major, L., 145
Maltsberger, J., 197, 201
Mandell, A., 147
Marholin, D., 167, 168, 175
Marks, P., 136
Marohn, R., 209, 215, 216
Marriott, S. A., 165
Marx, G., 66
Marx, K., 84, 94
Marzillier, J. S., 161, 162
Massimo, J. L., 173
Masters, J. C., 159, 161, 162, 166, 168, 171, 174, 175, 181, 243
Masterson, J., 115, 208, 215
Matthews, W., 204
Maughs, S. B., 7
Maxwell, D., 135
Mead, G. H., 86
Mednick, S. A., 12, 28, 31, 35, 36, 38, 40
Meeks, J., 210, 222
Meichenbaum, D., 164, 165
Milan, M. A., 171
Miller, F., 133
Millon, T., 21
Mills, C. M., 173, 179
Mills, C. W., 79, 86, 88
Modell, A., 272
Moffit, T., 12
Molnar, G., 143
Montgomery, D., 143
Montgomery, S., 143
Moore, D. R., 178
Moran, E., 134
Morgenthau, H., 269, 272
Moss, G. R., 167, 170, 179, 182, 183
Mowrer, O. H., 4, 5
Moyer, K., 132
Mukai, L. H., 178
Mullen, P., 143, 146
Murphree, O., 133
Muscettola, G., 138

Nay, W. R., 165
Neppe, V., 133
Ng, K., 133
Nietzsche, F. W., 94
Ninan, P., 143
Noam, G., 46, 57
Novaco, R. W., 165

Nunberg, H., 126

O'Brien, M., 136
O'Dell, S. L., 169
O'Donnell, C. R., 177
O'Gorman, T., 37
O'Leary, K. D., 177
Ollendick, T. H., 181
Oreland, L., 143
Orenberg, E., 133
Ovesey, L., 269

Padina, R. J., 171
Palaniappan, V., 143, 144
Palmer, H., 265
Parks, S., 46, 56
Parsons, B. V., 178, 179
Parsons, M., 46
Pasternak, S., 197
Patterson, G. R., 178
Paunonen, S. V., 17
Paxinos, G., 136
Peabody, D. L., 176
Pease, D., 33
Pepinsky, H., 194
Perez-Cruet, J., 133
Perry, J., 208
Perry, W. G., 45
Person, E. S., 129, 256–73
Persons, R., 194
Peterson, D., 28
Philipson, I., 90
Piaget, J., 45, 46, 47, 62
Pickar, D., 134
Pokorny, A., 135
Polakow, R. L., 176, 180
Post, R., 146, 148
Potts, L. J., 231–55
Powell, G., 134
Prentice, N., 57, 59
Pritchard, J. C., 78
Protter, B., 192

Quay, H., 28
Quevillon, R. P., 165
Quinlan, D., 57
Quinn, M. J., 9

Racker, H., 196
Raine, A., 3, 9
Raskin, D. C., 14
Regier, D., 29
Reich, C. A., 84
Reich, T., 35
Reich, W., 100, 122

Reid, W. H., 45n, 159, 160, 161, 204
Reis, O., 133
Reiser, D., 203
Renner, K. E., 7
Reppucci, N. D., 169
Rice, J., 29
Rice, L., 37
Richardson, J. S., 171
Rick, G. R., 167, 170, 179, 182, 183
Riesman, D., 84, 94
Rimm, D. C., 159, 161, 162, 166, 168,
    171, 174, 175, 181, 243
Rinsley, D., 115, 209, 214, 216, 218
Roberts, M., 171
Robins, L., 29, 30, 31, 40, 135
Robinson, M. J., 178
Rogers, L., 45n
Rosenberg, B., 82, 87, 88, 94
Rosenblum, M., 142
Rosenthal, D., 31
Rossman, P. G., 183, 241
Rotenberg, M., 12
Rowe, D., 37
Roy, A., 135, 143
Roy-Byrne, P., 143
Rushton, J., 41
Russell, R., 41
Rutter, M., 40

Sagarin, E., 78n
Samenow, S., 11, 12, 160, 161, 163–64,
    166, 241, 244, 245
Sánchez, J., 78–96
Sanders-Bush, E., 133
Sanger, D., 136
Saslow, G., 182
Saunders, J. T., 169
Scarr, S., 34
Schachtel, E., 47
Schalling, D., 24
Schiavo, R. S., 179
Schroeder, K. G., 17
Schroeder, M. L., 17
Schulsinger, F., 12, 33, 34, 37
Schumpeter, J., 260
Schupper, F., 121
Schwitzgebel, R. K., 167, 168
Schwitzgebel, R. L., 167, 168
Segal, D., 133
Seidman, E., 173, 176, 183
Selman, R. D., 66, 221–30
Selzer, M., 137
Shamblin, W., 208–20
Shapiro, L. N., 192, 202
Sharpless, N., 138

Sheard, M., 133, 147
Shemberg, K. M., 178
Shichman, S., 100, 130
Shoemaker, M. E., 181
Shore, M. F., 173
Siddle, D. A. T., 3, 9
Sigvardsson, S., 32, 35, 37
Silberman, C., 91, 92
Silverstein, H., 82, 88
Sjoerdsma, A., 133
Smith, R., 89, 90, 94
Snyder, J. J., 165
Sobo, S., 272
Sofia, R., 133
Sohn, D., 181
Sorokin, P., 258
Southwick, C., 135
Spitz, R., 134
Spitzer, R., 137
Stabenau, J., 37
Stambaugh, E. E., 170, 175
Stayer, S. J., 171
Steinberg, J., 146
Stern, J. A., 10
Stoff, D., 148
Stone, C. I., 163
Storrs, K., 159n
Strange, R., 137
Strasburger, L. H., 191–206
Stuart, J. E., 181
Stuart, R. B., 179
Stumphauzer, J. S., 166, 167, 168, 169,
    171, 173, 174, 175, 176, 179, 180, 182,
    183
Suedfeld, P., 191, 194
Sullivan, H., 74
Sulser, F., 133
Sutton, M., 134
Sutton, W., 63

Takahaski, S., 145
Taylor, M., 138
Templeman, T. L., 160, 161, 162, 164,
    166, 169
Tenen, S., 133
Tharpe, R. G., 177
Thoa, N., 133
Thomes, L., 171
Thoren, P., 132, 143
Tiffany, T., 28
Tillich, P., 82
Traskman, L., 132, 143
Trasler, G. B., 3, 9
Travin, S., 192
Tripodi, T., 179

Troughton, E., 28, 37
Tucker, D. M., 24
Tupin, J., 147
Tye, N., 136

Ulrici, D. K., 180

Vaillant, G., 36, 40, 56, 74, 192, 193,
    194, 196, 208, 209, 266
Valzelli, L., 133
Van Doorninck, W., 165
Van Dusen, K., 35
Van Praag, H., 143
Varendonck, J., 119
Varley, W. H., 165, 167, 168, 169, 174,
    175, 179, 181, 183, 184
Veloz, E. V., 175
Venables, P. H., 3, 9, 11
Vestergaard, P., 143
Vincent, K., 58
Vincent, L., 58
Vines, R., 146
Virkkunen, M., 29, 37, 142, 143
Vojnik, M., 143
von Knorring, A., 32, 35

Wagner, B. R., 165
Walter, T. L., 173, 179
Watkins, J. T., 162
Weathers, L., 179
Webber, P., 34
Weber, M., 94
Wehr, T., 138
Weinberg, R., 34
Weiner, I., 101
Weissman, A., 133
Wells, P., 41
Welsh, G. S., 6, 138
Werner, H., 46
West, D., 30, 31
West, L., 133
Wetzel, R. J., 177
Wheelis, A., 85, 86, 88
Whitaker, C., 197
White, M. J., 165
White, R., 127
Whitters, A., 28
Wichlacz, C. R., 171
Widmer, R., 28
Willerman, L., 34
Wills, C., 257
Wilson, E., 41
Winnicott, D., 201, 204
Winokur, G., 31
Wishnie, H., 198

Wittig, M., 34
Wolf, M. M., 173
Wolfgram, E., 29, 30
Wolfred, T. R., 173, 176
Wollersheim, J. P., 160, 161, 162, 164,
  166, 169
Wong, S., 21
Wood, G., 190
Woodhall, P. K., 98–130, 231–55

Wurtman, R., 138, 142

Yochelson, S., 11, 12, 160, 161, 163–64,
  166, 241, 244, 245

Zaleznik, A., 260*n*
Zelie, K., 163
Zuckerman, M., 136
Zung, B., 137

Subject Index

Achievement Place, 172, 173
activity therapy:
  for antisocial adolescents, 245–54
  art, 251–52
  assertiveness training, 249–50
  communication skills, 246–47
  creative-expressive, 251
  leisure skills, 250–51
  music, 252
  occupational therapy groups, 252–53
  problem-solving, 250
  self-awareness exercises, 247–49
  values clarified in, 247
Adaptive Regression In Service of the Ego,
  see ARISE
adolescents:
  abstract thinking in, 54–55, 75
  antisocial, see antisocial adolescents
  interpersonal organization in, 55, 69, 75
  intrapersonal organization in, 55–56, 75
  subject-object relationships in, 54–56
adoption studies:
  adoptee methods used in, 32
  antisocial personalities and, 32–37
  gene-environment interaction and, 33,
    36, 40
  genetic inheritance and, 33–37
  twins in, 31, 34, 37
aggression, 132–48
  animal models and, 132–36
  animal suicide and, 134–35
  CNS biochemistry and, 133–48
  memory capacity and, 135–36
  suicide linked to, 132, 135, 139–40, 141,
    147
aggressive/impulsive/suicidal behavior,
  studies in, 137–48
Alcoholics Anonymous, 75
American Psychiatric Association, 18
anaclitic depression, 134
antisocial adolescents:

activity therapy for, 245–54
behavioral and cognitive interventions
  for, 240–45
case studies of, 210–13, 231–55
family history of, 232–33
family intervention and, 236–40
hospital progress of, 234–35
inpatient treatment of, 208–20, 231–55
medical history of, 233
mental status of, 233
psychiatric hospitalization for, 213–20
psychotherapy issues and, 235–36
substance-abuse treatment and, 221–30
token reinforcement systems and, 241–45
  see also antisocial personality
antisocial personality:
  adoption studies and, 32–37
  definitions of, 18, 19, 21, 28–29
  DSM-III criteria and, 28, 29, 36, 38,
    103–4
  entrepreneur as, 159
  epidemiology of, 28–41
  family history and, 30–31
  genetic factors and, 33–38, 40–41
  in urban vs. rural population, 29–30
  see also antisocial adolescents
APD (Antisocial Personality Disorder), 18,
  19, 21
ARISE (Adaptive Regression In Service of
  the Ego), 119–21, 128
  adaptation and creativity in, 120–21
  global rating in, 121
  relaxation dimension in, 120
art therapy, 251–52
assertiveness training, 249–50
assessment procedures:
  comparisons in, 18–21
  in psychopathy, 7–18
autonomic responses, psychopath's, 7–8, 9–
  14
autonomous functioning, 124–26

autonomous functioning (*continued*)
  global rating in, 126
  impairment of primary functions and,
    125
  interference with secondary functions
    and, 125
avoidance learning:
  fear arousal and, 7
  punishment and, 4, 5

"baby boomers," 91, 92
BDI (Buss-Durkee Inventory), 138, 139
behavioral interventions, 161–62, 166–83
  for antisocial adolescents, 240–45
  aversive procedures, 168–69
  in combined treatment, 182–83
  community-level programs, 182
  contingency contracting, 176, 177, 179–
    80
  mediated treatment, 169, 177–78
  in Oregon Social Learning Project, 178
  probation, 176–77
  rights issues and, 167–68
  short-term systems therapy, 178–79
  systemic constraints on, 169–70
  system-level changes and, 167
  target behaviors and, 166–67
  token reinforcement systems, 170–76
behavior studies:
  animals vs. humans in, 134–36
  "state" vs. "trait" in, 134, 135
Black Panthers, 75
brain, language specialization in, 21–24
Briquet's syndrome, 30, 35
Buss-Durkee Inventory (BDI), 138, 139

California Psychological Inventory, 18
cardiovascular activity:
  in psychopaths, 9–11, 14
  sensory input and, 10–12
cerebrospinal fluid, *see* CSF
children:
  guilt created in, 54
  impulse-coordination in, 53
  monitoring activity of, 71, 72
  subject-object relationships in, 51, 52–54
  see also adolescents
classical conditioning paradigm, 5, 9
Cleckley psychopaths, 3–24
  characteristics of, 15–17
  semantic disorders in, 21–24
CNS (central nervous system) biochemistry,
    aggression and, 133–48
cognitive-behavioral interventions, 164–65,
    183

barb techniques, 165
  self-instruction training, 165
  stress inoculation, 165
cognitive interventions, 161–64, 166, 183
  for antisocial adolescents, 240–45
  cognitive-behavioral treatment packages,
    164–65
  rational-emotive therapy (RET), 162–63
  Yochelson and Samenow's approach,
    163–64, 241, 244
concrete thinking, in psychopaths, 62, 63,
    75
countertransference:
  problem-solving in, 203–4
  settings as problematic in, 202–3
  in therapists, 195–204
countertransference reactions, 195, 197–202
  denial, 200
  fear of assault, 197–98
  guilt, 198–99
  hatred, 201
  helplessness, 198–99
  invalidity, 199–200
  loss of identity, 199–200
  rage, 201–2
  rejection, 201
criminality, *see* delinquent behavior
CSF (cerebrospinal fluid), 138, 139
  neurotransmitter metabolite levels in,
    134, 135
  see also specific chemical components

DA (dopamine), 133, 134, 138, 139
David Copperfield (Dickens), 256
decentration, in mental organization, 47, 51
defensive functioning, 121–22
  failure and, 122
  global rating in, 122
  interference with adaptation and, 121–22
  success and, 122
delinquent behavior, 159–84
  causes of, 91
  genetic inheritance and, 34–36
  in juveniles, 91–93, 160
  studies of, 57–58
  see also aggression
developmental delay, sociopathy as, 45–76
divided visual field (DVF) technique, 22–23
dopamine (DA), 133, 134, 138, 139
Draper Correctional Center, 171
DSM-II (*Diagnostic and Statistical Manual
    of Mental Disorders*), 137
DSM-III (*Diagnostic and Statistical Manual
    of Mental Disorders*), 18, 20–21, 28,
    137, 254

DSM-III criteria, antisocial personality and, 28, 29, 36, 38, 103–4
DVF (divided visual field) technique, 22–23

EFA (Ego Functions Analysis), 100–101, 109, 119, 127, 130
  antidepressant medication and, 103
  rating methodology in, 101–2, 104
  results of, 104–5
  subjects in, 102–3
effective programs:
  breadth of, 218
  communication in, 217
  control in, 216–17
  evaluation in, 216
  psychiatric hospitalization and, 216–18
  staff teaching in, 218
  tolerance in, 217–18
egocentrism, in mental organization, 47, 51
ego dysfunctions, in psychopathic inpatients, 98–130
ego functions, 101, 106–28
embeddedness, in mental organization, 47, 51, 74, 75
Encyclopaedia Britannica, 272
entrepreneurs, 259–65
  as antisocial personalities, 159
  manipulativeness in, 256–73
  narcissism in, 259, 263, 264
  psychopaths vs., 257, 258–59, 269–70
Evolving Self, The (Kegan), 47

fear arousal:
  avoidance learning and, 7, 160
  of psychopaths, 8
  temporal gradient of, 7–8

GABA (gamma-amino-butyric acid), 133
gene pool, 40–41
  altruism in, 41
genetic inheritance:
  adoption studies and, 33–37
  alcohol abuse and, 35–37, 38
  antisocial personality and, 33–38, 40–41
  criminality and, 34–36

5HIAA (5-hydroxyindoleacetic acid), 134, 135, 136, 138, 139, 140, 141, 142, 143, 144, 145, 147, 148
Hopewell programs, 222–30
  behavioral principles in, 225–26
  components of, 223–24
  patients in, 222–23
  prosocial atmosphere in, 226
  special-groups familiarization in, 226–29

staff considerations and, 229–30
  therapeutic milieu in, 223–24
5HT (serotonin), 133, 134, 136, 138, 139, 142, 145, 147
1-5HTP (1-5-hydroxytryptophan), 146–47
HVA (homovanillic acid), 134, 138, 139, 141, 142, 143
Hypomia (*Ma*) scale, 6, 19, 20

impulsivity, suicide and, 135, 136
infants, anaclitic depression in, 134
internalization:
  by identification, 82–83
  psychopaths and, 80–81, 82–83

judgment, 109–11, 128
  adjustment to reality in, 110–11
  anticipation of consequences in, 109–10
  global rating in, 111

language, cerebral specialization for, 21–24
Lithium, 103, 147
Loxitane, 103
Ma (Hypomia) scale, 6, 19, 20
manipulativeness:
  cultural milieu and, 272–73
  in entrepreneurs, 256–73
  in psychopaths, 69–70, 73, 256–73
Manipulator, The (Bursten), 266
Mask of Sanity, The (Cleckley), 4–5, 99
mastery-competence, 127–28
  objective performance level and, 127
  subjective performance level and, 128
Mellaril, 103
mental organization:
  aspects of, 46–47, 60
  development of, 46–56
  embeddedness and, 47, 51, 74, 75
  subject-object relationships and, 47, 51, 52–54
  see also thought processes
Methadone, 103
MHPG (3-methoxy-4 hydroxyphenylglycol), 134, 138, 139, 141, 142, 143
Michigan Alcoholism Screening Test, 137
MMPI (Minnesota Multiphasic Personality Inventory), 6, 18, 20, 58, 138, 139, 143, 147, 233
music therapy, 252

narcissism:
  in entrepreneurs, 259, 263, 264
  societal, 90–91
Narcotics Anonymous, 223
National Institutes of Mental Health, 137

National Naval Medical Center, 137
NE (norepinephrine), 133, 134, 138, 139, 148
"New Kid, The" (Heyert), 65

object relations, 115–17, 128
  degree of closeness and, 115–16
  global rating in, 117
  object constancy and, 117
  people as independent entities and, 116–17
  relationship with elders and, 116
occupational therapy groups, 252–53
Oregon Social Learning Project, 178

PCPA (parachlorophenylalanine), 133
Pd (Psychopathic Deviate) scale, 6, 19, 20, 138, 141
"Protean Man" (Lifton), 88
psychiatric hospitalization:
  for antisocial adolescents, 213–20
  character diagnosis in, 214–15
  character pathology and, 215
  criteria for inpatient treatment in, 214
  effective programs in, 216–18
  improvement in, 219–20
  treatment stages in, 218–19
Psychopathic Deviate (*Pd*) scale, 6, 19, 20, 138, 141
psychopathic inpatients:
  ego dysfunctions in, 98–130
  substance abuse by, 102, 103
psychopaths, 7, 265–68
  action orientation by, 68, 75
  as adaptable personality types, 89
  adoptees as, 32
  cardiovascular activity in, 9–11, 14
  as childlike, 75–76
  Cleckley, 3–20
  concrete thinking in, 62, 63, 75
  criminal, 5–6, 7, 11
  definition of, 94
  ego deficiency in, 100
  electrodermal activity in, 5, 9, 11
  entrepreneurs vs., 257, 258–59, 269–70
  epistemological evolutions of, 55, 61–62
  features of, 60–61, 80
  goals lacked by, 67–68
  hollowness in, 68–69
  manipulation by, 69–70, 73, 256–73
  moral logic of, 67
  as morally arrested, 64–65
  nonpsychopaths compared with, 7, 24
  perceptual-cognitive factors and, 13
  semantic disorders in, 21–24, 98, 119

stress behavior of, 12–13
unstable superego of, 88
U.S. society and, 81, 82, 89–90, 92, 95
Psychopaths . . . (Harrington), 89
psychopathy:
  as adaptation to modern society, 93–96
  assessment procedures in, 7–18
  as developmental delay, 45–76
  global rating scales of, 8
  identification methods and, 6
  internalization and, 80–84
  legitimacy and, 80–84
  lie detection and, 14–15
  psychodynamic approach to, 99–100
  sociological perspective on, 78–96
  therapeutic pessimism and, 191, 196
psychopathy checklists, 15–18
  reliability of, 17

rating methodology, 129
  in EFA, 101–2, 104
  psychopaths vs. nonpsychopaths in, 8
rational-emotive therapy (RET), 162–63
reality sense, 111–13
  body awareness and, 112
  demarcation and, 112–13
  external events and, 111–12
  global rating in, 113
  individuality and, 112
  self-image and, 112
reality testing, 106–9, 128
  accuracy of external events and, 107–8
  accuracy of internal events and, 108
  global score in, 108–9
  inner vs. outer stimuli and, 107
regulation of drives, 113–14, 128
  control mechanisms in, 114
  global rating in, 114
  impulse expression in, 114
responses:
  autonomic, 7–8, 9–14
  defensive, 10
  orienting, 10
RET (rational-emotive therapy), 162–63

self-awareness exercises, 247–49
self-report psychopathy (*SRP*) scale, 18
semantic disorders, in psychopaths, 21–24, 98, 119
sensory input:
  cardiovascular activity and, 10–11
  modulation of, 10–12
serotonin (5HT), 133, 134, 136, 138, 139, 142, 145, 147
So (Socialization) scale, 18, 19

social structures, 78–96
  alienation and, 82, 94
  anomie and, 82, 88, 94
  changes in, during crises, 83
  credibility gaps and, 84, 88
  crises of confidence and, 83, 88, 95
  crises of conscience and, 86
  legitimacy and, 80–84
  narcissism and, 90–91
  personality related to, 85–86
  violent youth and, 91–93
socioeconomic status (SES), 57, 59
SRP (self-reporting psychopathy) scale, 18
START (Special Treatment and Rehabilita-
    tive Training) Program, 172
stimulus barrier, 123–24
  global rating in, 124
  sensory stimulation and, 124
  stimulus threshold and, 123–24
subject-object relationships:
  in adolescents, 54–56
  mental organization and, 47, 51, 52–54
suicide:
  aggression linked to, 132, 135, 139–41,
    147
  animal behaviors and, 134
  CNS biochemistry and, 139–48
  impulsivity and, 135, 136
superego:
  formation of, 82
  fragmentation of, 86
  in modern society, 82, 87
  in traditional society, 85
Synanon, 75

synthetic-integrative functions, 126–27, 128
  active relating of conflictual and non-
    conflictual issues in, 127
  global rating in, 127
  reconciliation of conflict areas and, 126–
    27
therapeutic interventions, *see*
  behavioral interventions; cognitive-behav-
    ioral interventions; cognitive interven-
    tions
therapists:
  characteristics of, 193–95
  countertransference in, 195–204
  feelings of, in treating antisocial syn-
    dromes, 191–206
thought processes, 117–19
  abstraction-concreteness and, 118
  adaptiveness and, 118
  conceptualization and, 118
  global rating in, 119
  language and, 118–19
  see also mental organization
token reinforcement systems:
  for antisocial adolescents, 172–73,
    241–45
  in behavior employment programs, 173
  as behavior interventions, 170–76
  generalization of change in, 174–75
  in prisons, 171–72
  problems in, 172, 173–74
  in psychiatric hospitals, 170–71
  in residential treatment, 172–73
  target behavior changes in, 170, 174, 175